THE ACTS OF THOMAS

Early Christian & Apocrypha

Julian V. Hills

Harold W. Attridge

Dennis R. MacDonald

VOLUME 1: *The Acts of Andrew*

VOLUME 2: *The Epistle of the Apostles*

VOLUME 3: *The Acts of Thomas*

THE ACTS
OF THOMAS

Harold W. Attridge

Edited by Julian V. Hills

POLEBRIDGE PRESS
Salem, Oregon

Cover and interior design and production by Robaire Ream

Library of Congress Cataloging-in-Publication Data

Acts of Thomas. English.
 The Acts of Thomas / [translated by] Harold W. Attridge and Julian V.
Hills.
     p. cm. -- (Early Christian apocrypha series ; v. 3)
 Includes bibliographical references (p.   ) and indexes.
 ISBN 978-1-59815-021-6 (alk. paper)
 I. Attridge, Harold W. II. Hills, Julian Victor. III. Title.
 BS2880.T4A3 2010
 229'.92505209--dc22
                        2010019290

CONTENTS

SERIES PREFACE

The series *Early Christian Apocrypha &* (*ECA&*), the first such publication by north American scholars, is designed as a study edition of early Christian apocryphal texts and related writings. These comprise the standard set of New Testament apocrypha (gospels, acts, epistles, apocalypses) along with other, some less well known, writings that emerged from the early Christian movement, such as homiletical, polemical, exegetical, and church order tracts. Writings reckoned "orthodox" and "heretical" by contemporaries and later authorities will be included.

The publisher and the editors have had several goals in mind. First, to provide quotable and lively renderings into modern U.S. English—satisfying both to the specialist and to the non-expert reader. Second, to offer full introductions and bibliographies that will situate the texts in question in their larger Christian and Greco-Roman contexts. Third, to supply brief commentary explaining technical aspects of the writing and the movement of the text—storyline or theological argument. Fourth, to add "verse numbers" where previous editions gave only larger section or chapter numbers.

Where appropriate, the texts will be annotated with cross-references, not only within the biblical canon but also outside it—in due course supplying a network of interconnected references to assist comparative study. A full index of texts, biblical and non-biblical, will conclude each volume.

Thanks are due to
Lisa Cullison, John Fortner, and Tim Henderson,
of Marquette University, for checking numerous references.

SIGLA, ABBREVIATIONS, CONVENTIONS

Aaa	Lipsius-Bonnet, *Acta apostolorum apocrypha*
ANF	Roberts-Donaldson, *Ante-Nicene Fathers*
BAGD	Bauer-Arndt-Gingrich-Danker, *Greek-English Lexicon*
CSD	Payne Smith, *Compendious Syriac Dictionary* (see also PSTS)
Gr	Greek version, further specified according to manuscripts ACDF, etc.; see Introduction
LPGL	Lampe, *Patristic Greek Lexicon*
LSJ	Liddell Scott Jones, *Greek-English Lexicon*
NHC	Nag Hammadi Codex, followed by codex and line number(s)
NHLE	Robinson, *Nag Hammadi Library in English*
NTApoc [2]	Schneemelcher, *New Testament Apocrypha*
PSTS	Payne Smith, *Thesaurus Syriacus* (see also CSD)
Syr	Syriac version, further specified as SyrB, SyrL; see Introduction
<and>	words supplied *ad sensum*
[then]	words supplied to fill whole or partial *lacunae* (gaps)
»	indicates the place where the principal reference list of passages related by a common theme or expression is to be found
†	a reference to a text in the Appendix, after the main translation

INTRODUCTION

The *Acts of Thomas* is one of numerous examples of early Christian narratives that relate the adventures and mission of the apostles and disciples of Jesus after the resurrection. *Thomas* is numbered among the five "major" acts, the others being the *Acts of Andrew*, the *Acts of John*, the *Acts of Paul*, and the *Acts of Peter*. Each document presents its own special problems of translation and interpretation, but all five present such challenges as assessing the original length and ordering of its episodes; collating the various recensions in several languages; retrieving quotations from patristic and medieval authors; and identifying multiple layers of editing in the course of transmission. It is also of importance to discover how these works were either appropriated by "unorthodox" groups and hence discredited along with other apocryphal writings, or were made theologically more acceptable to a later generation through a process of "catholicizing" redaction (that is, theological editing) that often included extensive omission of supposedly offensive material.

The *Acts of Thomas* relates the adventures of the apostle Judas Thomas as he preaches an ascetic or encratite form of Christianity on the way to and in India. Like other apocryphal acts combining popular legend and religious propaganda, the work attempts to instruct but also to entertain. In addition to narratives of Thomas's adventures, its poetic and liturgical elements (prayers, hymns, sacramental themes) provide important evidence for the study of early Syrian Christian traditions.

TRANSMISSION AND SURVIVAL

The principal witnesses to the *Acts of Thomas* are manuscripts in Greek and Syriac. The critical edition of the Greek by Maximilian Bonnet (1893) utilized twenty-one manuscripts, only two of which, designated P and U (see the list below), contain the complete narrative portion of the *Acts*. Only U contains, in addition, the famous *Hymn of the Pearl* (chaps. 108–13). Other Greek witnesses comprise various shorter recensions, here listed alphabetically by identifying letter (or *siglum*), manuscript name and number, century, and content by chapter numbers:

A	Parisiacus graecus 881; X cent.	1–29; 163–71
B	Par. gr. 1468; XI cent.	1–29 (= Acts 1–2)
C	Par. gr. 1454; X cent.	same as B
D	Par. gr. 1176; XII–XIII cent.	1–38; 42–61

F   Romanus Angelicanus B2.2; XI cent.   same as B
G   Escorialensis Y II; XI cent.   1–16 (= Act 1)
H   Escorialensis Y II 6; XII cent.   same as B
K   Romanus Chisianus R VII 51; XII cent.   156–71
L   Par. gr. 764; IX cent.   144–49; 163–69
M   Monacensis gr. 262; IX cent.   170–71 (the end of the work)
O   Oxoniensis Clarkianus 43; XI cent.   159–65
P   Par. gr. 1510; XI cent.   1–171
    (= complete narrative, but lacking the *Hymn of the Pearl*)
Q   Par. gr. 1485; XI cent.   1–29; 144–49
R   Par. gr. 1551; XIV cent.   1–29; 42–50; 62–66; 156–71
S   Par. gr. 1613; XV cent.   1–29; 144–49; 163–71
T   Par. gr. 1540; XI cent.   same as B
U   Romanus Vallicellanus B 35; XI cent.   1–171
    (= complete narrative, and the *Hymn of the Pearl*)
V   Vaticanus gr. 1190; XV cent.   1–16; 41–81; 149–71
X   Par. gr. 1173 A; XII cent.   same as B
Y   Vaticanus gr. 797; XI cent.   1–59
Z   Petroburgensis Caesareus 94; XII cent.   1–4; 17–29; 144–49; 163–71

The manuscripts give evidence of different editions or stages of translation. Among the witnesses to the first two acts (chaps. 1–29), there are two distinct recensions. One, comprising the manuscripts arranged by Bonnet (1893: xix) in groups comprising A, CD, FTX, PUY, QR, SV, is longer and closer to the Syriac. The other recension, comprising mss GHZ (Klijn, 1962: 5, adds M in error), is considerably abbreviated. Ms B stands alone as representing a "mixed" text—a common phenomenon in documents with a long and complex transmission history. The martyrdom (Act 13 = chaps. 159–71) also survives in two recensions. One of these (mss FLPSZ) is characterized by the placement at chap. 167 of a prayer of Thomas found in other manuscripts at chaps. 144–48 (ms Q follows FLPSZ but without the special placement of the prayer). This marks a distinct version of the martyrdom, probably based on an independent translation of the earlier Syriac (see below). The Greek is much smoother than that of the remaining manuscripts of this portion of the work (mss AKORUV).

The Syriac is attested by five manuscript witnesses, only one of which (SyrL: see the list below) contains the entire work, including the *Hymn of the Pearl*. The manuscripts are as follows, here by *siglum*, name, century, contents, and first editor's name (in parentheses):

SyrB   Sachau (Berlin) 222; XIX cent. (Bedjan)   complete
       (Bedjan prints SyrL and gives variants from SyrB in the apparatus,
       occasionally placing them in the text itself)
SyrC   Cambridge add. 2822; XIX cent. (see Bonnet, 1883)   lacking the *Hymn*

SyrL   British Museum add. 14, 645; 936 c.e. (Wright, 1871)   lacking the *Hymn*
SyrM   Mosul 86; 1711–12 c.e.   lacking the *Hymn*
SyrS   Sinai 30; V or VI cent. (Smith Lewis, 1904)   a palimpsest
          (contains portions of 17–19; 32–34; 40–44; 66–69; 83–85; 124–27; 128–36;
          137–39, 140–42; 154–58—suggesting that most of the narrative formed
          a literary unity by late antiquity)

    Because the work was popular in many parts of the Christian world, daughter versions exist—in Latin (a much abridged form of the work edited by Bonnet, 1883); in Armenian (edited by the Mekhitarists, 1904: two independent translations, from the Syriac and Greek, respectively); in Coptic (Leloire); in Arabic (fragmentary); and in Ethiopic (Budge, 1900. For an overview of all the versions, see Klijn, 1962: 1–13; though Klijn, 2003: vii, defers to the critical edition forthcoming in the Corpus Christianorum Series Apocryphorum).

ORIGINAL LANGUAGE

Since the first publication of the Syriac text, there has been considerable debate about the original language of composition. Scholars initially presumed that the Greek was primary (Wright, 1871: 1. xiv; Bonnet, 1892: 2/2. xv–xxvii). Subsequently many have argued that the extant Greek is itself a translation from the Syriac—but not the Syriac text as we know it from surviving manuscripts (Nöldeke, in Lipsius, 1883: 2/2. 423; Burkitt, 1900, 1901, 1902; Preuschen, in Hennecke, 1904b: 563; Devos, 1951: 123; Klijn, 1962: 5–7; Bornkamm, in Hennecke, 1964: 2. 428; Plümacher, 1978: 34). It is also possible that sources of the work, perhaps underlying the episodic miracle stories in the earlier chapters, were originally composed in Greek, translated into Syriac, and then back into Greek. Evidence for such a process, however, is hard to secure (for this hypothesis concerning the martyrdom, see James, 1924: 364). In any case, for the work as a whole several factors indicate the derivation of the current Greek witnesses from a Syriac source. This evidence consists not only of Semitisms in the Greek, but also clear cases of dependence of the Greek on corruptions within the Syriac textual tradition. Today, the priority of the Syriac is generally taken as a settled matter, although a few authorities remain unconvinced (Ysebaert, 1962: 4; LaFargue, 1985: 9; the arguments are reviewed in Attridge, 1990).

    The original language, then, was most likely Syriac; but none of the extant witnesses to the Syriac is the source of the Greek texts we possess. How are the differences to be accounted for? Some passages where the Greek appears to preserve an original reading involve what may well be mechanical errors—what sometimes amount to simple spelling mistakes—in the Syriac. In Ac-Thom 12:9, for example, Devos (1951: 123) proposes emending the Syriac to read ܪܚܡܬܢܐ ("bridegroom's friend, groomsman"; PSTS, s.v. [col. 4341; CSD,

p. 569a]) rather than ܪܒܝܬܐ ("singer, chorister"; PSTS, s.v. [col. 4027; CSD, p. 304a]) on the basis of the word παράνυμφοι ("members of the wedding party") in the parallel Greek text. Frequently, however, the differences between the Greek and the Syriac are recensional: conscious modifications of the narrative or liturgical elements that form a large part of the *Acts*. These changes generally push the Syriac version in "orthodox" directions by emphasizing human freedom and responsibility, over against Gnostics or Manichaeans (there are lengthy such additions in chaps. 33, 34, 39, 70); and by insisting on the reality of two natures in Christ, in conformity to the Chalcedonian definition. So, for example, in 10:8 Thomas's prayer includes the phrase, not found in the Greek, "You showed the glory of your divinity by your patience with our humanity"; similarly, chap. 48 emphasizes the full divinity as well as the reality of the incarnation; chap. 83 insists on the full humanity of the apostle. The motif of Thomas's twinship is sometimes eliminated, as in 31:7. The Syriac seems to avoid soteriological language that might be taken as, and might indeed have been, heterodox. Representative of this is 48:2, where the Greek invokes Christ as one "who gathers all <those of> his <own> nature [φύσις] into one place": the corresponding Syriac has "his possessions" instead of "his nature"; and though it is possible to explain the difference on the basis of the similarity in sound between ܩܢܝܢܐ ("possessions"; PSTS, s.v. ܩܢܝܢܐ [col. 3655; CSD, p. 511a]) and ܟܝܢܐ ("nature"; PSTS, s.v. [col. 1703; CSD, p. 213a]), it is more likely that the suggestion that Christ was saving part of *his own nature* was viewed as heterodox and so was "corrected" (so also Klijn, 1962: 242; 2003: 121. Bonnet, 1893: 164, allows the possibility of inner-Greek confusion, between κτῆσις ["possession"] and κτίσις ["creation"], but this doesn't account for the extant Greek "nature"). For similar cases, see the notes on 78:6 and 167:4–5. The Syriac also quietly conforms the text to a more orthodox perspective by eliminating the more distinctive hymnic or liturgical language referring to the Spirit as maternal (e.g., in 27:6; 39:17; 50:5). In this respect the baptismal and eucharistic prayers in chaps. 27; 49–50; 120–21; and 133 display numerous differences (see Whitaker, 1970: 13–19). Finally here, the Syriac seems to intensify the ascetical thrust of the text. Hence, for example, the added beatitudes in chap. 94: "Blessed are you continent, for you will rest and rejoice in spiritual things which do not pass away and do not dissipate. Blessed are you continent"; and the list of sins in 84:1–3, which includes in the Syriac a petition for deliverance from "shameful deeds, odious intercourse, and sordid sleeping."

SOURCES

Oral traditions about Thomas may underlie some of the acts. The *Acts of Thomas* manifests significant parallels to the *Acts of Paul* as well as allusions to traditions found in the New Testament. Some may have been added at later stages of redaction, but others are tightly woven into the fabric of the narrative (e.g., imagery borrowed from the NT gospel passion narratives in Act 5). In addition, several parallels recall earlier Syrian literature, particularly the *Odes of Solomon* and the *Gospel of Thomas.*

CONTENTS AND STRUCTURE

The Greek version consists of thirteen acts, concluding with the martyrdom of Thomas. The division into acts is fairly stable in the manuscripts, but some individual manuscripts have section or "chapter " divisions. "Verse" numbers in the present translation are an innovation intended to facilitate precise location and reference.

The first six acts are loosely connected episodes highlighting Thomas's miraculous powers; some of these stories may have circulated independently, analogously with the New Testament miracle accounts. Tissot emphasizes the composite character of the text, but on the basis of the examination of only a few selected pericopes, or sections. In summary, the contents are as follows:

Act 1 (chaps. 1–16) begins with the apostolic distribution of missionary territories, a common scene in the apocryphal acts (see Junod, 1981; with special reference to the *Acts of Thomas*, see Kaestli, 1981; and now Czachesz, 2007). Since Thomas is reluctant to undertake his assignment to India, his master and twin, Jesus, sells him to an Indian merchant, Chaban, who had come seeking a skilled craftsman. Thomas submits, and departs with his new owner. On the way to India they stop in a city, Sandrok (in Syriac; Andrapolis in Greek), where a royal wedding is in progress. At the wedding banquet, Thomas encounters a Hebrew flautist for whom he sings the *Hymn of the Bride* (chaps. 6–7). An insulting waiter soon meets a dire fate in accordance with the apostle's prediction. The prophecy brings Thomas to the attention of the king, who requires a nuptial blessing for his daughter. After Thomas prays for the bride and groom, Jesus appears to the couple and converts them to celibacy—to their parents' dismay. Before the king can react, Thomas departs.

In **Act 2** (chaps. 17–29), Thomas, now in India, has an audience with King Gundafar (so SyrB, the Greek form being Γουνδαφόρος, or "Gundaphorus"; in SyrL "Gudnafar"), for whom the apostle undertakes to construct a palace. With the king's abundant supplies, Thomas initiates a program of poor relief while preaching the gospel. Gundafar, on an inspection visit, discovers the truth of Thomas's activity. He imprisons the apostle with the merchant Chaban. While they languish in jail, the king's brother, Gad, dies and goes to heaven, where angels show him various mansions. He asks to dwell in one, but is told that it belongs to his brother. Gad obtains permission to return to earth to purchase the property, whereupon Gundafar finally understands the sort of palace Thomas has been constructing. Both royal brothers are converted and seek initiation. In the first major liturgical passage, then, Thomas anoints both royals, preaches, and celebrates the eucharist.

In **Act 3** (chaps. 30–38), Thomas, instructed by a nocturnal vision, discovers the corpse of a youth. A serpent claims responsibility and then sings of his diabolical lineage. At Thomas's command, the serpent sucks his poison from the youth and dies. The youth then hymns his deliverance. All of this prompts a series of homilies from Thomas advocating asceticism and promising forgiveness to the youth and other bystanders.

In **Act 4** (chaps. 39–41), Thomas is returned to the city by a talking foal, which claims descent from Balaam's ass. Upon arrival, the animal dies and Thomas orders a proper burial.

In **Act 5** (chaps. 42–50), Thomas, now back in the city, encounters a woman possessed. Thomas exorcises the demon, who complains at length before being expelled. After an elaborate prayer, Thomas baptizes the woman and celebrates the eucharist.

In **Act 6** (chaps. 51–61), Thomas is told of a youth who was crippled upon receiving the eucharist. Inquiry reveals that the young man had tried to convince a beloved prostitute to embrace celibacy; her refusal provoked him to kill her. Thomas prepares holy water to cleanse him, but he remains in despair. The apostle brings him to the victim's corpse, where, prompted by Thomas, the youth himself prays and revives the woman, who gives a graphic account of hell and the punishments in store for the wicked (chaps. 55–57). Inspired by this vision, Thomas preaches repentance and conversion to Jesus. Prayers of praise and requests for divine aid close the section.

The second half of the *Acts of Thomas* is a more integrated composition with a number of interlocking episodes. Here the work displays a typical Christian version of erotic motifs at home in the romantic novels of the Hellenistic and Roman periods. The dramatic tension increases as Thomas's ascetic gospel is accepted by two upper class women—to the consternation of their powerful husbands.

In **Act 7** (chaps. 62–67), Thomas encounters a character prominent in the rest of the work who will finally (chap. 169) be ordained a presbyter. He is a military commander, later identified as Sifor, who serves a King Mizdai. He seeks assistance for his wife and daughter, both of whom are possessed by demons. The apostle departs with him, after praying for his flock and appointing a deacon in his place.

In **Act 8** (chaps. 68–81), Thomas and Sifor travel together until their draught animals drop from exhaustion. Thomas sends Sifor to request assistance from a herd of wild asses, who readily comply. One, like the ass in Act 4, is endowed with speech. At Sifor's residence, Thomas prays and sends this beast to exorcise the demons possessing Sifor's wife and daughter. It does so, rendering the women unconscious. The demons try to strike a bargain with Thomas, but he sends them away. The asses then preach, urging the crowds to listen to the apostle. He utters a lengthy doxology to Christ, restores the women to consciousness, and dismisses the helpful beasts.

In the long **Act 9** (chaps. 82–118; the *Hymn of the Pearl*, in chaps. 108–13, is present only in Greek ms U and in SyrL), romantic drama and Thomas's ascetical or encratite theology become prominent. (It should be noted that the virtue ἐγκράτεια, that is, "self-control," was highly prized among all early Christian groups. The near technical use of the designation "encratite" by Irenaeus, Clement of Alexandria, and Hippolytus refers to those groups who reject wine, flesh-meat, and, commonly, marriage. For the actual term in the *Acts of Thomas*, see note on 20:6.) A noble woman, Mygdonia, wife of a high royal counselor, Carish, comes to hear Thomas preach. After hearing a sermon on chastity, humility, and related virtues, she asks to be baptized, and Thomas admonishes her to forsake the world. That night she refuses to eat or sleep with her husband, who has a symbolic dream about an eagle snatching a partridge from him. Mygdonia hints at the interpretation: the eagle is Thomas, and the partridge is herself. With a tense farewell, Carish goes to attend on the king, while Mygdonia seeks out Thomas. Later Carish confronts Mygdonia, and piteously entreats her to return to him. She instead prays to be delivered from him, and flees. After a bitter soliloquy, Carish complains to King Mizdai, who summons Sifor. While Thomas questions Mygdonia about her husband, the king questions the commander, who describes how Thomas healed his wife and daughter. The king authorizes Carish to arrest Thomas, who is interrogated, scourged, and imprisoned. The apostle offers a prayer of thanksgiving that echoes numerous gospel texts, then launches into a poetic reflection commonly entitled the *Hymn of the Pearl*. Carish returns home to find Mygdonia unkempt and in squalid attire. After emotional appeals to give up her religious folly, he tries to bargain Thomas's life for Mygdonia's love. She remains adamant. Still unbaptized and yearning to see Thomas, she takes money for bribes and hides from her husband.

In **Act 10** (chaps. 119–33), the conflict intensifies. While Mygdonia is in hiding with Marcia (or, in Syriac, Narkia), her nurse, Thomas comes to her. Marcia provides bread, water, and oil. Thomas blesses the oil, baptizes the two women, and celebrates the eucharist before returning to prison. Dawn finds Carish in a dramatic confrontation with Mygdonia while King Mizdai again interrogates Thomas. The king advises and Carish implores Thomas to convince Mygdonia to return to her husband. Thomas accompanies Carish to his home and advises Mygdonia to obey her husband, but she refuses. Thomas returns to Sifor, who requests baptism. The apostle preaches, baptizes, then celebrates the eucharist with Sifor and his family.

In **Act 11** (chaps. 134–38), Thomas gets into deeper trouble. Mizdai tells the story of Mygdonia to his own wife, Tertia, whom he urges to visit Mygdonia. Tertia complies, but Mygdonia preaches Thomas's gospel. Tertia, herself now enthralled, visits Thomas, then tries to evangelize the king. An exasperated Mizdai finds Carish, and together they seek to arrest Thomas.

In **Act 12** (chaps. 139–49), Thomas makes further important converts. Vizan, the king's son, assumes command of the soldiers guarding Thomas—only to have the apostle preach to him. Mizdai tries to interrogate Thomas under torture, but the instrument of torture, a set of hot slabs, is miraculously neutralized by a sudden flood, which threatens to submerge the area until stopped by Thomas's prayer. Thomas then bids his followers farewell and prays.

In **Act 13**, the final act (chaps. 150–71), which includes the **Martyrdom of Thomas** (chaps. 159–71), Vizan asks Thomas to visit his ailing wife. Mygdonia, Marcia, and Tertia, miraculously freed from imprisonment, come and—like the friends of Socrates—seek to take Thomas into exile. Tertia explains how they came to the prison, guided by a divine visitation. Thomas leads his visitors in prayer and song. Vizan, sent to bring necessities, meets his wife, Mnesara, miraculously healed and guided to the prison. All assemble at Vizan's house, where Mnesara recognizes Thomas as her healer. Thomas prays, blesses oil, then anoints and baptizes Vizan. Mygdonia baptizes Mnesara and Tertia. Thomas celebrates the eucharist, then returns to prison for a final farewell. After the guards report to Mizdai the strange comings and goings of the night, there follows another dramatic encounter between Mizdai and Thomas, reminiscent of that between Pilate and Jesus in John 18–19. The king orders Thomas to be removed and speared. Thomas compares his fate to that of Jesus, bids a final adieu to his friends, and prays before being slain. After his death he appears to several of his followers. Later still, Mizdai searches for Thomas's bones, with which he plans to heal his sick son. But they have been taken west; instead, the king uses dust from the tomb area to good effect. After Thomas appears to him, the king is brought to Sifor, now a presbyter, and requests prayers. The work ends on this happy note, when the persecutor is brought to the threshold of the persecuted community.

THE HYMNIC PASSAGES

Considerable attention has been devoted to the two major poetic sections, the *Hymn of the Bride* (chaps. 6–7) and the *Hymn of the Pearl* (chaps. 108–13). In both pieces, which were probably independent poems adapted to the *Acts of Thomas*, the rich but elusive symbolism has elicited a wide variety of readings.

The first poem, the *Hymn of the Bride*, which in the Syriac is an allegory of the church, begins with a description of a bride, the "daughter of light" (6:4), who is "glowing with radiant beauty" (6:5). The imagery becomes patently symbolic with the reference to her headgear consisting of "the King" (6:7) and "Truth" (6:8) (see in particular LaFargue, 1985). That the bride has some cosmic significance is suggested by the back of her neck, which is "like the steps which the First Craftsman made" (6:11), and of her hands, that "give signs and clues, heralding the blessed aeons' dance" (6:12). Together with seven groomsmen and bridesmaids she has twelve servants, all watching for the bridegroom in order to be admitted to "the banquet of the holy ones" (7:1–3). There they will put on royal garments and celebrate forever (7:4–7). In the meantime, they have received his ambrosial food and wine and have glorified "the Father of Truth and Mother of Wisdom" (7:8–10). The bride may indeed be meant to symbolize the community of the celibate faithful, although other interpretations are possible. In any case, she is probably related to the figure of Lady Wisdom (as in, e.g., Proverbs 7–8; Wisdom of Solomon 7–9), and to a forerunner of the Sophia-Pronoia (Wisdom-Insight) figure found in Gnostic writings. If so, she may represent the insight or the faith that enables its attendants to enter the heavenly banquet and put on the wedding garment.

The better known *Hymn of the Pearl* is introduced as a reflection by Thomas on his own fate. (The complex philological and interpretative issues are surveyed in Poirier, 1981; the most recent English translation of the Greek is in Layton, 1987: 366–75; Layton reads the poem as an allegory of the fate of the soul.) It tells of the quest by a prince who, as a child, is equipped and sent from an eastern kingdom to Egypt. His mission: to acquire "the one pearl which is there with the dragon, the devourer." His reward is to be invested with a special garment. So he travels to Egypt through Babylon (or to Egyptian Babylon, the Roman fortress at the site of Old Cairo) acquiring guides for the trip. In Egypt he disguises himself and takes an eastern prince as a companion. Although the prince warns his friend about Egyptian ways, he himself is overcome when the locals learn that he is a stranger. After tasting their food and drink, he enters the service of their king—forgetful of his mission. At home, the royal council hears of his plight and dispatches a letter recalling him to his task. This letter issues a dramatic summons: "Arise and awake from sleep . . . and remember that you are a son of kings. . . . Remember your splendid robe. . . . Recall the pearl for which you were sent to Egypt" (110:43–45). This sealed letter, which speaks and serves as an ambassador, evokes a response from the prince. He seizes the pearl and makes for home. At his approach, the promised royal garment appears. In it the prince perceives himself, and is reunited with his former glory. Suitably clad, he enters with the pearl into the presence of the king of kings.

Although the hymn is susceptible to various interpretations—many of which, the evidence shows, it received as it was adapted in successive contexts—probably its original purpose was as an allegory of the fate of the soul.

The soul (that is, the prince) is sent into the realm of materiality, where it experiences oblivion of its heavenly origin and destiny. Impelled by a message of heavenly origin, it completes its mission. In the royal garment, which the redactor who inserted the hymn may have associated with the wedding garment imagery of the earlier bridal hymn, the prince sees himself. Donning it apparently symbolizes reunion with the soul's heavenly counterpart or higher, pneumatic self. The poem reaches its climax when that salvific union is achieved.

LITURGICAL ELEMENTS

Initiation rituals figure in several episodes: in AcThom 25–27; 49; 121; 132; 157. In the first account, Thomas's preliminary prayer (chap. 25) refers to washing before anointing (25:4). The ritual itself consists only of an anointing, though perhaps two anointings are involved if the strange phrase, "sealing of the seal" (27:3), is meant to distinguish between the actions. After the anointing(s) comes an elaborate epiclesis (invocation of the divine) over the initiand. The Greek form specifically invokes the Spirit both in good Syrian style as "the merciful Mother" and, unusually, as "fellowship of the male." The next reference to initiation, in 49:3, is brief and provides little information. The last three cases (in chaps. 121; 132; 157) follow the common Syrian order of anointing *before* baptism.

The prominence given to the anointing, in the Syriac regularly called a "sign" (ܪܘܫܡܐ; PSTS, s.v. [col. 3987; CSD, p. 536a] gives a full range of technical and non-technical meanings), in the Greek a "seal" (σφραγίς) is striking. Slight differences in practice are apparent in these accounts, and this will occasion no surprise when it is noted that Syrian baptismal tradition will eventually distinguish as many as four anointings connected with baptism: first, the catechumenal "seal" (ܚܬܡܐ; PSTS, s.v. [col. 1410; CSD, p. 164a, b]); second, a "sign" or "mark" (ܪܘܫܡܐ) prior to the consecration of the water; third, the "anointing" proper (ܡܫܚ, ܡܫܝܚܘܬܐ; PSTS, s.vv. [col. 2241 ; CSD, pp. 305b, 306a]), just before the baptism; and fourth, the post-baptismal "imprint" (ܛܒܥ; PSTS, s.v. [col. 1429; CSD, p. 167a]; and see Brock, 1979: 23). But that system is not yet fully in place. Instead, the different anointings in the various sections of this writing may reflect different strata in the development of the baptismal ritual, an original anointing of the head later developing into an anointing of the entire body (so Winkler, 1978 and 1982; and see Brock, 1977). The differences may, however, be attributable to the gender of the initiands. As for the second, separate, whole-body anointing (see Myers, 1988), the elaborate description of a non-initiatory anointing involving the whole body in AcThom 5 apparently prefigures the religious initiations. This suggests that, at least at the final stage of redaction, the pre-baptismal anointing was understood to involve the whole body.

The significance of the initiation rite is expounded in various ways. (On the range of Syrian baptismal theologies, see Brock, 1979: 24–25, 37–69, 106–7). According to one explicit comment, it brings remission of sins, new birth, and participation in the spirit (132:1–2). Yet there are also indications of other interpretations. In the Syrian region the rite may originally have involved a bestowal of sonship or priestly status on the initiand, in imitation of Christ's own baptism. Later, under the influence of western ideas and practices ultimately inspired by Pauline theology, the rite was understood to be a purification through participation in the death and resurrection of Christ. In any case, the prayers accompanying the anointings in AcThom 121 and 157 associate the oil with Christ's cross, rather than with his messianic status, as does the epiclesis in AcThom 27. The anointing is said to cleanse and strengthen (AcThom 121). In some contexts, it serves an apotropaic function, that is, for the protection of the initiated from hostile forces (AcThom 25). All of these elements may be traditional. The primary significance of the pre-baptismal anointing within the theological perspective of the *Acts of Thomas* is suggested by the narrative of the wedding banquet scene in chap. 5. Although Thomas's action has a certain verisimilitude in the context of the "secular" banquet, the whole episode is patently symbolic of the true "bridal chamber" of celibacy to which Thomas calls converts. The pre-baptismal anointing may have been understood as a ritual connecting the initiand with the sacred marriage of the soul and its heavenly counterpart. (Bornkamm, 1933, stands as a landmark work in its insistence on the close relationship between narrative and actual ritual. For example, the "scented oil"—μύρον, as in Cant 1:3—can be shown in some instances to have strengthened the connection between baptismal and betrothal.)

The apostle celebrates the eucharist on various occasions (AcThom 27; 29; 49–50; 121; 133; 158). Wine is not regularly mentioned, appearing only in AcThom 158; indeed, at the request of Mygdonia, it is expressly excluded from the eucharist in AcThom 121, according to the Greek version. An epiclesis over the bread (50) repeats some of the unusual invocations of the epiclesis over the initiands in AcThom 27. Participation in the eucharist, like baptism, secures forgiveness of sins and spiritual empowerment (see AcThom 50; 133; 158).

THEOLOGICAL PERSPECTIVES

To sketch the theology of the work is a precarious undertaking, given the composite character of the whole and the constant redactional process evident in the *Acts of Thomas*. Yet while poems and liturgies have exotic elements, Thomas's teaching is generally familiar early Christian material. The major focus is the Savior, Jesus Christ, who combines divinity and humanity (see AcThom 48; 80), and who reduced himself to smallness (15; 123) to en-able humans to participate in the majesty of a new humanity (48). Through his prophetically proclaimed (59) suffering, death, and resurrection, he overcame the powers of death, entered Hades, and released its captives (10; 143; 156). He has come as the revealer of saving truth (25) and is expected as eschatological judge (28).

Acceptance of Christ and his apostle brings salvation from the inimical powers graphically portrayed in the exorcisms (AcThom 32), and ultimately from the punishments of hell described by one who had seen them (56–58). It also liberates the believer from ignorance and error (98), while providing knowledge of the origin and destiny of the self (15). The final goal of the soteriological process is frequently envisioned as eternal "rest" (e.g., in 27:8; 34:4; 39:10; 60:4).

Conversion entails a life of rigorous asceticism, particularly in sexual matters. The Christian rejects the transitory world and all its allurements in favor of the world above (AcThom 36–37). In particular, the Christian rejects the source of all ills, sexual intercourse, even in marriage (12; 28; 84; 126; 144). To be attached to Christ is to find the true bridegroom (14; 124) and is the basis for entry into the heavenly wedding feast. Although asceticism figures in most apocryphal acts narratives, the position taken in this work is extreme and probably reflects that of the encratite movement of which Tatian (active ca. 160 c.e.) and Julius Cassian (the author of a treatise *On Being a Eunuch*, of uncertain date) are the best known representatives. (On this dimension of the work, see further Tissot, 1980; Sfemani Gasparro, 1983; Burrus, 1987; P. Brown, 1988; and Wire, 1988.)

It is generally recognized that the classification of all the apocryphal acts as "Gnostic" (connected with the intellectual and religious movement) or even "gnostic" (emphasizing a saving *knowledge* rather than faith) is an oversimplification. The *Acts of Thomas* does have some elements that are gnostic in a general sense, such as the awareness of and eschatological union with one's true self (AcThom 15; also 113, in the *Hymn of the Pearl*). On the other hand, it lacks the cosmogonic myths characteristic of works that are Gnostic in the stricter sense. Instead, the work exhibits the mixture of theology, liturgy, and ascetical piety characteristic of Syrian Christianity of the third century.

THE "HISTORICAL" THOMAS:
PARTHIA AND INDIA

The *Acts of Thomas* is obviously a work of fiction, but it is reasonable to ask whether it has any historical basis and what connections it may have with Indian Christianity (on the whole topic, see L. Brown, 1982). It has long been noted that the first king whom Thomas encounters, Gundafar, bears the name of a historical individual (see already Gutschmid, 1864; Lipsius, 1883:

1. 278–81; Festugière, 1983: 45 n. 1). In fact, several kings bearing this name were members of a dynasty of Parthian origin that ruled in the Indus Valley region in the first century. The area over which Gundafar is said to rule may be of some significance, since it matches early traditions about the missionary assignment of Thomas, which was not India, but Parthia (Origen *Hom. 3 in Gen.*; Eusebius *Hist. eccl.* 3.1.1). The original setting of some of the adventures of Thomas was no doubt that eastern portion of Parthia, and represented an interest in such missionary activity by elements of the Syrian Church. Other figures in the text are less easy to connect with any particular locale, although the names of King Mizdai and his son Vizan would also be at home in Parthia.

Indications of other traditions can be seen in the document. It may be of significance that, after leaving Jerusalem, Thomas *sails* to his eastern destination, presumably from some Red Sea port. Such a route is quite compatible with conditions in the second century, when an active mercantile traffic connected Roman Egypt and the Malabar coast on the west side of India (see Dihle, 1963). The Alexandrian Christian teacher Pantaenus made the journey and discovered Christian communities in India supposedly founded by Bartholomew, not Thomas (Eusebius *Hist. eccl.* 5.10.3). What we may see in these acts is a symbolic appropriation of Bartholomew's mission field by Syrian Christians in the name of their hero, Judas Thomas. This hypothesis would also support dating the work to the third century, after the Egyptian-Indian connection had declined in importance for political reasons. It is impossible to say where, if anywhere, the historical Thomas conducted a mission, yet it is clear that Christianity spread to the realms envisioned in this story—Parthia and India—early in the history of the church. To that extent, at least, the work has a modicum of verisimilitude, if not historical veracity.

DATE

The major *Syriac* witness, B.M. add. [i.e., British Museum, addition] 14,645, was inscribed (that is, copied) in 936 C.E. The earliest Syriac manuscript, a fragmentary palimpsest—a text written "again" (*palin*) on a previously used piece of parchment, prepared by "rubbing" or "scraping" (*psēn*), as frequently in antiquity—and identified as Sinai 30 dates from the fifth or sixth century. The major *Greek* witnesses, P and U, date to the eleventh century, although there are partial Greek witnesses dating from the tenth. The work in some form was clearly circulating by the end of the fourth century, when testimonies begin. Epiphanius (*Pan.* 47.1; 60.1.5) records its use by Encratites; Augustine (*Serm. Dom.* 1.20.65; *Adim.* 17; *Faust.* 14; 22.79) attests to its use by Manichaeans; and allusions are found in the Manichaean psalms (*Manich. Psalm.* 192,15–16; 194,13 [Allberry]). Attestations continue sporadically until the ninth-century Byzantine patriarch Photius (*Bibliotheca*, cod. 114, on which see Junod, 1981) and the eleventh-century archbishop, Nicetas of Thessalonica, who paraphrased the work (see Bonnet, 1901: 159–64; Poirier, 1981: 300–301, 366–69).

The original composition is probably to be dated in the first half of the third century, slightly later than the *Acts of Peter*, *Acts of John*, and *Acts of Paul* (which are attested in the second century) and possibly later than the *Acts of Andrew* (which is also to be dated in the early third century; see most recently MacDonald, 2005: 7–9). Some sections, particularly the originally independent *Hymn of the Pearl*, presuppose conditions that obtained in the Parthian period, which ended with the establishment of the Sassanian empire in 226 C.E.

As mentioned previously, it is likely that this *Acts* underwent redactional development, including adaptation by Manichaeans, in the late third or fourth century. The extent of such Manichaean redaction has been variously assessed. The pioneering work on the subject was that of Bousset (1917–1918), who strongly influenced Bornkamm (1933). Subsequent studies have at least confirmed the use of the *Acts of Thomas* in Manichaean circles. The major elements reminiscent of Manichaean doctrine are found in the poetic compositions, and it is therefore possible that these were revised in the direction of Manichaeism prior to their incorporation into the work as a whole.

AUTHORSHIP AND PROVENANCE

According to Photius (in the *Bibliotheca*), all the major apocryphal acts (*Andrew, John, Paul, Peter*, and *Thomas*) were the work of one Leucius Charinus. While there may be reason to connect this otherwise unknown author with the *Acts of John* (Junod, in Bovon, 1981: 16–18), the other Acts are independent and anonymous compositions. Earlier studies conjectured some connection between the *Acts of Thomas* or the *Hymn of the Pearl* (AcThom 108–13) and the second-century Syrian theologian, Bardaisan (see Drijvers, 1966; Poirier, 1981: 38–166). But since the possible points of contact are few, the connection, though not inherently unlikely, is not demonstrable.

The work is clearly of Syrian provenance. Further, the hypothesis of an Edessan origin is not unreasonable, since Thomas was venerated there perhaps as early as the first half of the third century (see Klijn, 1962: 39–45). The martyrdom (AcThom 159–70) records the translation—the official removal—of his relics from India back to the West, presumably to Edessa. The celebrated pilgrim Egeria (or Etheria) writes of visiting his shrine there in the late 4th century (*Itin. Eger.* 17.1; 19.2; see Gingras, 1970; Wilkinson, 1981), and further evidence is provided by Ephrem (d. 373; see his *Carm. Nis.* 42.1). The *Acts of Thomas* has parallels in other Thomas literature of probable Syrian provenance, including the *Gospel of Thomas* (NHC II,5) and *The Book of Thomas the Athlete* (NHC II,7), discovered at Nag Hammadi, both of which rely on the notion that the apostle was Jesus' twin and both of which can be read as advocating a radical asceticism.

HOW TO USE THIS BOOK

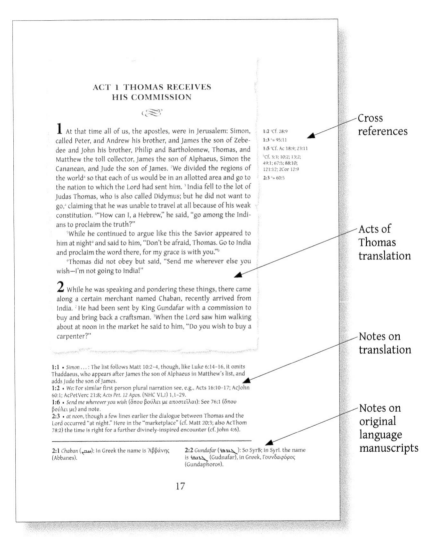

ACT 1 THOMAS RECEIVES
HIS COMMISSION

1 At that time all of us, the apostles, were in Jerusalem: Simon, called Peter, and Andrew his brother, and James the son of Zebedee and John his brother, Philip and Bartholomew, Thomas, and Matthew the toll collector, James the son of Alphaeus, Simon the Cananean, and Jude the son of James. ²We divided the regions of the world° so that each of us would be in an allotted area and go to the nation to which the Lord had sent him. ³India fell to the lot of Judas Thomas, who is also called Didymus; but he did not want to go,ᵃ claiming that he was unable to travel at all because of his weak constitution. ⁴"How can I, a Hebrew," he said, "go among the Indians to proclaim the truth?"

⁵While he continued to argue like this the Savior appeared to him at nightᵃ and said to him, "Don't be afraid, Thomas. Go to India and proclaim the word there, for my grace is with you."ᵇ

⁶Thomas did not obey but said, "Send me wherever else you wish—I'm not going to India!"

2 While he was speaking and pondering these things, there came along a certain merchant named Chaban, recently arrived from India. ²He had been sent by King Gundafar with a commission to buy and bring back a craftsman. ³When the Lord saw him walking about at noon in the market he said to him, "Do you wish to buy a carpenter?"

Cross references

Acts of Thomas translation

Notes on translation

Notes on original language manuscripts

1:2 ᶜCf. 28:9
1:3 ᵃ ᵇ 95:11
1:5 ᵃCf. Ac 18:9; 23:11
ᵇCf. 3:3; 10:2; 13:2;
49:1; 67:5; 88:10;
121:12; 2Cor 12:9
2:3 ᵃ ᵇ 60:5

1:1 • *Simon . . .* : The list follows Matt 10:2–4, though, like Luke 6:14–16, it omits Thaddaeus, who appears after James the son of Alphaeus in Matthew's list, and adds Jude the son of James.
1:2 • *We*: For similar first person plural narration see, e.g., Acts 16:10–17; AcJohn 60:1; AcPetVerc 21:8; Acts Pet. 12 Apos. (NHC VI,1) 1,1–29.
1:6 • *Send me wherever you wish* (ὅπου βούλει με ἀποστεῖλαι): See 76:1 (ὅπου βούλει με) and note.
2:3 • *at noon*, though a few lines earlier the dialogue between Thomas and the Lord occurred "at night." Here in the "marketplace" (cf. Matt 20:3; also AcThom 78:2) the time is right for a further divinely-inspired encounter (cf. John 4:6).

2:1 *Chaban* (ܚܒܢ): In Greek the name is Ἀββάνης (Abbanes).   **2:2** *Gundafar* (ܓܘܢܕܦܪ): So SyrB; in SyrL the name is ܓܘܕܢܦܪ (Gudnafar), in Greek, Γουνδαφόρος (Gundaphoros).

17

ACT 1 THOMAS RECEIVES
HIS COMMISSION

1 At that time all of us, the apostles, were in Jerusalem: Simon, called Peter, and Andrew his brother, and James the son of Zebedee and John his brother, Philip and Bartholomew, Thomas, and Matthew the toll collector, James the son of Alphaeus, Simon the Cananean, and Jude the son of James. ²We divided the regions of the world[a] so that each of us would be in an allotted area and go to the nation to which the Lord had sent him. ³India fell to the lot of Judas Thomas, who is also called Didymus; but he did not want to go,[a] claiming that he was unable to travel at all because of his weak constitution. ⁴"How can I, a Hebrew," he said, "go among the Indians to proclaim the truth?"

⁵While he continued to argue like this the Savior appeared to him at night[a] and said to him, "Don't be afraid, Thomas. Go to India and proclaim the word there, for my grace is with you."[b]

⁶Thomas did not obey but said, "Send me wherever else you wish—I'm not going to India!"

2 While he was speaking and pondering these things, there came along a certain merchant named Chaban, recently arrived from India. ²He had been sent by King Gundafar with a commission to buy and bring back a craftsman. ³When the Lord saw him walking about at noon in the market he said to him, "Do you wish to buy a carpenter?"

1:2 ᵃCf. 28:9
1:3 ᵃ» 95:11
1:5 ᵃCf. Ac 18:9; 23:11
ᵇCf. 3:3; 10:2; 13:2; 49:1; 67:5; 88:10; 121:12; 2Cor 12:9
2:3 ᵃ» 60:5

1:1 • *Simon...*: The list follows Matt 10:2–4, though, like Luke 6:14–16, it omits Thaddaeus, who appears after James the son of Alphaeus in Matthew's list, and adds Jude the son of James.

1:2 • *We:* For similar first person plural narration see, e.g., Acts 16:10–17; AcJohn 60:1; AcPetVerc 21:8; *Acts Pet. 12 Apos.* (NHC VI,1) 1,1–29.

1:6 • *Send me wherever you wish* (ὅπου βούλει με ἀποστεῖλαι): See 76:1 (ὅπου βούλει με) and note.

2:3 • *at noon*, though a few lines earlier the dialogue between Thomas and the Lord occurred "at night." Here in the "marketplace" (cf. Matt 20:3; also AcThom 78:2) the time is right for a further divinely-inspired encounter (cf. John 4:6).

2:1 *Chaban* (ܚܒܢ): In Greek the name is Ἀββάνης (Abbanes).

2:2 *Gundafar* (ܓܘܢܕܦܪ): So SyrB; in SyrL the name is ܓܘܕܢܦܪ (Gudnafar), in Greek, Γουνδαφόρος (Gundaphoros).

2:7 ᵃ» 143:6
2:11 ᵃ» 8:1; 106:7
3:1 ᵃCf. 30:3; 144:2;
Mt 6:10; Lk 22:42;
AJn 18:5
3:3 ᵃ» 1:5
3:6 ᵃCf. 147:2
3:7 ᵃCf. 17:5

⁴"Yes," he answered.

⁵Then the Lord told him, "I have a slave who's a carpenter, and I want to sell him."

⁶He showed him Thomas, some distance away, and settled with him on the price of three bars of unstamped silver. ⁷He drafted a bill of sale that read, "I, Jesus, son of Joseph the carpenter,ᵃ agree to sell my slave, Judas by name, to you, Chaban, a merchant of Gundafar, King of India." ⁸When the paperwork was complete, the Savior took Judas, called Thomas, and brought him to Chaban the merchant.

⁹When Chaban saw him he said to him, "Is this your master?"

¹⁰"Yes, he is, my lord," the apostle responded.

¹¹Chaban said, "I've bought you from him." The apostle kept quiet.ᵃ

3 Early on the following day the apostle prayed and begged the Lord: "All right—I'll go where you want, Lord Jesus; enact your will."ᵃ ²He went off to Chaban the merchant bringing nothing at all with him except his purchase price. ³For the Lord had given it to him and said, "Let your value, with my grace, be with you wherever you go."ᵃ

⁴The apostle caught up with Chaban as he was carrying his baggage onto the boat, so he began to give him a hand. ⁵When they had embarked and were settled, Chaban asked the apostle, "So, what kind of things do you make?"

⁶The apostle answered, "With wood I make plows,ᵃ yokes, scales, ships, ships' oars, masts, and wheels. ⁷With stone I make monuments, shrines, and royal residences."ᵃ

⁸The merchant Chaban said, "We certainly need such a craftsman."

⁹They then set sail with a favorable wind and proceeded rapidly until they reached Andrapolis, a royal city.

3:3 • *Let your value:* This comment, lacking in Syr, involves a wordplay between τίμημα ("price, purchase price," see v. 2) and τιμή ("value, honor"); see also 165:2.
3:6 • *plows, yokes:* In InfThom 13:1, Joseph is described as making such items.
3:9 • *Andrapolis* (Ἀνδράπολις), that is, "City of Men" (the name is given only here). The Syriac ܣܢܕܪܘܟ ("Sandrok") lacks the symbolic significance of the Greek. Ancient tradition told of an Indian ruler named Sandrocottus (Σανδρόκοττος) at the time of Seleucus Nicator (d. ca. 280 B.C.E.); he was head of the Gangaridae, or Prasii, on the banks of the Ganges. Plutarch (*Alexander* 62) and Appian (*Syria* 55) give his name without the initial "s," as *Androcottus*.

2:6 *three bars:* Syr "twenty pieces," except SyrB "thirty pieces." "Thirty pieces" recalls Matt 26:15 (from Zech 11:12; cf. Exod 21:32); for "twenty pieces," see Gen 37:28; AcAndGE 18b:42.

4 They disembarked and entered the city to the sounds of flautists, organists, and trumpeters. [2]The apostle asked, "What's the festival going on in this city?"

[3]The local people replied, "The gods have brought you to this city to be entertained. [4]For the king has an only child, a daughter—at this very moment he's giving her away in marriage. [5]What you see today is the joyful wedding celebration. [6]The king has sent heralds to make a general proclamation: Everyone is to attend the wedding—rich and poor, slave and free, aliens and citizens.[a] [7]If anyone refuses to attend,[a] that person will be answerable to the king."

[8]When Chaban heard this he said to the apostle, "We should go, too, so we don't offend the king, especially since we are strangers"; to which the apostle said, "Certainly."

[9]So after unpacking at the inn and resting for a while they went off to the wedding. [10]When the apostle saw everyone sit down to eat, he, too, joined their company, while everyone stared at him, a stranger come from a foreign land. [11]Chaban the merchant, since he was a master, sat down to eat elsewhere.

5 While everyone else ate and drank the apostle tasted nothing. [2]So the surrounding guests said, "Why did you come here if you're not going to eat or drink?"[a]

[3]"I've come here," he answered, "for something more important than food or drink[a]—to do the will of the king, of course. [4]Heralds announce the king's proclamation, and whoever doesn't obey the heralds is subject to the king's judgment!"

[5]When they had finished eating and drinking, garlands and precious oils were brought out. [6]Each guest took some lotion: one wiped his face with it, another his beard, others some other parts of their bodies. [7]The apostle wiped the top of his head, drew the lotion down to his nostrils, daubed it into his ears, applied it to his teeth, and carefully wiped the area around his heart. [8]He then took the wreath offered him, woven of myrtle and other flowers, and placed it on his head. [9]He also took and held in his hand a bamboo reed.[a] [10]Meanwhile a flute girl, instrument in hand, mingled with

4:6 [a]Cf. 83:3; 129:3; Gal 3:28

4:7 [a]Cf. Mt 22:1–14; Lk 14:16–24; Th (NHC II,2) 64: 44,10–35

5:2 [a]Cf. 96:6; Mt 11:18; Lk 7:33

5:3 [a]Cf. Mt 6:25; Lk 12:23; Jn 4:34

5:9 [a]Cf. Mt 27:28–29

5:3 • *the will of the king:* The comment is ironic, since Thomas has come to do the will of a heavenly king, not simply fulfill the command of an earthly king; cf. 18:13. Thomas and the other apostles are the "heralds" (5:4 οἱ κήρυκες) of their king.

5:5 • *garlands and precious oils . . . :* This anointing, although done with scented oil, likely foreshadows the initiation rituals in AcThom 26–27; 121; 132; 157.

6:1 [a] Cf. 116:1
[b] Cf. Mt 26:68; Mk 14:65; Jn 18:22; 19:3
6:2 [a] Cf. Lk 23:39–43
[b] » 8:10
6:6 [a] Cf. 6:14
6:7 [a] Cf. OdSol 1:1, 4; 5:12
[b] Cf. 7:8; 36:10; OdSol 1:5
6:8 [a] Cf. OdSol 1:2; 9:8
6:12 [a] Cf. AJn 94–102

the guests and played. [11]When she came to the apostle's place, she stood at his head and played for a full hour. Now, that flute girl was a Hebrew.

6 The apostle was still as he was, staring at the ground,[a] when one of the wine-pourers raised his hand and slapped him.[a] [2]The apostle looked up, stared at his attacker and said, "My God will forgive you this unrighteous act in the world to come,[a] but in this world he will manifest his wonderful powers: I'll soon see this hand that struck me dragged along by dogs!"[b] [3]And having said that he began to sing, intoning this poem:

> [4]The young woman is light's daughter;
>> the radiance of kings has come to rest on her.
> [5]Pleasant is the sight of her;
>> it glows with beauty bright.
> [6]Her garments, like the flowers of spring,
>> give off a fragrant scent.[a]
> [7]The king is stationed at her head:[a]
>> he feeds with his ambrosial food[b]
>> those stationed under him.
> [8]Truth also rests on her head,[a]
>> while with her feet she shows her joy.
> [9]Her mouth is open wide, as suits her well,
>> Two and thirty sing hymns to her.
> [10]Her tongue, a curtain at the door,
>> is shaken by all who enter.
> [11]Her neck lies like the steps
>> that the First Craftsman made.
> [12]Her hands—they give signs and clues
>> heralding the blessed aeons' dance.[a]
> [13]Her fingers point out
>> the city's gates.

6:9 • *two and thirty,* presumably the young woman's teeth. The significance of the symbol is obscure; Syr makes them twelve apostles (see 7:3) and seventy-two disciples.

6:4 *light's daughter:* Syr "my Church."
6:7 *under him,* reading ὑπ' αὐτοῦ for ἐπ' αὐτῷ ("on him"), with Syr.

¹⁴Her bridal chamber is full of light,
 of balsam, redolent of every fragrant spice,^a
 giving off sweet aromas from the myrrh
 and from the clove.
¹⁵It is strewn inside with myrtle
 and sweet petals of every kind;
 the doors decorated with bamboo reeds.

7 Around her are her groomsmen,
 in number seven, whom she chose.
²Her bridesmaids, too, are seven,
 and they dance before her.
³Twelve serve before her and support her,
 keeping watch and looking for the groom,
 so they may be illumined at his sight.
⁴They will be with him forever in joy eternal,
 and in that wedding feast
 where great ones are assembled.
⁵They will remain in that banqueting
 of which eternal ones are worthy.
⁶Royal garments they will don
 and put on gleaming stoles,^a
 and in joy and festive gladness both will be.
⁷They will glorify the Father of the worlds,
 whose exultant light they have received;
 yes, they have been illumined by their master's sight.

6:14 ^a» 6:6
7:6 ^aCf. 36:11;
108–110; APaTh 38:6;
GPh (NHC II,3) 59:
67,19–22

6:14 • *bridal chamber* (also in 12:9; 124:11): Wedding imagery appears in the NT, e.g., in Matt 9:15; 22:10; 25:1–12; Mark 2:19; Luke 5:34; John 2:1–11. The "bridal chamber" is a soteriological symbol in Hellenistic Judaism; see, e.g., *Jos. Asen.* 15.7 "(Penitence) has prepared a heavenly bridal chamber for those who love her" (note variant reading: "place of rest"). Christians followed in referring to the bridal chamber as the place of union between the soul and its heavenly spouse. That place was understood either as heaven or as the baptismal font; see, e.g., Thom (NHC II,2) 75: 46,11–13; *Gos. Phil.* (NHC II,3) 59: 67,9–26; 67–68: 69,4–70,4; 83: 74,12–24; *Tri. Trac.* (NHC I,5) 122,12–24; and Syrian sources such as Ephrem (d. 373) *De fide* 4.8.
7:1 • *Around her . . . :* This verse and the next involve astral symbolism in the Greek. The heavenly bridal chamber is surrounded by seven planets and the twelve signs of the zodiac.
7:4 • *assembled:* For the heavenly wedding banquet, inspired by Matt 22:1–14, see also 12:9; 146:7.

7:8 ªCf. 6:7

ᵇCf. Jn 6:27

7:9 ªCf. Jn 4:13

7:10 ª» 26:4

ᵇCf. 27:6; 39:17; 50:5; 110:41; 133:4

8:1 ª» 2:11

8:2 ªCf. AAnMt 28:9; APaMar 5:6

8:4 ªCf. APaTh 20:6

8:9 ªCf. Th (NHC II,2) 7: 33,23–28

8:10 ªCf. 6:2; AAnPas 22:5

ᵇCf. 115:8

9:3 ªCf. 68:4; 102:3; 105:2; APaTh 18:2

ᵇCf. 20:5; InTh 17:2; TAdd f.3a

[8]They have received His ambrosial food,[a]
    food that has no waste at all.[b]
[9]They have also drunk the wine
    that brings them no thirst or longing.[a]
        [10]They have given praise and glory, the spirit that is living,
        to the Father ever truthful[a] and the Mother ever wise.[b]

8 When he had finished singing this poem, all the guests looked at him; but he kept quiet.[a] [2]They noticed his changed appearance but did not understand what he had said, since he was a Hebrew and had spoken in Hebrew.[a] [3]The flute player alone understood everything, since she, too, was a Hebrew. [4]Standing apart from him she played for the others, but frequently glanced back at him and kept watching him,[a] for she loved him dearly as her fellow countryman. [5](He was also more handsome in appearance than anyone else present.) [6]When the flute girl finished playing, she sat down opposite him and stared at him. [7]For his part he did not look at or pay attention to anyone, but kept his eyes fixed on the ground, waiting for someone to release him from the spot.

[8]Now the same wine-pourer who had slapped him went down to the well to draw water. [9]A lion happened to be there—and it killed him, tore him apart, and left his limbs lying right there.[a] [10]Dogs immediately took his limbs away;[a] and one, a black one, holding the right hand[b] in its mouth, brought it into the banquet chamber.

9 Seeing this, everyone was amazed and asked who among them was missing. [2]When it became clear that the hand belonged to the wine-pourer who had slapped the apostle, the flautist broke her flutes and threw them down. [3]She went over to the apostle, sat at his feet,[a] and said, "This man is either a god or an emissary of God;[b] for I heard him say to the wine-pourer in Hebrew, 'I shall soon see the hand that struck me dragged by dogs.' [4]And that's precisely what you've now seen—it happened just as he said." [5]Now some people believed her, but others did not.

7:8 • *food that has no waste:* The notion that heavenly food produces no excrement is clearer in Syr. According to Valentinus, as quoted in Clement of Alexandria *Strom.* 3.7.59, Jesus did not defecate.
9:5 • *some people believed:* For the rhetorical "some" (rather than "all") believing, see also 141:6 (but cf. 163:8); AcJohn 18:3; 22:8; 30:7; and already Rom 11:14.

⁶When the king heard all this, he came in and addressed the apostle: "Get up, come with me, and pray for my daughter; she's my only child and today I shall give her away."

⁷The apostle did not want to go along with him, because the Lord had not yet appeared to him there, but the king led him off reluctantly to the bridal chamber, so he might pray for them.

10 The apostle stood, then, and began to pray:

> My Lord and my God,[a] who accompanies his servants,
>> who leads and guides those who believe in him;
> ²refuge and rest of the afflicted,
>> the hope of the poor[a] and redeemer of the imprisoned;
> ³the healer of souls laid low by disease
>> and savior of all creation,
>> who gives life to the world and strength to human souls:
> ⁴You understand what things are to be,

10:1 [a]Cf. 81:1; 144:5; 167:2; Jn 20:28
10:2 [a]Cf. Jb 5:16

10:2 • *refuge . . . rest . . . hope . . . redeemer:* καταφυγή, ἀνάπαυσις, ἐλπίς (cf. 1 Tim 1:1), λυτρωτής (twice in the Greek Bible: of God in Ps 18:15; 77:35; of Moses in Acts 7:35). The same four epithets appear together in 60:4, except with βοηθός ("helper"; cf. *1 Clem.* 36:1, and of God in Heb 13:6; *1 Clem.* 59:3) instead of ἐλπίς; similarly, 156:1. In 167:2, a nearly equivalent set of terms is found: ἐλπίς, λυτρωτής, ἡγεμών ("ruler, governor, prefect"), ὁδηγός ("guide"; cf. 10:1 " who guides"); and as in 10:1–2, the list is preceded by the invocation, " My Lord and my God."

10:3 • *healer of souls:* Jesus is referred to as "healer" in 37:7; 143:3; 156:3 (see also AcAndGE 33:7; AcJohn 22:3; 108:2), and in another three places as "healer of souls" (10:3; 95:8; 156:14; see also AcPetVerc 1:6, of Paul).

The concept of "the cure of the soul" (ἰατρεία ψυχῆς), found, e.g., in Aristotle, Plato, Plutarch, rather than, or in addition to, the cure of the body, quickly found its way into Christian usage, along with the simple epithet "physician" or "healer" applied to God or to Jesus Christ; for the latter see, e.g., Ignatius *Eph.* 7:2; *Diogn.* 9.6; Ps.-Justin *De res.* 10 "our physician, Jesus Christ"; Clement of Alexandria *Paed.* 1.2 "the paternal Word is the only Paeonian [= divinely healing] physician of human infirmities, and the holy charmer of the sick soul"; Origen *C. Cels.* 2.67 "our Savior Lord, like a good physician, came to us who were full of sins."

The full title, "*healer* of souls," or its equivalent is found in contemporary Hellenistic literature, e.g., Plato *Prot.* 313E "unless one happens to be schooled in the health of the soul (περὶ τὴν ψυχὴν ἰατρικὸς ὤν)"; Philo *Sac.* 70.7: God is "the only physician for the diseases of the soul (τὸν μόνον ἰατρὸν ψυχῆς ἀρρωστημάτων)"; Plutarch *De tranq.* 465D "physician of the soul (ψυχῆς ἰατρός)"; Diogenes Laertius *Lives* 3.45: Plato is the ἰητὴρ ψυχῆς. This epithet was gradually taken up by early Christian writers; see, e.g., Origen *Comm. in Matt.* 13.5.6 (commenting on the request in Matt 17:15, "Master, have mercy on my son") "the father of the epileptic prays the Physician of souls for his son"; Cyril of Jerusalem *Cat.* 10.13: Jesus is "physician of souls and bodies (ἰατρὸς ψυχῶν καὶ σωμάτων)"; 12.8; *Acts Pet. 12 Apos.* (NHC VI,1) 11,18; *Liturgy of St. Mark* (Brightman, 1896: 127).

10:5 ªCf. 27:7; 47:3;
165:3; Th (NHC II,2)
proem.: 32,10–14;
AAnGE 18b:26

10:6 ªCf. Mt 7:17–19;
Lk 6:43

10:8 ªCf. 60:4; 87:3;
136:6; Mt 16:16

ᵇ» 44:7

10:9 ª» 156:2

ᵇCf. 156:4; 1Pt 3:19

10:10 ª» 80:1

10:12 ªCf. 29:9; 49:1,
4; 54:4

ᵇ» 1:5

11:3 ªCf. AAnPas
47:1; APaTh 21:4

and bring them to completion through us;

[5]You, Lord, reveal hidden mysteries,

and disclose secret words;[a]

[6]You, Lord, tend the good tree,[a]

and through your hands

all good works are generated;

[7]You, Lord, are in all things, pervade all things,

are present in all your works,

and become manifest

through the activity of all things.

[8]Jesus Christ, compassionate Son and perfect Savior,

Christ, Son of the living God,[a]

undaunted power that has overthrown the enemy;[b]

[9]Voice[a] that has been heard by the rulers,

that has shaken all of their powers,

ambassador sent from on high

who has descended as far as Hades;[b]

[10]You who have opened the doors,

and led up from there those who for long ages

have been locked in the storehouse of darkness,

and have shown them the way that ascends on high:[a]

[11]I ask you, Lord Jesus, I bring my petition to you on behalf of these youths:

that you do what is helpful, suitable, and beneficial for them."

[12]He then laid his hands on them [a] and said, "The Lord be with you.[b]

Then he left them in that place and went on his way.

11 Now the king asked the wedding attendants to come out of the bridal chamber. [2]When everyone had come and the doors were locked, the groom lifted the veil of the bridal chamber to take the bride to himself. [3]But he saw, speaking with the bride, the Lord Jesus, in the guise of Judas Thomas[a]—the apostle who had just now blessed them and left them! [4]So the groom said to him, "Didn"t you leave before everyone else? How is it that you're still here?"

10:7 *... of all things:* Here Syr has additional material; see the Apendix.

[5]The Lord said to him, "I'm not Judas who is also Thomas; I'm his brother."[a]

[6]The Lord sat down on the bed, ordered them to sit on the chairs, and began to speak to them:

12 "Remember, my children, what my brother told you and to whom he commended you. [2]Know this, that if you abandon this sordid intercourse, you'll become holy temples,[a] pure, freed from afflictions and pains, both visible and hidden, and you'll not take on the troubles of livelihood or children,[b] the final result of which is destruction. [3]It's so, isn't it? If you have many children, because of them you become thieves and cheats, beating orphans and defrauding widows, and when you do such things you subject yourselves to dreadful punishments.[a] [4]Not only that, but most children turn out to be useless, afflicted by demons—some openly, some in secret: they're either epileptic, half-withered, lame, deaf, dumb, paralytic, or foolish. [5]And if they do happen to be healthy, they'll be unproductive anyway, doing useless or dreadful things. [6]Perhaps they'll be involved in adultery, murder, theft, or fornication; you, too, will be tormented by all these things. [7]But if you obey and keep your souls pure for God, you'll have living children—no harm can touch them.[a] [8]You'll also be carefree, living an undisturbed life, without grief or anxiety, waiting to welcome the imperishable, the true marriage. [9]You'll be members of the wedding party who go into that bridal chamber[a] which is full of immortality and light."

13 When the young people heard this they believed the Lord and pledged themselves as given to him: they refrained from filthy desire and spent the night in that place accordingly. [2]The Lord left their company, saying, "The grace of the Lord be with you."[a]

[3]At dawn the king entered, laid out a breakfast table, and set it before the groom and bride. [4]He found them sitting opposite one another, the face of the bride uncovered and the groom obviously happy. [5]But when her mother approached she said to the bride, "Why do you sit so, child, and show no shame but act as if you've lived with your husband for a long time?"

11:5 [a]Cf. 160:1
12:2 [a]Cf. 1Cor 3:16–17; 6:19; 2Cor 6:16; AAnPas 56:10
[b]Cf. 32:9; 88:6; 126:5
12:3 [a]Cf. 126:5; AJn 34:3; AAnPas 56:10
12:7 [a]Cf. 28:4
12:9 [a]» 6:14
13:2 [a]Cf. 1:5; 49:1; Rm 16:20; 1Cor 16:23; 1Ths 5:28

12:2 • *the final result of which is destruction* (ὧν τὸ τέλος ἀπώλεια): The Greek phrase likely derives from Phil 3:19; see also AcThom 33:2.
13:1 • *young people*, taking the masculine plural νεώτεροι to be of common gender but specific reference; otherwise "young men" or "young people (present)."

14:1 ᵃCf. AAnPas 23:6
14:7 ᵃCf. 124:13

[6]Her father added, "Is it because of your great love for your husband that you don't cover yourself?"

14 The bride responded, "Truly, father, I'm deeply in love.[a] [2]I pray to my Lord that the love I've felt tonight may remain with me, and I'll ask for the husband I recognized today. [3]So I'll no longer remain covered, since the garment of shame has been taken away from me. [4]I'm no longer ashamed or embarrassed, since the shameful and embarrassing deed has departed far from me; nor am I terrified, since there's no terror left in me. [5]Instead I'm joyful and glad, since the joyful day hasn't been disturbed. [6]I've come to despise this man, and this wedding celebration that fades before my very eyes, now that I've been united in another marriage. [7]I've not had intercourse with a husband who passes away—something that ends up in lewdness and bitterness of soul—because now I've been joined to a real husband."[a]

15 The bride went on in this vein.
[2]Then the groom joined in:

> I give thanks to you, Lord,
>   who were proclaimed through the stranger
>   and found among us;
> [3]who distanced me from corruption,
>   and sowed life in me;
> [4]who released me from this eternally lingering disease
>   that is so difficult to treat or cure,
>   and provided me with chaste health;
> [5]who showed yourself to me,
>   and revealed to me everything about my condition;
> [6]who rescued me from disaster,
>   and led me to what is better;

15:2 • *I give thanks:* For prayers of thanksgiving with εὐχαριστεῖν, see also 19:7; 60:6; 94:2; 107:2; 145:1 (v.l. ἐξομολογεῖσθαι) .
15:6 • *from disaster,* literally, "from the fall" (ἀπὸ τῆς πτώσεως). But here πτῶσις suggests misfortune (as in Sir 3:31; Luke 2:34; cf. πταῖσμα in AcAndPas 37:12)

14:3 *garment of shame:* The shorter Gr recension (mss A CD FTX PUY QR S), much abbreviated in this chapter, agrees with Syr in reading τὸ ἔνδυμα τῆς αἰσχύνης. The longer Gr recension has τὸ ἔσοπτρον τῆς αἰσχύνης, "mirror of shame" (cf. 112:76). For the "garment of shame" motif, see also Thom (NHC II,2) 37: 39,27–40,2 and the fragment of the *Gospel of the Egyptians*, quoted in Clement of Alexandria *Strom.* 3.91, which speaks of a time "when you have trampled on the garment of shame and when the two become one and the male with the female is neither male nor female."

15:14 ^aCf. AAnPas 65:1; APeVer 21:14

[7]who have released me from what is temporary,
    and instead have made me worthy
    of things that are immortal and exist forever;
[8]who humbled yourself to me and my smallness,
    so that, by introducing me to majesty,
    you might unite me with yourself;
[9]who did not withhold your mercy from me
    when I was perishing,
    but showed me how to seek after myself
    and to know who I was,
[10]who I am, and how I exist in the present,
    so that I might again become what I was.
[11]You whom I didn't know
    have sought me out;
[12]you whom I haven't grasped—
    you have taken hold of me.

[13]The one I've come to perceive—I can't forget him now. [14]His love throbs inside me, and I cannot speak as I should: all that I'm able to say is brief, altogether paltry, and inadequate to his glory.[a] [15]But I can't be blamed for speaking to him—shamelessly, it must seem—about things I don't really understand, because it's his love that makes me speak as I do.

16 When the king heard this testimony from the groom and the bride, he tore his clothing and said to his guards nearby, "Go out, quickly, and make the rounds of the whole city. [2]Arrest and bring

---

rather than a developed doctrine of "the fall." Its cognate, πτῶμα, which means both "fall" and "corpse" (for the second sense see AcThom 30:1), is used by contemporary writers to refer to Adam's sin, e.g., Hippolytus *De antichr.* 64 " 'Wherever there's a *corpse*, that's where vultures gather' [= Matt 24:28]. Now the *fall* took place in paradise"; Methodius *Symp.* 3.6 "Humankind suffered a terrible and destructive *fall*."

15:8 • *smallness, majesty:* This recurrent contrast of humanity and divinity (see also 80:6; 123:4; 143:7; 159:3) is common in Syriac sources; see, e.g., *Od. Sol.* 7:3; *T. Addai* f. 6a (Howard, 1981: 17; also quoted in Eusebius *Hist. eccl.* 1.13.20).

15:10 • *what I was:* The sentence recalls the often-quoted gnostic extract reported in Clement of Alexandria *Exc. Theod.* 78.2 "Who were we? What have we become? Where were we? Where have we been thrown? Where do we hasten? From what have we been set free?"; and the plot of the *Hymn of the Pearl*, in Ac-Thom 108–110.

16:1 • *tore his clothing* (τὸν ἐσθῆτα αὐτοῦ διέρρηξεν), possibly as a sign of grief (see Gen 37:29; Jdth 14:19; Esth 4:1) but more likely of anger (see Matt 26:65; Mark 14:65; Acts 14:14); see also AcThom 63:7.

16:2 • *that sorcerer:* The charge of being a sorcerer (φαρμακός) is frequent; see

me that sorcerer who by some ill chance has come to this city. ³To think that with my own hands I led him into my house!—and I myself told him to pray for my ill-fated daughter! ⁴To the man who finds and brings him to me I'll give whatever he asks."

⁵So they went out searching, but they did not find him, because he had sailed away. ⁶But when they went to the inn where he had lodged, they discovered the flute girl there, weeping and grieving because he had not taken her along with him. ⁷They related to her what had happened to the youths, and she heard this with great joy; so that, putting aside her grief, she said, "Now I, too, have found repose here." ⁸She got up to accompany them and was with them a long time, until they had informed the king as well. ⁹Many of the believers were still gathered there, until they heard a report that the apostle had been conveyed to the cities of India and was teaching there. ¹⁰At that they went off and joined him.

ACT 2 THOMAS'S AUDIENCE WITH KING GUNDAFAR

17 When the apostle came to the cities of India with Chaban the merchant, Chaban went to greet King Gundafar and told him of the carpenter he had brought along. The king was very pleased, and had him brought in. ²So when he arrived, the king asked, "What kind of craft do you know?"

³"Carpentry and construction," the apostle said.

⁴"What kind of things can you make in wood and in stone?" asked the king.

⁵The apostle said, "In wood I make plows, yokes, scales, pulleys, ships, oars, and masts; in stone monuments, temples—and royal residences!"ª

98:2; 99:7, 10; 107:3; 114:6; 116:6; 117:7; 123:7; 130:11; 134:3, 6; 138:3; 162:1, 5. For the charge of being a wizard (μάγος), see 20:4; also AcPaulThec 15:3; AcAndGE 12:14; 22:3. Perhaps in defiant tone the eucharist is termed "the medicine of life" (φάρμακον τῆς ζωῆς) in 135:7, though this term or its equivalent is already in common Christian use.

16:9 • *believers*: ἀδελφοί "brothers." But the Greek can include both men and women, and here denotes fellow-believers, i.e., Christians. See also 27:2; 29:7; 60:1; 66:1; 68:3; 88:1 (followed by "sisters"); 159:2 (see note); 169:7; 170:7, 10, 11. The plural participle, "believers," occurs only in 27:15 (see note).

18:4 ªCf. 121:7; 140:12; 141:1

⁶"Will you build me a palace?" the king said.

⁷"Yes, I'll build it, and do the finishing work," the apostle answered. "That's the reason I came <here>—to build and do carpentry."

18 The king took him along and went outside the city gates. ²On the way, he began to discuss with him the construction of the residence and how the foundations were to be laid, until they came to the spot where he wanted the building. ³Once there, he said, "Here's where I want the building to be."

⁴The apostle said, "Yes, this place is suitable for the building." Now that area was forested, and had water in abundance.ª

⁵So the king said, "Start building!"

⁶"I can't start building right away," the apostle replied.

⁷"When," the king asked, "will you be able to do so?"

⁸"I'll begin in October, and finish in April."

⁹The king said in amazement, "All building takes place during the summer! Can you build and establish a palace in winter?"

¹⁰To this the apostle said: "It must be so, and not otherwise."

¹¹"Well then," the king said, "if this is what you have decided, diagram for me how the work will go, since it will be some time till I come back."

¹²The apostle took a reed, measured the site, and made a diagram: he set the main doors on the east to look toward the light; the windows in the west toward the winds, the kitchen in the

---

17:7 • *finishing work* is a double entendre: Thomas "finishes" woodwork and "perfects" souls.

17:7 • *That's the reason I came <here>:* διὰ τοῦτο ἦλθον, in the NT only at John 1:31; 12:27.

18:4 • *water in abundance:* ὕδατα πολλὰ ἦν ἐκεῖ, as in John 3:23 of "Aenon, near Salim."

18:9 • *winter:* For symbolic exegesis of the seasons, see *Gos. Phil.* (NHC II,3) 4: 52,25–28 "Whoever sows in the winter reaps in the summer. 'Winter' means the world; 'summer' means the other realm. Let us sow in the world so that we may reap in summer. For this reason we ought not to pray in the winter."

18:8 *October:* Dios (Δίος; LSJ, s.v. [p. 435a]) is the first month of the Greek (Macedonian) year, equivalent to October-November. P reads Hyperberetaios (Ὑπερβερεταῖος; LSJ, s.v. [p. 1861a]), the last month of the Greek year, equivalent to September-October; Syr has *Teshri*, which can stand for one or more of the autumn months (PSTS, s.v. ܬܫܪܝ [col. 4514; CSD, p. 623b]).

April: Xanthikos (Ξανθικός; this spelling in, e.g., Diodorus Siculus 18.56; 2 Macc 11:30) or Xandikos (Ξανδικός; LSJ, s.v. [p. 1187b]) is equivalent to April in the Macedonian calendar; Syr has Nisan, "April" (PSTS, s.v. ܢܝܣܢ [col. 2363; CSD, p. 338b]).

18:12 ᵃCf. 28:9
18:13 ᵃCf. 5:3
19:7 ᵃ» 15:2
19:9 ᵃCf. 59:2;
APeVer 8:2
20:4 ᵃCf. 42:3; 69:6;
70:2; 73:1; 82:1;
101:4; 123:2; 165:6

south, the service aqueduct in the north.ᵃ ¹³When the king saw it, he said to the apostle, "So, you really are a craftsman, and it's fitting for you to serve kings!"ᵃ ¹⁴And having left him ample provisions, he went on his way.

19 From time to time he sent money and supplies to meet the basic needs of Thomas and the other workers. ²But Thomas took it and gave it away, traveling to the towns and surrounding countryside, bestowing gifts and giving alms to the poor and afflicted. ³He provided for their needs, saying, "The king knows that he has acquired his royal dues; now it's time for the poor to have relief."

⁴After a while the king sent an ambassador to the apostle, with the following letter he had written to him: "Describe for me what you have done, and what I'm to send you or what you need."

⁵"The palace has been built; only the roof remains," the apostle replied.

⁶When the king heard this, he sent Thomas gold coin and bullion, and wrote <this>: "If the palace structure is done, let it be roofed!"

⁷But the apostle said to the Lord, "I thank you,ᵃ Lord, for everything, because you were dead for a short while so that I might live eternally in you, and you sold me so that through me you might liberate many."

⁸Needless to say, he did not stop teaching and giving relief to the afflicted, saying: "The Lord has bestowed these things on you and provides to each person his nourishment. ⁹For he it is who feeds orphans and cares for widows,ᵃ and for all the afflicted he is relief and rest."

20 When the king came to the city, he asked his courtiers about the palace that Judas Thomas was building for him. ²They told him, "He hasn't built a palace—in fact, he's done nothing he promised to do! ³No, he goes around the towns and surrounding areas and gives all he has to the poor. ⁴He teaches a single new god,ᵃ heals the sick, casts out demons, and does many other marvels—we think he's a

---

20:4 • *a new god* (θεὸν νέον): From early times a commonplace in Greek tradition; see, e.g., Aristophanes *Birds* 848 "I want to sacrifice to the new god"; Aeschylus (6th–5th cent. B.C.E.) *Prom.* 450 "by the law of change a new god rules"; Euripides *Bacchae* 219 "this new god [Dionysus]"; Aristophanes (5th–4th cent. B.C.E.) *Birds* 848 "I want to sacrifice to the new god." Thomas will later be identified as God's "new apostle" (82:1; 136:3; 137:4), and be buried in a "new tomb" (158:10).

wizard. ⁵But his acts of mercy and the healings that freely come from him, as well as his simplicity, goodness, and the quality of his faith—all of this signifies that he's a righteous man or an emissary of the new god he proclaims.ᵃ ⁶Look, he's constantly fasting and praying, he eats only bread with salt,ᵃ drinks only water,ᵇ wears a single cloak in weather both fair and foul,ᶜ and takes nothing from anyone, but gives away to others whatever he has!ᵈ ⁷When the king heard this he rubbed his face with his handsᵃ and shook his head for a long time.

21 He sent for the merchant who had brought Thomas, and for the apostle himself, and to Thomas he said, "Have you built me the palace?"

²Thomas said: "Yes, I've built it."

³"So, when can we go and see it?" asked the king.

⁴The apostle answered, "You can't see it now, but when you leave this life—then you'll see it."

⁵The king became downright angry, and ordered both the merchant and Judas Thomas put in chains and thrown into prison until he could make inquiries and learn to whom the royal funds had been given; then he would execute the apostle and the merchant together.

⁶For his part, the apostle went away to the prison full of joy, saying to the merchant: "Don't be afraid of anything; only believeᵃ in the God I proclaim, and you'll be liberated from this world, and in the world to come you'll have life."ᵇ

⁷The king deliberated how they would be put to death,ᵃ and decided to have them flayed and burned alive. ⁸But that very night the

20:5 ᵃ» 9:3
20:6 ᵃCf. Nm 18:19; 2Chr 13:5
ᵇCf. 104:10
ᶜCf. 96:8; Mt 10:10; Mk 6:9
ᵈCf. 96:9
20:7 ᵃCf. AJn 30:4
21:6 ᵃCf. 69:4; 102:8; 103:5; 158:14; Mk 5:36; Lk 8:50; Jn 14:1, 27; AAnGE 27:3
ᵇCf. Mk 10:30; Lk 18:30
21:7 ᵃ» 141:8

wizard (μάγος): The same charge arises in 21:11; 96:3; 101:3, 8; 102:4; 104:1; 107:3; 152:3; similarly, AcAndGE 12:14; 22:3; AcPaulThec 15:3; 20:3.

20:5 • *freely* (δωρεάν), as in Matt 10:8 "Heal the sick, rise the dead, cleanse the lepers, drive out demons. You have received *freely, freely give*"; cf. 156:3; 2 Cor 11:7; AcAndGE 30:18.

21:6 • *Don't be afraid of anything, only believe* (μὴ φοβοῦ μηδέν, ἀλλὰ μόνον πίστευσον): Cf. 102: 8 μηδὲν φοβοῦ ἀλλὰ πίστευσον; 158:14 μὴ φοβεῖσθε ἀλλὰ μόνον πιστεύσατε. Mark 5:36 μὴ φοβοῦ, μόνον πίστευε; Luke 8:50 μὴ φοβοῦ, μόνον πίστευσον [v.l. πίστευε]. The distinctive pairing ἀλλὰ μόνον is not found in the NT with this exhortation; but it is used with another imperative in Matt 8:8.

20:6 *but gives away*... : Ms H lacks the entire concluding phrase, and instead reads uniquely "he teaches a new teaching [νέαν διδαχήν; cf. 126:1] concerning self-control [ἐγκράτεια] and virginity, and preaches that the one true God is Jesus Christ; because at his petition [ἐπίκλησις] he removes every disease." ἐγκράτεια and ἐπίκλησις are not found elsewhere in the writing.

21:11 ᵃ» 20:4
21:12 ᵃCf. 21:7
22:4 ᵃCf. Jn 14:2
22:10 ᵃCf. Lk
16:27–28
23:3 ᵃCf. Lk 15:32

king's brother, Gad, became ill, and because of the grief and anxiety that the king suffered he was much distressed. ⁹Sending for the king, he said to him, "My royal brother, I entrust to you my home and my children. ¹⁰I, too, am grieved at the insult that has happened to you, and I'm about to die. ¹¹If you don't punish that wizard,ᵃ you won't let my soul rest in Hades."

¹²The king said to his brother, "All night long I've been considering how to put him to death.ᵃ ¹³I've finally decided to have him flayed and burned alive, both him and the merchant who brought him."

22 While they were talking, the soul of his brother Gad departed. ²The king mourned Gad greatly, for he loved him dearly; so he ordered him to be laid out for burial in costly royal attire. ³While this was being done, angels took the soul of Gad, the king's brother, and brought it to heaven. ⁴They showed him the heavenly places and dwellings thereᵃ and asked him, "In what sort of place do you wish to dwell?" ⁵When they approached the edifice of Thomas the apostle that he had built for the king, Gad saw it and said to the angels, ⁶"Please, sirs, permit me to dwell in one of these apartments on the lower floor."

⁷They said to him, "You cannot dwell in this building."

⁸"Oh, and why's that?"

⁹"This palace is the one which that Christian built for your brother."

¹⁰"Please, sirs," he said, "let me to go to my brother,ᵃ to buy this palace from him—my brother doesn't know what sort of place it is and he'll sell it to me."

23 Then the angels released Gad's soul and while he was being clothed in the burial garment his soul reentered him. ²He said to those who stood about him, "Summon my brother, that I might make a request of him."

³They immediately told their king, "Your brother has come back to life."ᵃ

⁴The king, accompanied by a great crowd, ran and came to his brother. He went in and stood at his bed, as if terror-stricken, unable to speak to him.

21:11 • *punish*, literally, "come to vengeance on the head of," a Syriacism; see also 66:17; 76:4; 100:7; 101:8; 106:2.

24:7 ªCf. 9:3; 33:10;
41:2; 51:7; 54:6; 87:2
ᵇCf. 25:7

⁵His brother spoke: "I'm quite certain, brother, that if someone asked you for half of your kingdom, you'd part with it for me; so I think you'll do me the one favor I ask of you, and sell me what I request of you."

⁶"And what is it that you ask me to sell to you?"

⁷"Assure me with an oath that you'll turn it over to me."

⁸The king swore: "Any one of my possessions that you request I'll give you."

⁹Gad then said to him, "Sell me that palace you own in heaven."

¹⁰"And where," the king asked, "did I get a palace in heaven?"

¹¹Gad replied: "It's the one built for you by that Christian now in prison—the one the merchant bought from a certain Jesus and brought to you. ¹²I mean that Hebrew slave you intended to punish, on the grounds that you had suffered some insult from him. ¹³Because of the grief he caused I died, but I've now come back to life."

24 Then the king understood about the things that belonged to him and the eternal benefits that were to come, and he said, "I cannot sell you that palace, but I pray that I may enter it, dwell in it, and be worthy to be among its inhabitants. ²But if you truly wish to purchase such a palace, the man is still alive and will build for you one better than that." ³He straightway sent and had the apostle released from the prison along with the merchant who had been locked up with him. ⁴He said, "As a man who makes a request of the servant of God, I ask you to pray for me and to ask him whose servant you are that he might forgive and overlook what I've done to you and what I had in mind to do. ⁵I also ask that I might become a worthy resident of that dwelling for which I expended no labor—you alone built it for me by your labor, with the help of your God's grace. ⁶I also ask that I, too, may become an attendant and serve the God you proclaim."

⁷His brother also fell down at the apostle's feet ª and said, "I beg and implore you before your God to be made worthy of this dutyᵇ—⁸and to be judged worthy of the things shown me by his angels."

23:5 • *I'm quite certain:* οἶδα καὶ πέπεισμαι, as in Rom 14:14 (cf. Phil 1:25); the phrase is used again in 43:12.
23:5 • *half of your kingdom:* For the idea of trading half, e.g., of a house (1 Kgs 13:8) or one's goods (Luke 19:8) or realm (Esth 5:3, 6; Mark 6:23), for services rendered, see already Herodotus *Hist.* 9.34: a certain Melampus claimed "half the kingdom" (and an additional one-third for his brother, Bias) as his fee for restoring a portion of the Argive population to sanity.

25:1 ªCf. 39:7

25:5 ªCf. 26:5; 39:16;
67:4; 79:10; Mt 7:15;
10:16; Lk 10:3; Jn
10:12; Ac 20:29

25:6 ªCf. 37:7; 39:12;
Jn 4:14–15; 7:38;
Th (NHC II,2) 13:
34,30–35,14

25:7 ªCf. 24:7

25:8 ªCf. Jn 10:11, 14;
Hb 13:20; 1Pt 5:4

26:2 ª» 49:3
ᵇCf. Jn 10:14

25 The apostle, in joyous rapture, said, "I praise you, Lord Jesus, that you have revealed your truth among these men, for you alone are the true God[a] and no other, and you it is who knows all things that are unknown to the multitudes. ²You, Lord, are the one who shows constant pity and mercy to humankind. ³Because of their innate error they have neglected you, but you haven't neglected them. ⁴Now, at my earnest request, accept the king and his brother and include them in your flock, having cleansed them with your bath and anointed them with your oil from the error which encompasses them. ⁵Guard them also from the wolves,[a] supporting them in your meadows. ⁶Give them drink from your ambrosial fountain,[a] which is never muddied and never gives out. ⁷For they ask and beseech you and want to be your servants and ministers,[a] and for this reason they desire to be separated from your enemies and, for your sake, to be hated and mistreated by them and to die at their hands, ⁸just as you suffered all these things on our behalf, so that you might preserve us, being our Lord and truly our good shepherd.[a] ⁹Grant that they might have in you alone their boldness, as well as the aid for and hope of their salvation which comes from you, which they expect from you alone. ¹⁰Grant also that they may be confirmed in your mysteries, and that from your graces and gifts they may have the perfect good things and flourish in your service and will bear perfect fruit in your Father."

26 When King Gundafar and his brother Gad had thus been properly disposed by the apostle, they followed him, not hesitating at all, helping those in need, giving gifts and relief to all. ²They requested of him that they, too, might also receive the seal[a] of the word, saying, "Since our souls are ready and eager for God, give us the seal; for we have heard you say that the God you herald recognizes his own sheep[b] through his seal."

25:1 • *I praise you:* This prayer formula with ἐξομολογοῦμαι, comparable to opening lines in the Qumran *Hodayot* ("Thanksgiving Hymns"; eg., QHª VI, 23; X, 20, 31; XI, 37), is found in the OT (2 Sam 22:50; Dan 2:23; Sir 51:1) and in Matt 11:25; Luke 10:21. It reappears in 94:2; 107:1; and in one ms in 145:1 (v.l. for εὐχαριστεῖν).

25:3 • *innate error:* The force of "error" (πλάνη) is mentioned also in 37:6; 38:2; 44:5; 48:7; 67:3; 80:12; 98:4; 156:12. Cf. *Gos. Truth* (NHC I,3) 17,10–16 "Ignorance of the Father brought about anguish and terror. And the anguish grew solid like a fog so that no one was able to see. For this reason error became powerful."

25:4 • *oil:* The usual order (in 49:4; 121:2; 132:5; 157:14) in both Syr and Gr is anointing, then baptism; Syr here keeps that order.

³The apostle said to them, "I rejoice and ask you to take this seal and share with me in this, the Lord's eucharistic blessing, and be perfected by it. ⁴This is the Lord and God of all, Jesus Christ, whom I proclaim, and the very Father of Truth, in whom I've taught you to believe." ⁵And he ordered them to bring him oil,ᵃ so that through the oil they might receive the seal. ⁶So they brought the oil and they lighted many lamps, for it was night.

27 The apostle stood up and sealed them.ᵃ ²The Lord was revealed to them through a voice saying, "Peace to you,ᵃ brethren."ᵇ ³They only heard the voice, and did not see his form,ᵃ for they had not yet received the sealing of the seal. ⁴The apostle took the oil, poured it over their heads, smeared it, anointed them, and then said:

⁵Come, holy name of Christ, which is above every name.ᵃ
Come, power of the Most Highᵇ
and the perfect compassion.
⁶Come, highest charism.
Come, merciful Mother.ᵃ
⁷Come, fellowship of the male.ᵃ
Come, Lady who reveals the hidden mysteries.ᵇ
⁸Come, Mother of the seven houses,ᵃ
so that your rest might be in the eighth house.
⁹Come, you who are older than the five members—
mind, conception, thought, reflection, reason—
and commune with these young men.
¹⁰Come, Holy Spirit,
cleanse their minds and hearts, and seal them
in the name of the Father, Son, and Holy Spirit.ᵃ

¹¹When they had been sealed, a youth appeared to them carrying a lighted lamp, so that even the lamps became faint by the approach of its light.ᵃ ¹²He exited and became invisible to them. ¹³The

26:5 ᵃCf. 25:5
27:1 ᵃ» 49:3
27:2 ᵃCf. 70:4; Jn 20:19, 21, 26; AAnMt 3:5; 4:8; AJn 110:2; 115:2; APeVer 5:27, 29
ᵇ» 16:9
27:3 ᵃCf. Ac 9:7; AJn 98:3; 99:2; APaTh 7:3
27:5 ᵃCf. Phl 2:9
ᵇCf. Lk 1:35; 24:49
27:6 ᵃ» 7:10
27:7 ᵃCf. 50:2
ᵇ» 10:5
27:8 ᵃCf. Prv 9:1
27:10 ᵃCf. 49:4; 70:3(k)†; 96:4; 121:7; 132:7; 157:16; Mt 28:19; APeVer 5:25
27:11 ᵃCf. AJn 87:2; APa 7.4:8; APeVer 5:27

26:4 • *Father of Truth* (πατὴρ τῆς ἀληθείας), already used in 7:10, is not a NT title; but see *2 Clem.* 3:1; 20:5; *Gos. Truth* (NHC I,3) 16,33; *Hyp. Arch.* (NHC II,4) 86,21; *Treat. Seth* (NHC VII,2) 50,11; 53,3; *Test. Truth* (NHC IX,3) 43,26; *Val. Expos.* (NHC XI,2) 28,22; Origen *C. Cels.* 8.12 "We worship the Father of truth, and the Son, who is the truth"; *De Prin.* 2.6.1.

27:6 *Come, merciful Mother:* Syr "Come, Mercy."
27:7 *Come, fellowship of the male:* Syr "Come, sharer of blessing."

27:13 ªCf. APeVer
21:8

27:15 ª107:1; Mt 5:12;
1Pt 1:8; 4:13; Rv 19:7

ᵇCf. Ac 5:14

28:4 ªCf. 126:7

28:5 ªCf. Mt 6:34

apostle said to the Lord, "Lord, your light is incomprehensible to us, and we cannot bear it, for it's too great for our vision."ª

¹⁴When the light appeared and day dawned, he broke bread and made them partakers of the eucharist of Christ. ¹⁵They rejoiced and were glad, and many others were added as believersª and came to the refuge of the Savior.

28 The apostle did not cease preaching to them: "Men and women, boys and girls, young men and women, people in your prime and senior citizens, whether slaves or free, refrain from sexual immorality, greed, and gluttony, for all vice falls under these three heads. ²Sexual immorality, you see, blinds the mind, darkens the eyes of the soul, and is an impediment to the governance of the body, since it renders the whole person weak and subjects the whole body to disease. ³Covetousness, residing inside the body, reduces the soul to fear and shame; when it steals the property of others it is apprehensive, lest, when it restores to their owners what belongs to them, it be shamed. ⁴Gluttonyª casts the soul into cares, concerns, and sorrows, as it worries lest it lack something, and it reaches for things that are far off. ⁵When you have been freed from these vices, you become free of worry, grief, and fear, and what was said by the Savior pertains to you: 'Don't fret about tomorrow; let tomorrow fret about itself.'ª ⁶Also remember this saying, spoken previously: 'Observe the ravens and look to the birds of heaven, that they neither sow nor reap nor gather into barns, and

---

27:15 • *many others were added as believers* (πολλοὶ δὲ καὶ ἕτεροι πιστεύοντες προσετίθεντο) is more than just an echo of Acts 5:4: μᾶλλον δὲ προσετίθεντο πιστεύοντες τῷ κυρίῳ. . . .

28:2 • *eyes of the soul:* See also 53:6; 65:6 "eyes *of the mind* [or *of thought*] (τῆς ἐννοίας)"; similarly 166:2 "eyes *of the mind* [or *of understanding*] (τῆς διανοίας)," where the shorter recension has τῆς καρδίας "of the heart" (as in Eph 1:18; *1 Clem.* 36:2; 59:3; *Mart. Pol.* 2:3); in 143:7 this distinction is present in the implicit contrast with "bodily eyes" (also "ears of the flesh" in AcPetPas 10[39]:5). AcPetBG 2:17 reports that after his healing, Ptolemy "saw with the eyes of his flesh and the eyes of his soul"; see also AcAndPas 57:9; AcJohn 113:4; AcPetVerc 21:2–4.

The image, already at home in Greek thought (e.g., in Aristotle and Plato), became popular among Christian writers, e.g., *1 Clem.* 19:3 "let us gaze with the eyes of our soul on his long-suffering purpose"; Justin *Dial.* 134.5 "the eyes of your souls are excessively weak"; Clement of Alexandria *Paed.* 2.9 "understanding is the eye of the soul" (cf. *Strom.* 7.16 "if one is curable . . . let him lend the ears of the soul"); Origen *C. Cels.* 2.54; 7.39; Methodius *Symp.* 11.3; Augustine *Conf.* 7.10.

28:3 *lest,* reading the conjunction μή for the article ἡ ("the").

28:4 *reaches for,* reading θιγγάνει (already used in

12:7) for θεαθῇ ("it sees"), with Syr; see Bonnet, *Aaa* 2/2. 144 n. 15.

God takes care of them. How much more important are you, who have such little faith?'[a] [7]But await his coming, set your hopes in him, and believe in his name. [8]For he is the judge of the living and the dead,[a] he will render to each person according to that person's deeds,[b] and at his coming and his final appearance no one, when about to be judged, will be able to offer the excuse that he hadn't heard. [9]For his heralds are making their proclamation in the four corners of the world. [10]Repent, therefore, and believe the proclamation, and accept the gentle yoke and the light burden,[a] so that you may live and not die. [11]You have acquired these things; guard them. [12]You have come from the darkness, so that the light may receive you.[a] [13]Come to the one who is truly good, so you may receive grace from him and you will place his sign in your souls."

29 When he had said these things some of those present said to him, "It is time for the bondsman to receive the debt."

[2]He replied, "The creditor always wants to receive an excessive amount, but let us give him what is his due." [3]After blessing them he took bread, oil, an herb, and salt, blessed them, and distributed to them. [4]But he remained fasting, because the Lord's Day[a] was about to begin.

28:6 [a]Cf. Mt 6:26; Lk 12:24; Th (NHC II,2) 27: 38,17–20

28:8 [a]Cf. 30:4; Ac 10:42; Rm 14:9; 2Tm 4:1; 1Pt 4:5; AAnMt 14:5; APeVer 17:31; 28:12

[b]Cf. Ps 62:12; Prv 24:12; Mt 16:27; Rm 2:6; 2Tm 4:14; 1Pt 1:17; Rv 2:23; 2Clem. 1:1; AJn 113:10

28:10 [a]Cf. Mt 11:30; Th (NHC II,2) 90: 48,16–20

28:12 [a]Cf. Jn 8:12; 12:35–36

29:4 [a]Cf. 31:9; Rv 1:10; AAnPas 13:2; AJn 106:2; APa 7.4:6; APeVer 29:4; APeMar 1(30):1

28:8 • *the excuse*, literally, "word of defense" (λόγον ἀπολογίας): The second noun is found only here; cf. 1 Pet 3:15 ἕτοιμοι ἀεὶ πρὸς ἀπολογίαν παντὶ τῷ αἰτοῦντι ὑμᾶς λόγον. See also Ps.-Philo *L.A.B.* 11.2; *Pre. Pet.* 4 (*apud* Clement of Alexandria *Strom.* 6.6.48).

28:9 • *four corners* (τέσσαρα κλίματα): The four regions, zones, or directions (see also 1:2; 18:12; *EpPetPhil* [NHC VIII,2] 140,24–25); the same phrase refers to the four cardinal points (N., S., E., W.) in, e.g., Strabo (d. 21 c.e.) *Geogr.* 10.2.12.

28:10 • *Repent, therefore, and believe the proclamation* (μετάγνωτε οὖν καὶ πιστεύσατε τῇ ἐπαγγελίᾳ): In meaning, but with some striking verbal difference, this corresponds to Jesus' first preaching in Mark 1:15 "Repent, and believe in the gospel (μετανοεῖτε καὶ πιστεύετε ἐν τῷ εὐαγγελίῳ)"; μετανοεῖν ("to repent") does not occur in the AcThom; εὐαγγέλιον only at 139:14, where, however, Syr differs (see note); cf. also AcPaul 7.1:7.

29:1 • *It is time . . . :* This saying is usually taken to be a proverb about eating: the context is a meal, and contemporary writers refer to eating as paying a debt; see Klijn, 1962: 221. But the reference may be to impending death; see 127:7.

29:2 • *creditor*, literally, "lord of the debt," a Semitism; see also the debt-collecting demon in 32:3.

29:4 • *the Lord's Day* (ἡ κυριακή), or "Sunday," as commonly in ECL; see also 31:9 (τῇ κυριακῇ ἡμέρᾳ), where Syr has "first day of the week," another standard idiom.

  about to begin, literally, "about to dawn." But the use is metaphorical in both Gr and Syr. The day begins in the evening; for the same Jewish reckoning, see Matt 28:1.

29:4 *remained fasting:* In Syr, Thomas does *not* fast, because of the day to follow.

29:5 ᵃCf. AJn 48:1–2

29:6 ᵃ» 44:7

29:7 ᵃ» 16:9

ᵇCf. 66:1

29:9 ᵃ» 10:12

29:10 ᵃCf. 51:5; 1Cor 11:29

30:2 ᵃ» 15:6

30:3 ᵃCf. AJn 48:5

ᵇ» 3:1

30:4 ᵃ» 28:8

30:5 ᵃCf. 67:2

30:7 ᵃ» 44:7

ᵇCf. Mt 13:25, 28

31:1 ᵃCf. AJn 71:1

[5]When night came and he went to sleep, the Lord stood at his head and said, "Thomas, arise early, bless everyone after the prayer and the service, and go along the eastern road for two miles.[a] [6]There I shall display my glory through you; for because of the matter for which you are going out many will seek refuge in me, and you will rebuke the nature and power of the enemy."[a]

[7]Thomas rose from sleep and said to the believers[a] present, "Children and brothers,[b] the Lord wishes to accomplish something through me today. [8]Let us only pray that we not hinder him, but that both now and always whatever we do may be in accord with his desire and will." [9]When he had said this, he laid his hands on them[a] and blessed them. [10]He broke the eucharistic bread and gave it to them, saying, "May this eucharist produce compassion and pity and not judgment and retribution."[a]

[11]They said, "Amen!"

ACT 3 A DEADLY SERPENT

30 The apostle set out for where the Lord had commanded. [2]When he came near the end of the second mile, he veered slightly from the road and saw lying there the body[a] of a handsome young man. [3]He said, "Lord, so was it for this that you made me come out here, to see this trial?[a] Very well, then, enact your will."[b]

[4]He began to pray: "Lord, judge of the living and the dead,[a] the living who are standing and the dead who are lying down, master and Father of all; [5]but Father, not of the souls that are in bodies[a] but of those that have gone out of them—for you are master and judge of the souls that are in defilements: [6]Come, right now, when I call on you, and show your glory to this man lying here."

[7]Turning to those who followed him, he said, "This thing hasn't happened in vain, but the enemy[a] has been active and has done this[b] to launch an attack through him. [8]Notice—he didn"t use any other form, nor was he active through any beast other than the one that serves him."

31 When he had spoken, a great serpent[a] came out of a den, shaking its head and rattling its tail over the ground. [2]It cried out in a loud voice to the apostle, "I'll tell you to your face why I killed this man, since you were coming to punish my deeds."

[3]"Yes—so speak on," said the apostle.

[4]The serpent said, "There is a certain beautiful woman in this place opposite here. [5]When she passed by me I saw her, fell in love with her, followed her, and watched for her. [6]Then I found this youth kissing her, and he had intercourse with her and did other shameful things with her. [7]It would be easy for me to show all this to you, <but I dare not>; I know well enough that you're the twin of the Christ,[a] who always destroys our nature. [8]But since I didn't wish to disturb this woman, I didn't kill him at that very hour; no, I waited for him until the evening, when he'd come by. [9]Then I struck and killed him—and I did it particularly because he dared to do his deed on the Lord's Day."[a]

[10]The apostle interrogated him: "Tell me from what sort of seed you were sown and to what species you belong."[a]

32 The serpent said:

I am a crawler, with a crawler's nature,
    and a harmer with a harmer's nature.
[2]I am the son of him who harmed
    and struck down the four standing brothers.[a]
[3]I am the son of him who sits on a throne[a]
    over what is under heaven,
    who takes back his own
    from those who have borrowed them.[b]
[4]I am the son of him
    who girds the sphere.[a]
[5]I am kin to him who is around the ocean,
    whose tail lies in his own mouth.
[6]I am the one who entered through the fence in Paradise
    and told Eve
    what my father commanded me to say to her.[a]

31:7 [a]Cf. 39:2; 50:4
31:9 [a]» 29:4
31:10 [a]Cf. 74:10
32:2 [a]Cf. 165:8
32:3 [a]Cf. 1Kgs 22:19; 2Chr 18:18; Ps 47:8; Is 6:1; Sir 1:8; Rv 4:2
[b]Cf. 29:2
32:4 [a]Cf. Job 1:7
32:6 [a]Cf. 33:6; 76:6; Gn 3:1–5; Jn 8:44; AAnPas 21:4; APeVer 28:54

31:4 • *"There is a certain beautiful woman . . .":* The serpent's story is reminiscent of the lustful judges' plot against Susanna (see especially Sus 1–4, 7–8, 21, 36–40).
32:1 • *I am a crawler . . . :* The serpent responds in an aretalogy, a hymnic form (often with repeated "I am" statements) in which a deity recounts its powers or achievements (ἀρεταί).
32:2 • *four standing brothers:* This verse, not in Syr, may refer to a Jewish legend about four killed by the primal serpent; see *b. Shabb.* 55a; *b. B. Bat.* 17a.
32:6 • *the one who entered through the fence . . . :* Cf. *y. Pe'ah* 16b, which also features a talking snake.

31:7 *but I dare not* is added from Syr.

32:7 ªCf. Gn 4:7;
AAnPas 40:3

32:8 ªCf. Gn 3:18

32:9 ªGn 6; *1En* 6

ᵇ» 12:2

32:10 ªCf. Ex 4:21;
9:12; APeVer 8:21

32:11 ªCf. 66:6; Ex 32

32:12 ªCf. Mt 26:57;
27:13; Jn 18:28–32

32:13 ªCf. 84:1; Mt
26:14–16; Mk 14:10–
11; Jn 13:26–27;
18:2–3

32:15 ªCf. Mk 3:13;
13:20; Lk 6:13; Jn
6:70; 13:18; 15:16, 19;
Ac 1:2

32:16 ªCf. Rv 13:2–8

[7]I am the one who incited and inflamed Cain
 so that he slew his own brother.[a]
[8]Because of me,
 thorns and thistles grew on the earth.[a]
[9]I am the one who cast the angels down from on high
 and bound them with lust for women,[a]
 so that they might beget earthly children[b]
 and I might accomplish my will through them.
[10]I am the one who hardened the heart of Pharaoh,[a]
 so that he murdered the children of Israel
 and enslaved them with the hardest of yokes.
[11]I am the one who led astray the multitude in the desert
 when they made the calf.[a]
[12]I am the one who inflamed Herod
 and incited Caiaphas in his false slander to Pilate;[a]
 for this was fitting for me.
[13]I am the one who incited Judas and bought him,
 so that he might deliver Christ to death.[a]
[14]I am the one who dwells in the abyss of Tartaros
 and who possesses it.
[15]The Son of God cheated me against my will
 and chose for himself those who are mine.[a]
[16]I am kin to the one who is to come from the east,
 to whom power is given
 to do what he wishes on the earth.[a]

32:12 • *Herod:* This may be an allusion to the slaughter of the innocents by Herod the Great (38–4 B.C.E.; see Matt 2:16–18). Otherwise, his second son, Herod Antipas (tetrarch of Galilee and Perea, 4 B.C.E.–39 C.E.) is meant; see Luke 23:6–7 and Acts 4:27, where Herod and Pilate are mentioned together.
32:14 • *Tartaros,* i.e., Hades, the netherworld, or (as here) the place of torment and abode of the devil.
32:14 • *who possesses it,* or possibly, "who acts as a restraint"; cf. 2 Thess 2:7.
32:16 • *from the east* is not a standard element in early Christian reflection on the devil. Hippolytus predicts that the *antichrist* will come from Gad (*De antichr.* 14); Ps.-Athanasius (*Quaest. Ant.* 109) writes that he will come from Galilee, in fulfillment of Deut 33:22 ("Dan is a lion's whelp, that leaps froth from Bashan"). But in the 6th–7th century, Andreas of Caesarea in Cappadocia is explicit: "the antichrist is coming from the eastern parts of Persia, where the tribe of Dan is" (*Comm. in Rev.* 51).

32:9 *bound them* (καταδήσας): Syr ܐܘܣܪ ("inflicted pain, corrupted"; PSTS, s.v. ܐܣܝ [Aphael, col. 2734; CSD, p. 391a]), perhaps in error for ܐܣܪ ("bound"; PSTS, s.v. ܐܣܪ [col. 320; CSD, p. 24b]); so Burkitt, 1900: 284.
32:12 *Pilate* is lacking in P and Syr.

33 When the serpent had said all these things in the hearing of all the crowd, the apostle raised his voice and shouted: [2]"Now cease, most shameless one,[a] and be ashamed, since you have been slain; for your end, destruction,[b] has overtaken you. [3]Don't dare to say what I shall accomplish through those who are obedient to you. [4]In the name of that Jesus, who up till now has been conducting the struggle against you for the sake of his people, I command that you suck the poison which you have injected into this man, draw it out and take it from him."

[5]The serpent said, "The time of our end has not yet come,[a] as you have said; so why do you force me to take what I injected into this man and thus die before my time? [6]For when my father[a] draws up and sucks out what he cast into creation, then he will be finished."[b]

[7]"So then," the apostle said to him, "show your father's nature."

[8]The serpent approached, put his mouth on the young man's wound, and sucked out the poison from it. [9]Gradually the youth's purple complexion became white and the serpent swelled up. [10]When the serpent had drawn into itself all the poison, the young man leaped up, then ran and fell at the feet of the apostle.[a] [11]The swollen serpent burst apart and died and his poisonous bile poured out, and at the place where his poison poured out, a great chasm formed and that serpent was swallowed up.[a] [12]The apostle said to the king and his brother, "Send workers and fill up this place; lay the foundations and construct buildings above it as lodging for strangers."

34 The young man tearfully addressed the apostle:

What wrong have I done you? [2]For you are a man with two forms,[a] and you will be found wherever you wish, and are restrained by no one, as I can see. [3]For I saw that man who stood next to you and said to you, 'I have many wonders to

33:2 [a]Cf. 44:1; 74:4;
AJn 49:2; AAnPas
49:3

[b]» 12:2

33:5 [a]Cf. 45:2; 76:5;
Mt 8:29

33:6 [a]» 32:6

[b]Cf. Mk 3:26

33:10 [a]» 24:7

33:11 [a]Cf. 42:2

34:2 [a]» 44:3

33:12 • *lodging for strangers:* This disposition of the land, together with the description of the serpent's death in v. 11, is reminiscent of the NT accounts of Judas Iscariot's death; see Matt 27:7; Acts 1:18.

33:1 *When the serpent had said all these things:* Here Syr adds a short speech by the crowd, affirming Thomas's proclamation and begging him to destroy the serpent.

34:3 *who stood,* reading ὃς παρέστηκεν for ὡς παρέστηκα ("when I stood"); so Bonnet, *Aaa* 2/2. 151 n. 2.

34:5 ª» 44:7
34:8 ªCf. Eph 5:14
34:17 ªCf. AJn 76:9

make known through you and many great deeds to accomplish, through which you will receive a reward. ⁴You will make many people come to life and they will rest in eternal light as children of God. ⁵You, then,' he said to you, speaking about me, 'bring to life this youth who has been struck by the enemy,ª and always be his guardian.' ⁶You have done well, then, to come here and you will do well to return to him, since he will not ever leave you.

⁷I was without care or reproach.
⁸He shoneª on me in the midst of the care
    that comes by night;
    and I was given rest from the labor of the day.
⁹I was released from the one who goaded me
    to do these things;
    I sinned against him who taught me to do the opposite.
¹⁰I destroyed that one, the kin of night,
    who forced me to sin in his activities.
¹¹I found that luminous one who is my kinsman,
    I destroyed him who brings darkness
    and gloom on his subjects,
¹²so they can't know what they're doing
    and hold back from their deeds for shame,
    and their actions come to an end.
¹³I found that one whose deeds are light,
    whose actions are truth,
    and whose performance one will not regret.
¹⁴I was released from the one whose falsehood is constant,
    whom the cover of darkness precedes,
    behind whom follows shame, brazen in indolence.
¹⁵I found the one who reveals to me
    the things that are beautiful,
    so that I might receive them:
¹⁶The son of truth, kinsman of concord,
    who disperses the mist and shines on his own creation,
    who heals wounds and overturns its enemies.
¹⁷But please, man of God,ª let me gaze on him again and see him who is now hidden to me, so that I may hear his voice. ¹⁸I can't tell you how marvelous it sounded, for it's not the kind of sound that our physical mouth produces.

35 The apostle answered him, "If, as you have said, you've been released from the things which you have come to understand, and you know who it is that accomplished these things in you; ²and if you learn and become obedient to the one you now seek with a passionate love, you'll see him and be with him forever; you'll rest in his rest and in his joy. ³But if you neglect him and revert to your former actions,ᵃ if you abandon the beauty and forget that gleaming visage that has just been shown to you and its luminous radiance that you now desire, you'll lose not only this life but also the life to come. ⁴You will depart to the one you claim to have destroyed and you'll no longer see the one you claim to have found."

36 When the apostle had spoken, he came to the city holding that youth by the hand and saying to him, "The things that you've seen, child, are but a few of the many things which God has. ²For he proclaims good news to us not about these things that are manifest, but promises us things greater than these. ³As long as we're embodied, we can't say or express what he is to give to our souls. ⁴If we say that he provides us light, we mean this visible light and we already have it. ⁵If we speak of wealth that exists and appears in this world, we can identify it, but we don't want it, since it was said, 'It's difficult for the rich to enter Heaven's domain.'ᵃ ⁶If we speak about clothing, which the wealthy wear in this life, this, too, has been pointed out—here is what was said about it <back then>: 'Those who wear soft clothing are in the houses of kings.'ᵃ ⁷If we speak about costly dinners, we have received a command to abstain from them, 'not to be weighed down with intoxication, drunkenness and worldly concerns,'ᵃ <a command> spoken about things that do occur. ⁸It's also said, 'Don't fret about your life—what you're going to eat and drink, or about your body—what you're going to wear; there's more to living than food and clothing, isn't there?' ᵃ ⁹If we speak about worldly rest, the judgment about this, too, has been set out <for us>. ¹⁰But <instead> we speak about the world above, about God, angels, watchers, and holy ones, about ambrosial foodᵃ and the drink of the true vine;ᵇ ¹¹about permanent garments, which don't grow old,ᵃ about 'what eye has not seen, nor has ear heard, nor has entered into the heart of sinful people, what God has prepared for those who love him.'ᵇ These things are what we speak and preach. ¹²You too, then, believe in him so that you may live, and have confidence in him so you shall not die. ¹³For he is not persuaded by gifts, so that you should make an offering to him, nor does he need

35:3 ᵃCf. 37:4; 38:2; 48:10; 58:2; 59:9

36:5 ᵃCf. Mt 19:23–24; Mk 10:23–25; Lk 18:24–25

36:6 ᵃCf. Mt 11:8

36:7 ᵃCf. Lk 21:34

36:8 ᵃCf. Mt 6:25; Lk 12:22–23

36:10 ᵃ» 6:7

ᵇCf. Jn 15:1

36:11 ᵃCf. 7:6; 37:5; 88:3, 5; 108–110; 124:14; 135:9; 147:4; Lk 12:22–33

ᵇCf. 1Cor 2:9

36:7 *spoken . . . occur:* Possibly a scribal gloss, since there is nothing the participle "spoken" or "speaking" clearly modifies.

36:15 ªCf. 80:2; 149:3;
160:5; AJn 73:2

37:2 ªCf. Lk 19:4

37:3 ªCf. Jn 3:14;
12:32

37:4 ªCf. 1Jn 4:20

ᵇ» 35:3

37:5 ª» 36:11

ᵇCf. APa 7.3:7

37:6 ª» 25:3

37:7 ª» 25:6

ᵇ» 130:8;

ᶜ» 10:3

38:1 ª» 34:17

ᵇCf. Jn 3:20

38:2 ª» 35:3

ᵇ» 25:3

ᶜCf. 35:3; 58:3; 135:2;
Rm 3:25; AAnGE
18b:44; AJn 54:5

38:3 ªCf. 58:2–3; 59:9;
Ac 3:17; 17:30; AJn
107:12

sacrifices, so that you should make a sacrifice to him. [14]Instead, look to him, and he'll not overlook you; turn to him, and he'll not abandon you. [15]His charm and beauty[a] will give you the desire to love him, and he won't let you be turned away."

37 When the apostle finished speaking to that youth, a large crowd assembled. [2]The apostle looked up and saw them—they were straining to see him and moving up to higher ground[a] as he addressed them: [3]"People who have come to Christ's assembly and who wish to believe in Jesus, take a lesson from this situation and see that if you're not lifted up,[a] you can't observe me, although I'm small, and can't look on me, although I'm one like yourselves. [4]So, if you can't see me, though I'm like you, unless you lift yourselves a little from the earth, how will you be able to see him who lives on high[a] and now is found in the depth, if you don't first raise yourselves up from your previous behavior[b] and unprofitable activities—[5]<from> desires that don't last, wealth that's left behind here below, property that grows old on earth, clothes that wear out [a] beauty that ages and vanishes,[b] and what's more, the whole body in which all these things are stored, that when antiquated becomes dust and returns to its own natural state?—for the body supports all these things. [6]Instead, believe in our Lord Jesus Christ, whom we proclaim, so that your hope may be in him and you may have life in him forever and ever, and so that he may be your companion in this place of wandering[a] and a harbor for you in this stormy sea. [7]For you will have as well a fountain gushing out[a] in this parched place,[b] a bin full of food in the place of the hungry, rest for your souls, and a healer for your bodies."[c]

38 Then, as the assembled multitude heard, they wept and said to the apostle, "Man of God,[a] we dare not say that we belong to the God you proclaim, because the deeds that we've done are alien to him and don't please him.[b] [2]But if he has mercy on us, pities, and saves us, overlooking our former activities,[a] frees us from the evils that we have done in our error,[b] and neither makes a careful accounting with us nor remembers our former sins,[c] we shall become his servants and shall do his will to the end."

[3]The apostle answered, "He does not condemn you nor reckon up the sins that you committed in your ignorance, but he overlooks the transgressions that you perpetrated in ignorance."[a]

ACT 4 A TALKING ASS

39 While the apostle was still standing on the highway and speaking to the crowd, the foal of an ass approached and stood before him. It opened its mouth and said:

> ²Twin of Christ,ᵃ apostle of the Most High
> > and initiate into the hidden message of Christ,
> ³You who have received his hidden sayings,
> > the collaborator of the Son of God;
> ⁴You who though free became a slave,ᵃ
> > and, by being sold into slavery,
> > have led many to freedom;
> ⁵You who are a member of the great family
> > that has vanquished the enemy,ᵃ
> > and redeemed its own members;
> ⁶You who have become for many the cause of life
> > in the land of India,
> > for you came to people gone astray;
> ⁷and through your miraculous appearance and divine words,
> > they are now turning toward the God of Truthᵃ
> > who sent you;ᵇ
> ⁸Get up, sit on me,
> > and rest until you come to the city.

⁹The apostle answered:

> O Jesus Christ,
> > you who are spiritual and full of perfect compassion,ᵃ
> > O respiteᵇ and quiet,
> > you who now speak through dumb animals;ᶜ

Marginal notes:

39:2 ᵃ» 31:7
39:4 ᵃCf. Phl 2:6–7
39:5 ᵃ» 44:7
39:7 ᵃCf. 25:1; 70:3(a)†
  ᵇ» 76:5
39:9 ᵃ» 50:2
  ᵇCf. 50:4
  ᶜCf. 70:3(p)†

39:1 • *the foal of an ass* (πῶλος ὀνάδος): Similarly Matt 21:2 ὄνον . . . καὶ πῶλον; 21:5 ὄνον καὶ . . . πῶλον υἱὸν ὑποζυγίου (cf. Zech 9:9); Mark 11:4 (= Luke 19:30) πῶλον; John 12:15 πῶλον ὄνου. See also AcThom 78–79.
39:6 • *cause of life* (πρόφασις τῆς ζωῆς; similarly 42:4; 48:6; 136:2; 141:6): In slightly later church typology, "Eve" and "Mary" would become respectively the "cause of death" and "cause of life" (see Epiphanius *Haer.* 3.469.9, commenting on Rom 5:12).

39:8 *to the city* (εἰς τὴν πόλιν): U εἰς τὸν τόπον ("to the place"); the same v.l. is found in Deut 21:19 (τοῦ τόπου/τῆς πόλεως); Sir 36:18(15) (τόπον/πόλιν).

39:11 ªCf. 42:4
39:12 ª» 25:6
39:13 ª» 44:7
39:14 ªCf. 50:3; 85:6
39:16 ªCf. Jn 10:11
ᵇ» 25:5
39:17 ª» 7:10
ᵇCf. 70:3(b)†
40:4 ªCf. Nm 22:21
40:5 ªCf. Mt 21:1–9;
Mk 11:1–10; Lk
19:28–38

¹⁰O hidden rest, you who are made manifest through action,
  our Savior and nourisher,
    preserving us and giving us rest in other bodies;
¹¹The Savior of our souls,ª
  the sweet and everlasting spring;
¹²The firmly established, pure,
  and never-disturbed fountain,ª
    the defender and helper of his servants in their struggle;
¹³The one who wards off the enemyª
  and drives him away from us,
    the one who competes in many contests on our behalf,
    and who makes us victorious in all;
¹⁴Our true and unconquered athlete,ª
  our holy and victorious general;
¹⁵The glorious one who supplies to his own
  a joy that never ceases,
    and a respite that contains no tribulation whatsoever;
¹⁶The good shepherd, who gives himself up for his sheep,ª
  who has conquered the wolf,ᵇ redeemed his own lambs,
    and led them to good pasture:
¹⁷We praise and hymn you, your unseen Father,
  and your Holy Spirit, and the Motherª of all creations.ᵇ

40 When the apostle finished speaking, all the multitude present looked at him, waiting to hear how he would answer the foal. ²For a full hour, the apostle stood as if dumbfounded; then, looking up to heaven, he said to the foal, "Who are you, and who do you belong to? ³The things your mouth has uttered are astonishing—marvelous things, hidden from most people."

⁴The foal answered, "I am of the lineage that attended Balaam.ª ⁵Your lord and teacher also sat on one from that lineage, who was related to me.ª ⁶ I've now been sent to give you rest as you take your seat on me. ⁷And <I've been sent> that they might gain faith, and

---

39:14 • *athlete:* Athletic imagery is applied to Christ in the NT, e.g., in Heb 12:1–3; to ascetics, e.g., in AcAndGE 18b:11, 14; *Thom. Cont.* (NHC II,7) title, colophon; and martyrs, e.g., Eusebius *Hist. eccl.* 5. *proem.* 4. The term "unconquered [or invincible] athlete" (ἀθλητὴς ἀήττητος) reappears in AcThom 85:6.

general: This title is used of Sifor, a major character in the latter half of the Acts; see 62:1; 65:1; 68:3; 69:1.

40:7 • *faculty:* μερίς ("portion" or "part"), presumably the faculty of speech. Alternatively, it is the portion of faith, just referred to, sufficient for or appropri-

---

39:17 *Mother:* Syr "the one who hovers over" (cf. Gen 1:2 in the historic ᴋᴊᴠ translation: "broods").

40:2 *Who,* reading τίς for τινός ("whose"), with Syr.

that this faculty might be bestowed on me, which I acquired for the sake of the service that I performed for you. [8]When I've finished serving you, it will be taken from me."

[9]The apostle said to him, "He who bestowed this favor on you is capable of preserving it in you until the end, as well as in animals of other species; I'm weak and feeble in regard to this mystery." [10]He did not wish to be seated on him, but the foal, with an oath, earnestly requested a blessing from him. [11]Finally the apostle mounted and took his seat. [12]The people accompanied him, some going on ahead and some following behind,[a] and everyone ran, wanting to observe the amazing event and see how he would release the foal.

41 When he approached the gates of the city, the apostle dismounted and said, "Depart and keep yourself where you were."[a] [2]At once the foal fell onto the ground at the feet of the apostle[a] and died.[b]

[3]Everyone there was despondent, and they said to the apostle, "Give him life! Raise him up!"

[4]The apostle responded, "I could have raised him through the name of Jesus, but this <outcome> is altogether beneficial. [5]For the one who gave him the power of speech was able to bring it about that he not perish. [6]I'm not raising him up—not because I'm unable to, but because this is appropriate and beneficial for him."[a] [7]He commanded those present to dig a pit and bury his body, and they did as he commanded.

ACT 5 A DEMON WHO DWELT
IN A WOMAN

42 The apostle went into the city, and the whole crowd followed along. [2]He intended to go to the parents of the youth he had

ate to the foal's task; cf. Rom 12:3 ἑκάστῳ ὡς ὁ θεὸς ἐμέρισεν μέτρον πίστεως.

for the sake of . . . you: The preposition διά, in the mss followed by the genitive (τῆς σῆς ὑπηρεσίας), governs an accusative case in the sense adopted here; otherwise "through your service," i.e., service of you.

40:7 *they might gain,* reading ἵνα λάβωσιν for ἵνα λάβω ("I might obtain").   *I acquired,* reading κέκτημαι for μέλλω κτᾶσθαι ("I am to acquire"), with Syr.

40:12 [a]Cf. 70:5; Mt 21:9 Mk 11:9

41:1 [a]Cf. APeBG 1:16

41:2 [a]» 24:7

[b]Cf. Ac 5:10; APeVer 12:14

41:6 [a]Cf. APeVer 12:5

42:2 ᵃCf. 33:11
42:3 ᵃ» 20:4
42:4 ᵃCf. 39:11
ᵇ» 44:7
ᶜ» 39:6
42:6 ᵃ» 44:7
43:8 ᵃ» 44:3
43:12 ᵃ» 23:5

resuscitated, who had been slain by the serpent,ᵃ because they had earnestly entreated him to visit them and to come into their house. ³But suddenly a very beautiful woman uttered a loud cry, "Apostle of the new Godᵃ who has come to India, and servant of that holy and unique good God—⁴for through you he is proclaimed, the savior of the soulsᵃ that come to him, and through you the bodies of those tormented by the enemyᵇ are healed, and you are the cause of lifeᶜ for all who turn to him—⁵allow me to be brought before you, so that I can tell you what has happened to me and thus perhaps gain some hope from you, and so that those present can become more confident in the God you proclaim. ⁶You see, for five years I've been greatly tormented by the hostile one.ᵃ ⁷Previously I lived quietly, as women do; peace surrounded me on all sides; I was concerned for nobody, and gave a thought for no one else.

43 "But one day, as I was getting out of my bath, someone, apparently disturbed and very agitated, confronted me. ²His speech seemed to me to be indistinct and weak. ³Confronting me he said, 'You and I shall be lovers; let us have relations with one another as a man does with a woman.' ⁴I answered him, 'I've not been with my betrothed, since I'm trying to avoid marriage. ⁵So how could I give myself to you, who want to have adulterous intercourse with me?' ⁶When I said this I left the place, but to the servant girl who accompanied me I said, 'Did you see the impertinence of that youth! How boldly he dared speak with me!' ⁷She answered, 'But I saw an old man conversing with you.' ⁸When I got home and had finished dinner, I became suspicious, especially because he had appeared to me in two forms.ᵃ ⁹With this on my mind, I fell asleep and in that very night he came to me and communed with me in his filthy intercourse. ¹⁰Sometimes I also saw him during the day, and then I'd flee from him; but when he came to me at night, which was his customary time, then he abused me. ¹¹As you see me now, I've been tormented by him for five years, and still he won't leave me alone. ¹²But I know and believeᵃ that demons, spirits, and ghosts are subject to you and are terrified by your prayer. ¹³Pray for me, then, and drive from me the demon that torments me, so that I might be free, be restored to my original nature, and receive the gift that has been given to my kindred."

43:3 • *relations:* The term used here frequently for sexual relations is κοινωνία, which, like "communion," has a different set of connotations in, e.g., the epiclesis of chap. 49.

44 The apostle said,

O wickedness uncontrollable,
    O shamelessness[a] of the enemy;[b]
[2]O torment never idle,
    O ugly one who overcomes the beautiful;
[3]O you of many forms,
    you appear however and wherever you wish,
    but your nature cannot be changed;[a]
[4]O you who are from the deceitful and faithless one,
    O bitter tree, whose fruits are like you;[a]
[5]O you who are from the devil,
    who fights for those who are alien,
    O you who are from the error[a] that employs insolence;
[6]O you who are from the wickedness
    that crawls like a serpent,
    and are from his kind.

[7]When the apostle had finished speaking, the malevolent one came and stood before him, but no one saw him except the woman and the apostle. [8]He did, however, utter a loud cry, which everyone heard:

45 What do you want of us, apostle of the Most High?[a]
    What do you want of us, servant of Jesus Christ?[b]

44:1 [a]» 33:2
[b]» 44:7
44:3 [a]Cf. AJn 84:1; APeVer 8:16–32
44:4 [a]Cf. APeVer 8:19
44:5 [a]» 25:3
45:1 [a]Cf. Mt 8:29; Mk 5:7; Lk 8:28; AAnGE 17:1
[b]Cf. Rm 1:1; Phl 1:1; Jude 1

44:1 • *The apostle said:* What follows may reflect exorcistic rituals. There are similar sets of invocations in AcJohn 84; AcPetVerc 8.
44:3 • *you of many forms* (ὁ πολύμορφος): A very frequent motif in this writing (though the specific term occurs only here in AcThom, see also 34:2; 43:8; 48:3; 153:1) and other apocryphal acts, though of considerable antiquity. See Plato *Rep.* 2.462; Irenaeus *Adv. haer.* 1.10.3; AJn 85:3; AcPetVerc 21:12–13.
44:7 • *the malevolent one* (δυσμενής), only here in the writing; but similarly "the hostile one" (ὁ ἐναντίος) in 42:6; 157:14; "the evil one " (ὁ πονηρός) in 48:2; 94:11; 106:1; 144:4; and the more frequent "enemy" (ὁ ἐθχρός) in 10:8; 29:6; 30:7; 34:5; 39:5, 13; 42:4; 44:1; 49:3; 85:6; 86:1. The latter term is used once (in 106:1) of the apostle Thomas, by his adversary Carish.
45:1 • *What do you want of us* (τί ὑμῖν καὶ σοί;)? The wording recalls a demoniac's cry in Mark 1:24 and Luke 4:34, where Jesus is addressed as Ἰησοῦ Ναζαρηνέ; also Jesus' response to his mother in John 2:4 (τί ἐμοὶ καὶ σοί;).

44:3 *you appear:* The verse has been conformed throughout to the second person ("you"), with Syr.

44:6 *are,* reading ὑπάρχων (nominative) for ὑπάρχοντος (genitive).

45:2 ª» 33:5
45:6 ªCf. Hb 13:5
46:2 ªCf. Mt 3:17; Mk
1:11; Lk 3:22

²What do you want of us, counselor of the holy Son of God?
> Why do you wish to destroy us?
>> —our time has not yet come.ª

³For what purpose do you wish to usurp our authority?
> For up to this present hour
> we have had hope and time left for us.

⁴What do want of us?
> You have authority among your own kind,
> and we among ours.

⁵For what purpose do you wish
> to exercise tyrannical power against us,
> especially since you teach others
> not to exercise such power?

⁶For what purpose do you need possessions of others, not
> being satisfied with your own?ª
> For what purpose have you become like the Son of God,
> who did us wrong?

⁷You seem very much like him,
> as if you were his offspring.

⁸And we thought that we would make him our subject, just like everyone else, but he turned around and held us in his power. ⁹But we didn't recognize him: he deceived us by that most ugly form of his, and by his poverty and need. ¹⁰For when we saw him like that we thought that he was a flesh-clad man, not knowing that he is the one who gives life to all humankind. ¹¹But he gave us power among our own and for the present time he has granted us not to leave our own, but to operate in them. ¹²Yet you wish to oppress us and to get more than what is necessary and due to you.

46 After saying this, the demon cried out, "I leave you, my most beautiful companion, whom I found long ago and took delight in. ²I leave you behind, my brave sister, my dearest love in whom I'm well pleased.ª ³I don't know what to do, or who to call on to defend me. ⁴Yes! I know what I'll do: I'll go away to some places where the renown of this man has not been heard and perhaps instead of you I'll call another my dearest love." ⁵He raised his voice and said, "Remain in peace; take refuge in one greater than I. ⁶I'll go away and

46:2 *my dearest love* . . . : Syr lacks this demonic parody.

seek one like you, and if I don't find someone, I'll return to you again.[a] [7]For I know that while you are near this man you have in him a refuge, but that when he departs, you'll be as you were before he appeared. [8]You'll forget him and I'll have my chance for boldness; but for now I fear the name of the one who has saved you." [9]When the demon finished speaking he vanished; only fire and smoke were seen there when he left, and all the bystanders were astonished.

47 When the apostle saw it all he said to them, "This demon hasn't made any strange or unusual manifestation, but has only shown his nature, by which he will be burnt. [2]For the fire will consume him and the smoke from him will be scattered."

[3]And he began to speak:

> Jesus, the hidden mystery[a] which has been revealed to us,
> > you are the one who reveals to us all sorts of mysteries;[b]
> [4]The one who set me apart from my companions,
> > and said to me three words by which I am inflamed,
> > but which I cannot tell others;[a]
> [5]Jesus, a man slain, dead, buried;
> > Jesus, God of God, Savior,
> > who brings the dead to life and heals the sick;
> [6]Jesus, who is in need as if <the one to be saved>,
> > and who saves as one who has no need;[a]
> [7]Who catches the fish for breakfast and for dinner,[a]
> > who fills everyone with a little bread;[b]
> [8]Jesus, who rests from the weariness of travel as a human,[a]
> > and who walks over the waves as God;[b]

48 [1]Jesus Most High,
> > Voice[a] that has arisen from perfect mercy,[b]
> > Savior of all;

46:6 [a]Cf. Mt 12:42–45; Lk 11:24–26

47:3 [a]Cf. Eph 3:9; Col 1:26

[b]» 10:5

47:4 [a]Cf. 131:5; Th (NHC II,2) 13:34,30–35,14

47:6 [a]Cf. APaTh 17:2

47:7 [a]Cf. Jn 21:6, 11, 12

[b]Cf. Mt 14:15–21; 15:32–38; Mk 6:35–44; 8:1–9; Lk 9:12–17

47:8 [a]Cf. Jn 4:6

[b]Cf. 66:4; Mt 14:25; Mk 6:48; Jn 6:19

48:1 [a]» 156:2

[b]Cf. 50:2; AJn 24:2

47:6 • *one who has no need:* That the divine has no need is a Hellenistic theological and philosophical commonplace. See, e.g., Aristotle *E.N.* 8.10 "a king needs nothing"; *Met.* 10.4 "The complete needs nothing"; *Ep. Arist.* 211 "God does not want anything"; 2 Macc 14:35; Philo *Deus* 56; Josephus *Ant.* 8.111; *Sent. Sextus* (NHC XII,1) 382: 33,22–24 "God does not need anything, but rejoices over those who give to the needy"; Plotinus *Enn.* 3.8.11 "the Good needs nothing (τὸ δὲ ἀγαθὸν οὐδένος δεῖται)"; 3.6.6 "Since it [Being, or νοῦς] is complete it has no need of anything for its preservation and existence"; 3.8.11.

47:4 *three words:* Syr lacks "three."   **47:6** *the one to be saved:* Sense requires some such restoration; Syr lacks the clause.

48:2 ª» 44:7

48:3 ª» 34:2; AJn 88–93

48:4 ªCf. 60:1; 122:4; Jn 1:14

ᵇCf. Rm 8:29

48:6 ª» 39:6

48:7 ªCf. Mt 27:63; Rv 12:9

ᵇ» 25:3

48:10 ª» 35:3

48:11 ªCf. Eph 4:22; Col 3:9, 10

49:1 ª» 10:12

ᵇ» 1:5

49:3 ª» 44:7

49:4 ª» 10:12

ᵇ» 25:4

ᶜ» 27:10

²Right hand of the light,
>   who subjects the evil oneª with his proper nature,
>   and who gathers all <those of> his <own> nature
> into one place;

³The one who takes many forms;ª

⁴Who is the only-begotten,ª
>   the firstborn of many brothers and sisters;ᵇ

⁵God from God Most High;
>   the Man despised until now, Jesus Christ,
>   who does not ignore us when we call on you;

⁶Who became the cause of human life for all,ª
>   who on our behalf is judged and tormented in prison,
>   and who releases all those who are in bonds;

⁷Who is called a deceiver,ª
>   and <yet> who redeems his own from error:ᵇ

⁸I beseech you for those who stand here and believe in you,
>   for they need to receive your gifts,
>   confident of your aid and with a refuge in your majesty.

⁹They hold their ears,
>   ready to hear the words that we speak.

¹⁰Let your peace come on them and dwell in them,
>   let it renew them from their previous activities,ª

¹¹and let them put off the old humanityª with its activities,
>   and put on the new, which is proclaimed to them by me.

49 He laid his hands on themª and blessed them, saying, "The grace of our Lord Jesus be with you forever."ᵇ

²And they said, "Amen."

³The woman made a request of him: "Apostle of the Most High, give me the seal, so that that enemyª may not return to me again."

⁴Then he made her come near him, laid his hands on her,ª and sealed herᵇ in the name of the Father, Son, and Holy Spirit;ᶜ and many others received the seal along with her. ⁵The apostle then

---

49:3 • *seal:* For σφραγίς, in AcThom (see also 26:1; 27:1; 50:9; 51:9; 54:1; 87:5; 118:5; 120:1; 121:9; 131:4; 150:1; 152:8; 161:1) Syr commonly has ܪܘܫܡܐ ("sign"); but note Rev 13:17, for χάραγμα; and elsewhere in the NT, σφραγίς is rendered, e.g., ܐܬܘܬܐ (Rom 4:11; 1 Cor 9:2; 2 Tim 2:19); ܛܒܥܐ (Rev 5:1).

48:2 *own* is added from Syr. Although it refers to "possessions" rather than to nature, it is clear that what is in view is what is "co-natural" with

Jesus. See also 78:10.

48:5 ... *despised until now:* Here Syr has additional material; see the Appendix.

ordered his deacon to prepare a table, and they put up a bench which they found there. [6]He spread out a linen cloth on it and set out the bread of blessing. [7]The apostle stood by and said, "Jesus who deemed us worthy to partake of the eucharist of your sacred body and blood, now we make bold to approach your eucharist and to call on your holy name. Come and partake with us."

50 And he began to speak:

[2]Come, perfect compassion;[a]
Come, fellowship of the male;[b]
[3]Come, Lady,
    you who understand the mysteries of the chosen one,
Come, Lady,
    you who share in all the contests of the noble athlete,[a]
[4]Come, Respite,[a]
    you who reveal the magnitudes of every greatness,
Come, Lady, you who make manifest what is secret
    and render visible what is hidden;
    the sacred dove which gives birth to twin nestlings.[a]
[5]Come, hidden Mother;[a]
Come, Lady, you who are manifest in your own activities,[b]
    and who furnish joy and repose
     to those who cleave to you;
[6]Come and share with us in this eucharist
    that we make in your name,
    and in the love by which we are united
    at your summons.

[7]When he had spoken, he marked the sign of the cross[a] on the bread, broke it, and began to distribute it. [8]He gave it first to the woman, saying, "May this be for the remission of sins and eternal transgressions." [9]And after her he distributed also to the others who had received the seal.[a]

50:2 [a]Cf. 39:9; 48:1; 132:6; 156:8
[b]Cf. 27:7
50:3 [a]» 39:14
50:4 [a]Cf. 39:9
[b]» 31:7
50:5 [a]» 7:10
[b]Cf. Mt 11:19
50:7 [a]Cf. AAnMt 19:3; 29:5; AAnGE 9:2; APaTh 22:3
50:9 [a]» 49:3

50:1 • *fellowship of the male:* The same unusual phrase appears in the epiclesis in chap. 27.
50:6 • *love,* or "love feast" (ἀγάπη), a common meal shared by early Christians; see also AcPaulThec 25:1.
50:8 • *for the remission of sins* (εἰς ἄφεσιν ἁμαρτιῶν), including the preposition εἰς ("for, resulting in"), as in 133:5; 157:14; 158:3. But see 132:1.

ACT 6 A MURDEROUS YOUTH

51:2 ªCf. 1Cor 11:30;
APeVer 2:4
51:5 ª» 29:10
51:7 ª» 24:7
51:9 ª» 49:3
51:12 ª» 95:11
52:4 ªCf. Jn 4:10–11;
7:38; *Did.* 7:1

51 There was a youth who had committed an unspeakable deed. [2]When he approached and took the eucharist to his mouth his two hands shriveled up, so that they were no longer able to reach his mouth.[a] [3]Bystanders who saw him reported the event to the apostle. [4]So he called the young man and said, "Tell me, child—and don't be ashamed—tell me what you've done and how you came to be here. [5]The eucharist of the Lord has indicted you;[a] for when this gift comes to most people, especially those who approach it in faith and love, it heals them; but it has caused you to shrivel up. [6]What has taken place did not occur without some divine influence."

[7]The youth, convicted by the Lord's eucharist, approached, fell at the apostle's feet,[a] and implored him: "I've done a wicked deed. You see, I was seeking to accomplish something noble. [8]I fell in love with a certain woman who lives outside the city in an inn, and she loved me. [9]When I heard of you and came to believe that you proclaim the living God, I approached and received the seal[a] from you along with the others. [10]'Whoever has intercourse in a defiling union,' you said, 'especially in adultery, will not have life with the God I proclaim.' [11]So since I loved her dearly, I begged her and tried to persuade her to be my companion in purity and in a chaste way of life, the sort that you teach. [12]But she didn't want to;[a] and since she was unwilling, I took a sword and killed her, for I couldn't watch her commit adultery with someone else."

52 When the apostle heard this story he said, "O insane intercourse, how far into shamelessness you go! [2]O unrestrained desire, how did you move this man to do these things? O work of the serpent, how you rage among your own!"

[3]The apostle then ordered water to be brought to him in a basin. [4]When it arrived, he said, "Come, waters from the living waters,[a] realities from what is real and that have been sent to us; rest that has been sent us from rest; salvific power that comes from the power which conquers all and subdues all things to its own will—[5]come and dwell in these waters, so that the gift of the Holy Spirit might be brought to perfect completion in them."

51:8 • *in an inn:* The woman is apparently a prostitute.

[6] He said to the youth, "Go and wash your hands in these waters."[a]

[7] When he had washed, his hands were restored and the apostle said to him, "Do you believe in our Lord Jesus Christ, that he is able to do all things?"

[8] The youth said, "Even if I'm the least of all people, I do believe. But I did what I did, intending to do something good. [9] For I begged her, as I told you, but she didn't wish to be persuaded by me and keep herself chaste."

53 The apostle said to him, "Come, let's go to the inn where you did this deed, and let's see what happened." So the youth led the apostle on the way.

[2] When they arrived at the inn, they found her lying down. The apostle was distressed at the sight—she was a lovely young woman—and he ordered her brought to the center of the hospice. [3] They put her on a pallet, brought her out, and placed her in the center of the courtyard of the inn. [4] He placed his hand on her and began to speak: "Jesus, who are always becoming manifest to us—for this is what you wish, that we always seek after you—you yourself have given us the authority to ask and receive. [5] You've not only allowed this, you've also taught us to pray.[a] [6] You're not seen with bodily eyes, but you're not entirely hidden from the eyes of our soul.[a] [7] You're hidden from direct sight, but manifest to us in your works. [8] We've recognized you in your many activities as we have the capacity to do so,[a] and you've granted us your gifts without measure, saying, 'Ask and it shall be given to you; seek and you shall find, knock and it shall be opened to you.'[b] [9] Therefore, aware of our sins, we beseech you and ask you not for wealth, gold, silver, any possession, nor anything else that is on earth and returns to earth.[a] [10] No, we ask and request that by your holy name and power you raise up this woman who's lying here, for <your> glory and for the faith of those who are here."

54 He put the seal[a] on the youth and said to him, "Go, take her hand, and say to her, 'By my hands I murdered you with an iron <sword>, and by my own hands I raise you up in the faith of Jesus.'"

[2] The youth then approached the woman, stood over her, and said, "I've come to believe in you, Christ Jesus." [3] He looked to Judas Thomas the apostle, and said to him, "Pray for me, that the Lord

52:6 [a]Cf. 2 Kgs 5:10, 14; Jn 9:7

53:5 [a]Cf. Mt 6:5–9; Lk 11:2

53:6 [a]» 28:2

53:8 [a]Cf. APeVer 20:12

[b]Cf. Mt 7:7; Lk 11:9; AJn 22:6

53:9 [a]Cf. Sir 40:11; AJn 22:7

54:1 [a]» 49:3

53:10 *your* is added from Syr.

54:4 ª » 10:12
54:6 ª » 24:7
55:3 ª Cf. 64:4

I invoke will come to my aid." [4]He laid his hand on her hand[a] and said, "Come, Lord Jesus Christ. Grant to this woman life, and to me the pledge of your fidelity."

[5]As soon as he took her hand, she jumped up, took a seat, and looked at the great crowd standing about; she also saw the apostle standing opposite her. [6]She jumped off of her pallet, fell at his feet,[a] grasped his garments, and said, "Please, sir, where is that other person who was with you, who did not allow me to remain in that dreadful and terrible place, but delivered me to you saying, 'Take this woman so that she might be perfected and afterwards be gathered to her own place'?"

55 The apostle then said to her, "Tell us where you were."

[2]She answered, "You, who were with me, to whom I was delivered—you want to hear from me?" [3]And she began to tell her story: "A certain man took me; he was odious in his appearance, all black,[a] and his clothing was thoroughly soiled. [4]He brought me to a place in which there were many pits—there was a horrible stench, and noxious fumes coming out. [5]He made me look into every pit, and I saw in the <first> pit fire burning. [6]Wheels of fire were running about there and souls were suspended on those wheels and they were dashing against one another. [7]Crying and lamentation was there in abundance, but no one was released. [8]That man said to me, 'These souls are your kin; for a certain number of days they have been given over to punishment and chastisement. [9]Then others are brought in in their stead, while in like fashion they also go to another place. [10]These are the souls who have exchanged the intercourse of men and women.' [11]And when I looked in I saw infants piled up on one another and lying on one another struggling. [12]He said to me, 'These are the infant children of these souls and therefore they have been placed here as a testimony against them.'

56 "He led me to another pit. Looking in I saw a pit with worms gushing out. [2]There souls were being rolled about, and a great moaning was heard from them. [3]That man said to me, 'These are

---

55:3 • *her story:* The woman narrates a "tour of hell," a form common in apocalypses.
55:10 • *exchanged the intercourse* is presumably a reference to homosexual activity; cf. Rom 1:26–27.

55:5 *first* is added in conformity with Syr.

the souls of women who have left their husbands and committed adultery with other men and have been brought to this torment.' [4]He showed me another pit; I looked into it and saw some souls hanging by their tongues, others by their hair, others by their hands, others by their feet with their heads down; they were blackened with smoke and brimstone. [5]The man who was with me told me this about them: 'The souls that are hung by their tongues are slanderers; without shame they have uttered false and despicable words. [6]The shameless ones hung by their hair are those who have exercised no modesty and have gone about in the world with their heads uncovered. [7]Those hung by their hands are people who have pilfered and stolen the property of others, who have never given any alms to the poor, nor offered any succor to the oppressed, but have done everything thinking only of gain and giving no thought at all to what is right or just. [8]The ones who are hung upside down by their feet are people who have run with merry abandon down evil ways and undisciplined paths, not looking after the sick nor participating in the funeral processions for the departed. [9]So each individual soul receives requital for what it has done.'

57 "He led me on and showed me a cave that was quite dark and reeking with a foul smell. [2]Many souls tried to peek out, wanting to get a little air, but their guards did not allow them. [3]My companion said, 'This is the prison of the souls you saw. [4]When they have completed their punishments for the things which each one has done, others afterwards take their place. [5]But some are completely consumed; others are given over to other punishments.' [6]Those who guarded the souls in the dark cave said to the man who took me along, 'Give her to us, so we can bring her in to the others as long as the time is set for her to be given over to punishment.' [7]He answered them, 'I will not give her to you, for I fear the one who gave her over to me; I was commanded not to leave her here. [8]I shall take her back with me, until I receive instructions about her.' [9]He took me and led me off to another place, in which were men who were tormented bitterly. [10]The one who was like you took me and delivered me to you, saying, 'Take this woman, since she is one of the creatures that have gone astray.'[a] [11]I was received by you and stand before you now; I earnestly beseech you therefore that I not go back to those places of punishment that I saw."

57:10 [a]Cf. AJn 74:7

57:10 *creatures:* Syr "sheep."

58:2 ª» 35:3

ᵇ» 38:3

58:3 ª» 38:2

58:4 ªCf. Eph 4:22;
Col 3:9–10

58:5 ªCf. Gn 3:17–19;
Eph 4:28; 2Ths 3:10

58:6 ª» 84:1

58:7 ª» Eph 4:25;
Col 3:8

ᵇCf. Prv 20:22; Rm
12:17; 1Ths 5:15;
1Pt 3:9; AJn 81:6;
APa 2:13; Plato
Crito 49C

58:9 ªCf. Lv 19:2; Mt
5:48; Lk 6:36; Plato
Theat. 176B

ᵇCf. 68:5

59:2 ªCf. Ac 6:2; AJn
59:1

ᵇ» 19:9

59:3 ªCf. Ac 18:28

58 The apostle said, "You have heard what this woman has re-lated; and these are not the only punishments—there are others worse than these. ²As for you, if you don't return to the God I pro-claim, and refrain from your former deeds[a] and the activities you performed without knowledge,[b] you will end up in these punish-ments. ³Believe, then, in Christ Jesus. He will forgive you the sins done before this time,[a] will purify you from all your bodily desires that remain on earth, and will heal you from the failings that fol-low, accompany you, and are found before you. ⁴Each one of you, then, put off the old self and put on the new;[a] leave behind your former behavior and way of life. ⁵Let thieves no longer steal, but let them live by work and toil.[a] ⁶Let adulterers no longer commit sexual immorality, so that they might not render themselves liable to eternal punishment; for adultery is more serious in the eyes of God than the other sins.[a] ⁷Lay aside greed, falsehood,[a] drunkenness and slander, and don't requite evil with evil.[b] ⁸All these things are foreign and alien to the God I proclaim. ⁹Live instead in faith, gen-tleness, holy chastity, and hope, in which God rejoices, so that you may become like him,[a] accepting from him the gifts that only a very few receive."[b]

59 All the people believed, and they made their souls docile to the living God and to Christ Jesus, rejoicing in the good works blessed by the Most High and in his holy service. ²They provided money[a] in abundance for the care of the widows, for he had them assembled in the cities and dispatched provisions, both clothing and funds for food, to all of them through his own servants.[b] ³He himself did not cease preaching, speaking to them, and demonstrat-ing that Jesus is the Christ about whom the scriptures made their proclamation,[a]—he who came, was crucified, and raised from the dead after three days. ⁴Then, beginning with the prophets' state-

---

58:9 • *holy chastity*: ἀγιωσύνη, "sanctity"; Syr ﺭﺩﺣﺍﺱﺩﺗﺍ implies chastity. For similar connotations see 85:3; 86:4; 97:3; 104:3; 131:3; 139:13. Festugière (1983: 85 n. 28) cautions that *LPGL* (s.v. 5 [p. 19b]) cites only AcThom (97:3; 104:3) for this specific meaning.

59:3 *he who came, . . . after three days* (ὃς ἐλθὼν σταυροῦται καὶ ἐγείρεται διὰ τριῶν ἡμέρων ἐκ νεκρῶν) is a creedal summary of possible antiq-uity. The prepositional phrase ("after three days") is the same as in Jesus' "destroy this temple" say-

ing (Matt 26:61; Mark 14:58; contrast John 2:19 ἐν τρισὶν ἡμέραῖς). P has a fuller statement: "who was crucified, and was buried, and on the third day (τῇ τρίτῃ ἡμέρᾳ) arose, and is seated at the right hand of the Father."

ments[a] about the Christ, he again demonstrated that it was necessary for him to come and that in him were fulfilled all that had been foretold about him. [5]His renown spread throughout all the cities and outlying districts, and all who had relatives ill or distressed by unclean spirits brought them forward.[a] [6]Some they placed in the road on which he was going to pass and he healed everyone with the Lord's power.[a] [7]Then all who had been healed said with one voice in chorus, "Glory to you, Jesus, who has afforded healing on an equal basis through your servant and apostle Thomas. [8]Rejoicing in our health we ask you to become members of your flock and to be numbered among your sheep. [9]Receive us then, Lord, and don't take account of our transgressions and the previous errors[a] that we committed in ignorance."[b]

60 The apostle said,

Glory to the only-begotten of the Father.[a]
 Glory to the firstborn of many brothers and sisters,[b]
[2]Glory to you, the defender and helper
 of those who come to you for refuge.
[3]The sleepless one who awakens those who are asleep,[a]
 the Living One[b] who gives life to those who lie in death,
[4]God, Jesus Christ, Son of the living God,[a]
 redeemer and helper, refuge and rest[b]
 of all those who are weary with your labor;[c]
[5]You who provide healing to those who,
 for the sake of your name,
 bear the burden and the heat of the day;[a]
[6]To you we give thanks[a]
 for the gifts that have been given to us
 and bestowed on us with your help,
 and for the guidance that has come to us.

61 Now bring these gifts to perfect completion for us,

 so we may have confidence in you.
[2]Look on us, because for your sake
 we have left our homes and our parents,[a]
 and for your sake
 we readily and willingly have become strangers.

59:4 [a]Cf. 70:3(e)†; Lk 24:27
59:5 [a]Cf. Lk 6:18
59:6 [a]Cf. Ac 5:15
59:9 [a]» 35:3
[b]» 38:3
60:1 [a]» 48:4
[b]» 16:9
60:3 [a]Cf. 110:43; 153:7; Eph 5:14
[b]Cf. 118:5; 147:11; Rv 1:18; Th (NHC II,2) *proem.*: 32,10
60:4 [a]» 10:8
[b]» 10:2
[c]Cf. Mt 11:28
60:5 [a]Cf. 73:2; 78:2; Mt 20:12
60:6 [a]15:2
61:2 [a]Cf. Mt 19:27; Mk 10:28; Lk 18:28; AAnMt 2:4; AAnBod f.103,5

60:1 • *The apostle said:* Syr lacks the clear NT allusions in this chapter.

61:4 ªCf. Mt 19:29;
Mk 10:29–30; Lk
18:29–30

ᵇCf. Mt 12:46–50; Mk
3:31–35; Lk 8:19–21;
Hb 3:6

61:7 ªCf. Jn 15:4–10

62:1 ªCf. Mt 10:8;
1Cor 9:18; 2Cor
11:7–9

62:5 ªCf. AJn 20:4

³Look on us, Lord, because we have left our own property
 for your sake,
  to have you as an inalienable possession.
⁴Look on us, Lord, because we have left our kinsfolkª
 to be joined to your family.ᵇ
⁵Look on us, Lord,
 who have left our fathers, mothers, and nurses,
 to see your Father
 and be filled with his divine nourishment.
⁶Look on us, Lord, because for your sake
 we have left our earthly spouses,
 to share in that steadfast and true communion
⁷and bear true fruits, the nature of which is supernal,
 which no one can take from us,
 in which we abide as they abide in us.ª

ACT 7 GENERAL SIFOR

62 While the apostle Judas Thomas was proclaiming the word of God throughout India, a certain general of King Mizdai came to him and said, ²"I've heard that you don't accept pay from anyone,ª but you provide to those in need whatever you do have. ³Now if you did accept pay, I would have sent money in abundance and I myself wouldn't have come here. The king, you see, does nothing without me. ⁴Furthermore, I have many possessions and am, in fact, quite wealthy, one of the richest men in India. ⁵I've never wronged anyone,ª but, to the contrary, I've been wronged. ⁶I have a wife and I had a daughter by her. I feel deep affection for her, as of course nature demands, and I have no experience of any other woman. ⁷Now there happened to be a wedding in our city, and the hosts were dear friends of mine. So they came and asked my permission to invite my wife and daughter. ⁸Since they were good friends, I couldn't refuse. ⁹So I sent her, even though she didn't want to go, and I sent along many of my retainers with them. ¹⁰So off they went, richly adorned, both my wife and daughter.

62:1 • *a certain general:* He is finally named in 100:8: Σιφώρ ("Sifor"); for the form, see Bonnet, *Aaa* 2/2. 215 line 7.

 Mizdai: In Greek the name is "Misdaios" (Μισδαῖος); in Syr he is unnamed until chap. 87.

63 "When dusk fell and it was time to leave the wedding banquet, I sent lamps and torches to greet them; I even stood in the road watching, to see when she would come, so I could see her and my daughter. [2]Standing there I heard the sound of lamentation: 'Too bad for her!' was heard from every mouth. [3]The slaves, their clothes torn, came to me to tell what had happened. [4]They said: 'We saw a certain man, and with him a child; the man laid his hand on your wife, and the child did likewise to your daughter. The women fled from them. [5]We tried to smite them with swords, but our swords fell to the ground;[a] but at that moment the women fell gnashing their teeth and beating their heads on the ground. [6]So when we saw this we came to tell you.' [7]I tore my clothes[a] when I heard this, then struck my face with my hands and ran down the road like a maniac. [8]When I arrived, I found them sprawled out in the marketplace. I took them and brought them home, and after a long time they awoke and sat up, restored.

64 "I began to question my wife, 'What happened to you?' [2]She said to me, 'Don't you know what you have done to me? I begged you not to make me go to the wedding, since I was out of sorts. [3]While going along the road I came near an aqueduct in which water was flowing. [4]I saw a black man[a] standing opposite me motioning to me with his head, and a child like him standing at his side. [5]I said to my daughter, 'Look at these two ugly men, with teeth like milk, but lips like soot.' [6]We left them at the aqueduct and went on. [7]When dusk fell and we had left the wedding, as we went along with our lads and came near the aqueduct, my daughter saw them first and, fleeing their gaze, ran to me. [8]Afterwards I, too, saw them coming toward us and we fled from them, as <did> the boys who were with us. [9]They struck us and threw me against my daughter.'

[10]"When she had related this story to me, the demons attacked them again, and threw them down. [11]From that moment they have been unable to go out, but are locked up in one house or another. [12]Because of them I've suffered a lot and I'm in great distress, for

63:5 [a]Cf. AJn 49:3
63:7 [a]Cf. 16:1
64:4 [a]Cf. 55:3
65:6 [a]» 28:2
65:7 [a]Cf. Mk 9:24
66:1 [a]Cf. 29:7
[b]» 16:9
66:4 [a]Cf. 47:8; Mt 8:23–26; Mk 4:35–41; Lk 8:22–25; Jn 6:16–21

63:4 *they said*, reading φασίν for φησίν ("he says/said"), with Syr; see Bonnet, *Aaa* 2/2. 179 n. 18.
64:4 *motioning* is supplied from Syr. Gr has ὑπογρυλίζοντα, a participial form of ὑπογρυλίζειν, a word apparently not found elsewhere in extant literature; *LPGL* (s.v. [p. 1446b]) offers the definition, suggested by this context, "reprove gently." The simple γρυλίζειν means "to grunt (of a pig),"

which is difficult with the phrase "with his head." But LSJ (s.v. [p. 361a]) detects its use with reference to a person in Procopius (6th cent. c.e.) *Arc.* 17.
64:8 *did* is added from Syr. This clarifies the antecedent of the subject pronoun "they " in the next clause; otherwise the lads strike the women.

66:5 ªCf. Ac 20:5
66:6 ªCf. 32:11; Ex 32
66:8 ªCf. 1Cor 3:5, 22

they cast them down wherever they happen to be and they strip them naked. ¹³I urge you, I beg you before God, help me and have pity on me; it has been three years since a table was set in my house at which my wife and daughter would sit. ¹⁴I'm particularly grieved over my daughter, who has never seen anything good in this world."

65 When the apostle heard this from the general, he was quite saddened. ²He said to him, "Do you believe that Jesus will heal them?"

³"Yes," said the general.

⁴The apostle replied, "Entrust yourself to Jesus and he will heal them and give them his aid."

⁵The general said, "Show him to me, that I may ask him and believe in him."

⁶The apostle said, "He does not appear to these bodily eyes, but is found with the eyes of the mind."ª

⁷The general then raised his voice and said, "I believe in you, Jesus, and I ask and beseech you, aid the little faith that I have in you."ª

⁸The apostle commanded Xanthippos, the deacon, to bring everyone together. ⁹When all the crowd was assembled, the apostle stood in their midst and said <this>:

66 "My children, brothersª and sistersᵇ who believe in the Lord, remain in this faith, preaching the good news of Jesus whom I proclaimed to you, and place your hope in him. ²Don't abandon him, and he won't abandon you. ³While you lie in the sleep that burdens sleepers, he who is sleepless guards you. ⁴When you sail on the sea and you're in danger and no one is able to help you, he who walks on the waters supports you and gives you aid.ª ⁵For I'm departing from you and it's unclear whether I'll see you again in the flesh.ª ⁶So don't be like the people of Israel, who stumbled when their shepherd was away for a short time.ª ⁷I leave behind for you Xanthippos, the deacon, in my place; for he, too, proclaims Jesus as I do. ⁸Neither am I nor is he important; the only thing that counts is Jesus.ª ⁹For I'm a man clothed with a body, a human being like

66:9 • *human being*, literally, "son of man."

65:8 *Xanthippos:* In Greek, the name is Xenophon (Ξενοφῶν).
66:6 *when their shepherd was away,* reading

ἀπιόντος τοῦ ποιμένος for ἀπιδόντες τοὺς ποιμένας ("looking at their shepherds"), with Syr; see Bonnet, *Aaa* 2/2. 183 n. 6.

one of you. [10]I don't have, as do some people, wealth, which, being altogether without any useful quality, produces reproach for those who possess it, and is left on the earth from which it is extracted. [11]It brings along the transgressions that people commit because of it and the defilement due to sins. [12]Rarely are wealthy men found involved in acts of mercy,[a] but the merciful and humble of heart shall inherit the kingdom of God.[b] [13]For human beauty doesn't last; those who rely on it are thrown into shame when old age suddenly overtakes them. [14]Everything has its season: there is a time for love and a time for hate.[a] [15]So let your hope be in Jesus Christ, the Son of God, who is always to be loved and desired. [16]Remember us as we remember you. [17]For we ourselves, if we don't bear the burden of the commandments,[a] aren't worthy to be heralds of this name, and shall later pay the penalty."

67 He prayed with them, remaining in prayer and supplication for a long time. [2]Entrusting them to the Lord, he said, "Lord, ruler of every soul that is in a body,[a] Lord, Father of the souls that have their hopes in you and anticipate your mercies—[3]you who redeem your own people from error,[a] who free from slavery and decay those who are obedient to you and who come to your refuge: [4]Be among the flock of Xanthippos and, having anointed it with the sacred oil, heal them of their wounds and keep the flock from the wolves[a] that despoil it." [5]Laying his hand on them,[a] he said, "May the peace of the Lord be with you[b] and may it accompany us on our way."

ACT 8 A HERD OF WILD ASSES

68 The apostle then went out and took to the road. [2]Everyone sent him off with tears in their eyes, but they made him promise to remember them in his prayers and not forget them. [3]The general mounted the carriage and took a seat, while all the believers[a] remained behind. [4]He came up and roused the driver, saying, "I prayerfully ask to be worthy to sit at his feet.[a] [5]I'll be his driver on this road, so that he might be my escort on that road that few travel."[a]

66:12 [a]Cf. Sir 44:10
[b]Cf. Mt 5:4; 11:29
66:14 [a]Cf. Ecc 3:1, 8
66:17 [a]Cf. Mt 11:29
67:2 [a]Cf. 30:5
67:3 [a]» 25:3
67:4 [a]» 25:5
67:5 [a]» 10:12
[b]» 1:5
68:3 [a]» 16:9
68:4 [a]» 9:3
68:5 [a]Cf. 58:9

66:17 • *pay the penalty*, literally, "pay the penalty of our own head"; see note on 21:11.

69:4 [a] » 21:6
[b] Cf. Jn 1:50
69:6 [a] » 20:4
[b] Cf. 70:2; Mt 21:3; Mk
11:3; Lk 19:31; AJn
113:2
70:2 [a] » 20:4
[b] » 69:6
70:4 [a] » 27:2
70:5 [a] » 40:12
70:7 [a] Cf. AAnMt
15:14–15; AJn 61:4

69 When they had gone about two miles the apostle requested the general to sit by his side, allowing the driver to take his proper seat. [2]When they had gone some way along the road the animals became exhausted from the excessive heat and could not be budged. [3]The general became quite annoyed and thoroughly discouraged. [4]He considered running back on foot himself and bringing other animals that the carriage needed, but the apostle said, "Don't let your heart be disturbed or afraid, but believe in Jesus Christ,[a] whom I have proclaimed to you, and you will see great marvels."[b] [5]He looked up and saw a herd of wild asses grazing by the road and said to the general, "If you believe in Christ Jesus, go to that herd of wild asses and say, [6]'Judas Thomas, the apostle of Christ, the new God,[a] says to you, "Let four of you come—we have need of you." ' "[b]

70 The general went off in trepidation, for there were many wild asses. [2]As he approached they came to meet him, and when they were near he said to them, "Judas Thomas, the apostle of the new God,[a] commands you, 'Come here, four of you—I need you.' "[b] [3]Hearing this, the wild asses all stampeded toward him, and when they reached him they fell down and did obeisance to him.

[4]The apostle said to them, "Peace to you.[a] Yoke up four in the place of these beasts that have been removed." [5]Each of them approached and pressed to be yoked up. But there were four stronger asses, and they were yoked; as for the rest, some went ahead and some followed.[a] [6]After they had gone a little way, the apostle released the asses, saying, "I say to you, inhabitants of the desert, go off to your pastures. [7]If I had needed all of you, you could have come along with me, but now go, return to the place where you live."[a] [8]And off they went, quietly, until they were out of sight.

71 The apostle was seated alongside the general and the driver. [2]The wild asses drew the carriage gently and evenly, so as not to disturb God's apostle. [3]When they neared the city gate, they turned

---

70:2 • *I need you* (ὧν χρείαν ἔχω), literally, "of whom I have need"; cf. Matt 21:3 = Mark 11:3 = Luke 19:31, 34 ὁ κύριος αὐτοῦ [Matthew: αὐτῶν] χρείαν ἔχει; and AcThom 39:1 "the foal of an ass."

70:3 *. . . did obeisance to him:* Here Syr has additional material; see the Appendix.
71:1 *was seated,* reading καθεζομένου for

ἀπερχομένου ("going away"); see Bonnet, *Aaa* 2/2. 187 n. 7.

aside and stood before the doors of the general's house. ⁴He said, "I'm not permitted to tell what has happened, but when I see the outcome I shall speak."

⁵Everyone in the city came when they saw the wild asses in harness; they had also heard the reputation of the apostle who was going to stay there.

⁶The apostle asked the general, "Where is your dwelling, and where are you leading us?"

⁷He answered, "You yourself know that we stand before the doors and these \<beasts\> who have come with you at your command understand better than I."

72:4 ᵃCf. Ac 20:28; 1Cor 6:20; Gal 3:13

72:5 ᵃCf. Mt 16:26; Mk 8:36–37; Lk 9:25; Jn 10:11; 15:12; *2Clem.* 1:1–4

73:1 ᵃ» 20:4

73:2 ᵃCf. 60:5; 78:2; Mt 20:6
ᵇCf. Mk 14:41; Jn 12:23; 13:1

73:4 ᵃCf. Mt 12:25; Mk 3:23–25; Lk 11:17–18

72 So saying, he dismounted from the carriage.

The apostle exclaimed:
Jesus Christ, whose knowledge is rejected in this country;
    Jesus, whose renown is alien to this city;
²Jesus, you who have taken all the apostles
    into every country and in every city,
    and all who are worthy of you are glorified by you;
³Jesus, you who have taken on \<human\> form,
    and have come to be a human and appeared to all of us
    so that you might not keep us apart from your love;
⁴It is you, Lord, who have given yourself for us,
    bought us by your blood, ᵃ
    and received us as a high-priced possession.
⁵So what can we give you, Lord,
    as a recompense for your life that you have given for us?ᵃ
⁶You give us what we desire, that is,
    to ask for you and live.

73 After he finished speaking, many people gathered from all around to see the apostle of the new God.ᵃ ²He spoke again: "Why do we stand idle?ᵃ Lord Jesus, the hour is come.ᵇ ³What do you require to happen? Command, then, that what ought to happen take place."

⁴The general's wife and daughter were sorely burdened by demons to the point that the members of their household believed that they could no longer stand.ᵃ ⁵For \<the demons\> did not allow

---

72:1 *Jesus . . . country,* following SyrB. P has an awkward literal rendition of SyrL: "Jesus, who is blasphemed through knowledge of you in this country"; V deals with the difficulty by reading "blasphemed through ignorance."

74:4 ª» 33:2
74:8 ªCf. AJn 84:7

them to partake of any food, but cast them on their beds, unable to recognize anyone, until the day the apostle came there. ⁶The apostle said to one of the wild asses yoked on the right side, "Go, stand in the courtyard, call out to the demons, and say to them, 'Judas Thomas, the apostle and disciple of Jesus Christ, says, "Come out here." ' ⁷For I've been sent on account of you and those who belong to your race, so that I might destroy you and pursue you to your realm until the time of consummation when you will go to your dark depth."

74 The wild ass entered, accompanied by a great crowd, and said:

> I speak to you, enemies of Jesus who is called Christ;
> ²I speak to you who make eyes blind
>   so that they may not see the light,
>   for the most evil nature is not capable
>   of being changed into good;
> ³I speak to you, offspring of Gehenna and of destruction,
>   of him who unceasingly pursues evil
>   to this very moment,
>   who ever renews his activities
>   and the things proper to his nature;
> ⁴I speak to you, most shameless creatures,ª
>   who perish of your own accord.
> ⁵What things I should say about your final destruction,
>   or what I should relate, I don't know.
> ⁶They are many, far too numerous to hear:
>   However great your torments may be,
>   they are less than you deserve.
> ⁷I speak to you, demon, and to your son who follows you,
>   for now I have been sent to you.
> ⁸For what purpose should I describe at length
>   your nature and root,ª
>   which you yourselves know
>   and of which you are unashamed?

73:7 • *time of consummation* (καιρὸς συντελείας): Similar expressions appear in 85:7 (τὸν καιρὸν τῆς ἀπολυτρώσεως); 159:4 (ὁ καιρὸς τῆς ἀπαλλαγῆς); and see Acts 3:20 (καιροὶ ἀναψύξεως); AcJohn 22:2 (καιρὸς ἀναψύξεως).

74:6 *they are less than you deserve:* The translation follows SyrB. Gr, with extremely awkward syntax, reads "But your actions are greater than the punishment which is reserved for you."

⁹But Judas Thomas, the apostle of Christ Jesus speaks to you,
  he who was sent here by an immense loving will.
¹⁰In the presence of the entire multitude here,
  come out and tell me the race to which you belong.ᵃ

75 Immediately the woman came out with her daughter, in disarray, nearly dead. ²When he saw them, the apostle was saddened, especially because of the child, and said to the demons, "Let there be no favor or pity for you—you understand neither pity nor mercy. ³But in the name of Jesus, come out of them and stand aside."

⁴When the apostle had spoken, the women fell down as if dead, for they had no breath and made no sound. ⁵The demon responded in a loud voice, "Have you returned here, you who mock our nature and race? Have you returned, who blots out our traces? ⁶As I see it, you won't let us to remain on the earth at all. But you cannot accomplish this now." ⁷The apostle presumed that this was the demon that had been expelled from that <other> woman.ᵃ

76 The demon said,

I beg of you, command me and I'll go and live wherever you wish,ᵃ and take orders from you. ²I don't fear the authority who has power over me. ³For as you have come to preach the good news, so I, too, have come to destroy. ⁴In your case, if you don't do the will of the one who sent you,ᵃ he'll punish you. ⁵Likewise in my case, if I don't do the will of the one who sent me,ᵃ then before the appropriate and ordained timeᵇ I will be returned to my own nature:
  ⁶As Christ helps you in what you do,
    so my fatherᵃ helps me in what I do.
  ⁷As <Christ> constructs vessels for you
    that are worthy for you to inhabit,
    so <my father> seeks out vessels for me
    through which I might perform his activities.
  ⁸As <Christ> nourishes and provides for his subjects,
    so he prepares torments and punishments for me
    along with those in whom I dwell.

74:10 ᵃCf. 31:10
75:7 ᵃCf. 42–50
76:1 ᵃCf. 1:6
76:4 ᵃ» 76:5
76:5 ᵃCf. 39:7; 76:4;
79:8; 168:1; 171:1;
Jn 4:34; 5:30; 6:38, 40
ᵇ» 33:5
76:6 ᵃ» 32:6

76:4 • *he'll punish you*, literally, "he will inflict punishment on your head"; see note on 21:11.

75:5 *our traces*, reading τὰ ἴχνη ἡμῶν for τὴν τέχνην ἡμῶν ("our craft"), with Syr.

78:2 ᵃ» 60:5

⁹As <Christ> gives you life eternal
    as a reward for your activity,
    so he prepares eternal destruction
    as a requital for my deeds.
¹⁰As you by your prayer and good deeds find refreshment
    in your spiritual chants,
    so I, too, find refreshment in murder, adultery,
    and the sacrifices performed with wine on the altars.
¹¹As you turn humankind to life eternal,
    so I turn those who obey me
    to destruction and eternal punishment:
¹²You take along your people
    as I take along mine.

77 When the demon had said these and other similar things, the apostle responded, "Through me Jesus orders you and your child to go no longer into human habitations, but get out, away with you, and dwell far from where humans live."

²The demons said to him, "It's a harsh command you give us. What will you do to those who are now hidden from you? ³Those who fashion all the wooden idols delight in them rather than you— ⁴there are many who worship these numerous idols and do what they want, sacrificing to them, bringing them foods with libations, and making offerings with wine, water, and incense."

⁵The apostle said, "They, too, are now going to be destroyed, along with their activities."

⁶Suddenly the demons disappeared, and the women lay like corpses on the ground, making no sound.

78 The wild asses stood next to one another and did not move away. ²While all the others silently wondered what to do, the ass to whom the power of the Lord had given speech said to the apostle,

Why do you stand idle,ᵃ apostle of Christ, the Most High, since he expects you to ask him for the noblest teachings? ³Why delay? Your teacher wishes to display his great deeds through your hands. ⁴Why do you stand, herald of what is hidden? Your <master> wishes to reveal the things that have been unspoken, since he keeps them for those who are worthy to hear them. ⁵Why stay quiet, you who perform great deeds in the name of the Lord? Your master urges you on, and gives you courage. ⁶So don't be afraid: he will not abandon the soul that belongs to your family. ⁷Begin, then, to call on him; he'll readily hear you. ⁸Why do you stand wondering at all his activities and effects? For the things he has displayed by them are trifling. ⁹What will you say about his great gifts? You won't be able to recount them! ¹⁰Why wonder about the healings that are performed physically, especially since you understand that true, firm, and lasting healing <that> he supplies to <those of> his own nature? ¹¹Why consider this temporal life, and not think about eternal life?

79:7 ᵃCf. Lk 2:24
79:8 ᵃ» 76:5
79:9 ᵃCf. Mt 24:5, 24; 2Pt 2:1
79:10 ᵃ» 25:5

79 I say to you throngs who are standing about expecting those who are cast down to be raised up:

> ²Believe in the apostle of Jesus Christ;
>   believe in the teacher of truth.
> ³Believe in the one who shows you the truth;
>   believe in Jesus.
> ⁴Believe in Christ, who was born
>   so that those who have been born might live
>   through his life.
> ⁵He was raised as a child
>   so that perfect adulthood might be manifest
>   through his manhood.
> ⁶He taught his own teacher,
>   for he is the teacher of truth
>   and the sage among the wise.
> ⁷He brought his gift into the temple
>   to show how to sanctify every offering.ᵃ
> ⁸This is his apostle, the one who reveals the truth,
>   this is the one who does the will of him who sent him.ᵃ

⁹There will come false apostles and lawless prophets—whose end is like their deedsᵃ—preaching and encouraging people to flee from impieties, while they themselves are ever found in sin. ¹⁰They are disguised in sheep's clothing, but inside they are voracious wolves.ᵃ ¹¹Not content with one wife, they destroy

---

78:6 *he will not abandon . . . :* Syr changes the reassurance to read "he will not abandon you, and his divinity will not cause your humanity any sorrow."
78:10 *that* (ἥν) is added to complete the sense.
  his own nature: For φύσει ("nature") possibly read κτήσει ("possession"), with Syr; see Bonnet, *Aaa* 2/2. 193 n. 18. See also 48:2.
79:6 *his own teacher,* reading τὸν ἴδιον διδάσκαλον for τοὺς ἰδίους μαθητάς ("his own disciples"), with Syr. Cf. the incidents in Luke 2:41–52; InfThom 6–8; 14–15; *Ep. apost.* 4.

79:11 ªCf. 1Tm 3:2,
12; 2Tm 3:6; Titus 1:6

79:14 ªCf. Rm 2:1

80:2 ª» 36:15

80:3 ªCf. 136:9;
Lk 16:15; Jn 2:25;
Ac 1:24; 15:8; Rm
8:27; APaTh 24:3;
Herm. *Mand.* 4.3.4;
Hippolytus *Ap.Tr.* 3.4

80:6 ª» 15:8

80:7 ªCf. Rm 8:3;
Phl 2:7

80:10 ªCf. 10:10;
Hb 2:10

80:11 ªCf. Mt 19:28;
Lk 22:30

many women;ª and saying that they despise children, they destroy many youths, for which they will pay the penalty. ¹²Not content with their own property, they desire that all useless things be made to serve them alone, proclaiming themselves his disciples. ¹³They say one thing with their mouth but think something else in their heart; they bid others guard themselves from evils, but they themselves do nothing good. ¹⁴They think themselves moral and bid others refrain from sexual immorality, theft, and greed; but they do all these things secretly, while teaching others not to do them.ª

80 When the wild ass had finished speaking, everyone looked at him. ²And when he was quite silent the apostle said, "I don't have any way to think of your beauty,ª Jesus, or anything to say about you; I'm unable to do it. ³For I don't have the capacity to tell them, my Christ, you who have achieved rest and who alone are wise, who know what is in the heartª and understand the workings of the mind:

⁴Glory be to you, merciful and restful one,
  Glory be to you, wise word;
⁵Glory be to your mercy, brought forth for us,
  Glory be to your pity, spread out over us;
⁶Glory be to your majesty, made small on our account,ª
  Glory be to your kingdom on high,
  made low on our account;
⁷Glory be to your strength,
  which became weak on our account,
  Glory be to your divinity,
  which appeared on our account
  in the likeness of humankind;ª
⁸Glory to your humanity, which died on our account
  so that it might give us life,
⁹Glory to your resurrection from the dead,
  for through it resurrection and rest come to our souls;
¹⁰Glory and praise to your ascent into the heavens,
  for through it you have shown us the way on high,ª
¹¹promising us to be seated at your right hand,
  and to judge the twelve tribes of Israel.ª

80:4 ... *wise word:* Here Syr has additional material; see the Appendix.

[12]You are the heavenly word of the Father:
You are the hidden light of reason
that reveals the way of truth,
dispels darkness, and obliterates error.[a]

81 When he had finished speaking, the apostle stood over the women and said, "My Lord and my God,[a] I don't doubt you, nor do I call on you in disbelief, you who are ever my help, protector, and restorer, who infuse your own power into us, encourage us, and provide to your own servants freedom to speak with love. [2]I ask you, let the souls that have been healed be raised, and let them be as they were before being struck by the demons."

[3]When he had spoken, the women returned and took their seats. [4]The apostle ordered the general that his servants take the women and bring them inside. [5]When they had gone in, the apostle said to the wild asses, "Follow me." [6]At his command they followed him outside the gates, and after they had exited, he said to them, "Go in peace[a] to your pastures." [7]The wild asses went away willingly, and the apostle stood and watched them so that they would not be harmed by anyone, until finally they were far off and went out of sight. [8]He then returned with the crowd to the general's house.

ACT 9 MYGDONIA, THE WIFE OF CARISH

82 It happened that a certain woman by the name of Mygdonia, the wife of Carish, a close relative of the king, came to observe the new name and new God[a] being proclaimed and the new apostle[b] who had come to visit their country. [2]She was carried by her own slaves, but because of the large crowd and the narrow street they were unable to bring her to him.[a] [3]So she sent a request to her husband to dispatch more men to assist her. [4]They came and went ahead of her, forcefully pushing the people aside. [5]When the apostle saw this, he said to them, "Why do you turn away those who have come so eagerly to hear the word? Is it the case that you want to be near me, but have been kept away? [6]It's just as was said about the crowd that came to the Lord: 'Having eyes you do not see,

80:12 [a]» 25:3
81:1 [a]» 10:1
81:6 [a]Cf. 88:8; Lk 7:50; 8:48; AAnPas 34:1
82:1 [a]» 20:4
[b]Cf. 136:2; 137:4
82:2 [a]Cf. Mt 9:2; Mk 2:3–4; Lk 5:18–19

82:4 *went ahead of her*, reading προῆλθον αὐτῆς for προσῆλθον αὐτῇ ("approached her"), with Syr; see Bonnet, *Aaa* 2/2. 197 n. 19.

82:6 ᵃCf. Ps 115:3–8;
135:15–18; Jer 5:21;
Mt 13:13; Mk 8:18;
APa 7.1:8

82:7 ᵃCf. Mt 11:15;
Mk 4:9; Th (NHC II,2)
8: 34,2–3; 21: 37,19

ᵇCf. Mt 11:28

83:3 ᵃ» 4:6

83:7 ᵃCf. Tb 4:15; Mt
7:12; Lk 6:31; Did. 1:2

84:1 ᵃCf. 58:6; 1Tm
6:10; ISmyr 7:2; Pol.
Phil. 4:1; OrSib 2.111;
3.235, 641; 8.17

ᵇCf. 32:13; Mt 27:5;
Jn 12:6

and having ears you do not hear.' "ᵃ ⁷And he said to the crowds, "Let him who has ears for hearing listen," ᵃ and "Come to me all you who labor and are burdened, and I shall give you rest."ᵇ

83 He looked at those who were carrying the woman and said to them, "This encouraging beatitude that was proclaimed to them is directed at you who are burdened now. ²You're the ones who carry burdens that are difficult to bear and are swept along by her command. ³And those who have authority over you place loads on you men as if you were dumb beasts, thinking that you're not men as they are, whether you are slaves or free.ᵃ ⁴But property will not benefit the rich in any way, nor will poverty save the poor from judgment. ⁵We have not received any command that we cannot do. ⁶Neither has he laid on us difficult burdens that we cannot bear, neither <to construct> the sort of dwelling that people build, nor to cut stones and fashion houses, as your craftsmen do in their skill. ⁷This, rather, is the command we have received from the Lord, that what does not please us when done by another, we are not to do to anyone else.ᵃ

84 "Refrain, therefore, first, from adultery, for this is the origin of all evils,ᵃ then from theft, which enticed Judas Iscariot and led to his hanging.ᵇ ²For those who live in greed don't see the things that they bring about. ³Refrain also from arrogance and from all shameful activities, especially those of the body, which earn eternal condemnation; for this is the capital city of all evils. ⁴Likewise it leads the haughty into tyranny, drawing them into a pit and holding them in its power so that they may not see what they are doing, and so their deeds are unclear to them.

83:1 • *and said to them:* In the sermon that follows, through chap. 85, U and P differ considerably; the translation follows U. Syr differs from both and is more tightly organized.

84:3 • *capital city* (μητρόπολις; also in 85:4): A similar saying is attributed to the Cynic philosopher Diogenes of Sinope (404–323 B.C.E.): "The love of money (φιλαργυρίαν) is the *capital city* of all evils" (Diogenes Laertius *Lives* 6.50). In various eras and contexts, numerous vices and states have been identified as the greatest or worst of evils, e.g., Herodotus *Hist.* 7.15.7 "Of all evils slander is the most terrible"; Plato *Gorg.* 522E "to go to death with the soul full of injustice"; Cicero *Off.* 3.29 "dishonesty is the greatest of all evils"; ibid., *2 Phil.* 44 "slavery, the greatest of all evils"; Plutarch *Cat. Min.* 32.5 "It would be the greatest of all evils to abandon the commonwealth."

83:6 *to construct* is added from Syr.

85 "You, however, must be pleasing to God in all forms of goodness, in meekness, and peacefulness, for God cares for these things and they offer eternal life and destroy death. ²Also in gentleness, which accompanies all good things, overcomes all enemies, and alone receives the crown of victory. Also in peacefulness, in liberality to the poor, and in meeting the need of those in want, providing and giving to the needy. ³It is particularly fitting for you to live in holy chastity,ᵃ for that is favored in God's eyes and it leads to eternal life. ⁴It is the capital city of all good things in the eyes of God.ᵃ ⁵Those who don't compete in Christ's stadium won't receive <the prize> of holy chastity. ⁶Holy chastity was revealed by God: it destroys sexual immorality, overturns the enemyᵃ and pleases God, for it is an unconquered athlete,ᵇ having honor from God and esteemed by many. ⁷It is the ambassador of peace, proclaiming peace; if anyone acquires it, that person remains carefree, pleasing the Lord, expecting the time of redemption.ᵃ ⁸It does nothing improper but affords life, rest, and joy to all who acquire it.

86 Meekness, moreover, has subdued death,
    making it subject to its authority:
    meekness has enslaved the enemy.ᵃ
²Meekness is a good yoke;ᵃ
    meekness fears no one
    and yet does not contradict others;
³Meekness is peace and joy,
    and the enjoyment of rest.
⁴Remain, therefore, in holy chastity,ᵃ receive tranquility, and be near meekness, because the Christ I proclaim is characterized by these chief traits. ⁵Holy chastity is the temple of Christ, and the

---

85:3 ᵃ» 58:9
85:4 ᵃCf. 139:13
85:6 ᵃ» 44:7
ᵇ» 39:14
85:7 ᵃ» 73:7
86:1 ᵃ» 44:7
86:2 ᵃCf. Mt 11:30
86:4 ᵃ» 58:9

85:2 • *the crown of victory* (τὸν στέφανον τῆς νικῆς): Not in the NT, but equivalent expressions occur, e.g., 1 Cor 9:25 ἄφθαρτον (στέφανον); Jas 1:12 τὸν στέφανον τῆς ζωῆς (also Rev 2:10); 1 Pet 5:4 "unfading crown" (see notes on AcThom 142:4; 158:8); Rev 4:4 στέφανους χρυσοῦς (also 9:7; 14:14); cf. Rev 12:1. For "crown of victory," see also 147:11; AcPhil 38(144); *Interp. Know.* (NHC XI,1) 21,32; Tertullian *Cor.* 15; Cyprian *Ep.* 8; *Mart. Habib* (Cureton, 1864: 78).

85:1 *in all forms*, reading the dative for the genitive ("*of* all forms").
85:2 *liberality,* literally, "stretching out the hand," a Syriac idiom. The infinitive (ὀρέγειν) is read for the participle (ὀρέγοντι) here and in the next

phrase.
85:3 *It is particularly fitting for you* is added from Syr; otherwise, the cardinal virtue is simply a characteristic of the most deserving poor.

86:7 ªCf. Mt 4:2;
Lk 4:2
86:9 ªCf. Jn 18:11
86:10 ªCf. Mt
26:52–53
87:2 ª» 24:7
87:3 ª» 10:8
87:5 ª» 49:3
ᵇCf. 1Cor 3:16–17;
6:19; 2Cor 6:16
88:1 ª» 16:9
ᵇCf. Jn 1:14
88:3 ª» 36:11
88:5 ªCf. 36:11; 37:5;
APa 7.3:7
88:6 ª» 12:2

person who dwells in it receives it as a habitation. ⁶Self-denial is the resting place of God. ⁷For forty days and forty nights he fasted, tasting no food.ª ⁸The person who observes this will dwell in it as on a mountain, and meekness is his boast. ⁹For he said to Peter, our fellow apostle, "Put your sword back and replace it in its sheath.ª ¹⁰If I'd wished to do this, wouldn't I have been able to get more than twelve legions of angels from my Father?"ª

87 When the apostle had finished speaking and all the crowd was listening, they shoved and trampled one another. ²The wife of Carish, the king's kinsman, leapt from her seat, cast herself on the ground before the apostle, grasped his feet,ª and implored him: ³"Disciple of the living God,ª you've come to a barren country, for we dwell in a desert, like dumb animals in our way of life. But now we shall be saved at your hands. ⁴I beg of you, take thought for me and pray for me, so that I can have mercy from the God you proclaim, ⁵become his habitation, be transformed by prayer, hope, and faith in him, receive the seal,ª and become a holy temple where he may dwell."ᵇ

88 The apostle said, "I pray and request for all of you, brothers,ª who believe in the Lord, and for you, sisters, who hope in Christ, that the word of God might tabernacleᵇ in you all and dwell in you; for we don't determine these things." ²He began to speak to Lady Mygdonia: "Get up off the ground and remember who you are. ³This transitory world, you see, will be of no benefit to you, nor will the beauty of your body, nor your garments.ª ⁴Neither the renown of your rank nor the authority of this world nor the filthy intercourse with your husband will aid you if you're deprived of true communion. ⁵Indeed, a beauteous appearance is dissolved; the body ages and is transformed;ª clothes grow old; authority and power depart after being subject to judgment for what people have already done.ª ⁶The intercourse that produces children vanishes, since it has been condemned.ª ⁷Jesus alone remains forever, along with those who

88:1 • *sisters* (ἀδελφιδῶν), from ἀδελφιδή, usually translated "niece" (refs. in LSJ, s.v. [p. 20b]). This and a passage from Ephrem (where the given meaning is "nun") are the only early Christian refs. for this word in *LPGL*, s.v. (p. 30a).

86:6 *Self-denial is the resting place of God* is added from Syr.
88:5 *after*, reading μετὰ τό for μετ' αὐτῶν ("with them"), with Syr.
for: The Greek relative phrase (ἐν ᾧ) awkwardly translates the Syriac conjunction.

hope in him."ª ⁸Then he said to the woman, "Go in peace,ª and may
the Lord make you worthy of his mysteries."

⁹"I'm afraid to go away," she responded. "Perhaps you'll leave
me and go off to another nation."

¹⁰The apostle said to her, "Even if I do go away, I shan't leave you
alone: Jesus, through his mercy, will be with you."ª

¹¹At this, she fell down, did obeisance to him, and departed for
her house.

89 Carish, the kinsman of King Mizdai, bathed, went up, and re-
clined for dinner. ²He asked where his wife might be, for she had
not come from the bedroom to greet him, as was her custom. ³Her
servants told him, "She is feeling ill."

⁴So he leapt up, went into the bedroom, and found her lying
on the bed, covered over. ⁵He uncovered her, kissed her, and said,
"Why are you despondent today?"

⁶"I'm feeling out of sorts."

⁷"Why didn't you act like a free woman and stay at home instead of going out to listen to foolish talk and watch magic tricks?
⁸Get up and eat dinner with me; I can't eat without you."

⁸She responded, "Today I beg to be excused—I've not been well."

90 When Carish heard this from Mygdonia, he did not want
to go in to dinner; instead, he ordered his servants to bring it in,
so that he could eat dinner with her. ²When they brought it in, he
asked her to eat with him, but she refused. ³Since she was unwilling, he ate alone and said to her, "On your account I refused an
invitation to dine with King Mizdai, and you don't want to eat with
me?"

⁴ She said, "It's because I'm feeling out of sorts."

⁵Carish then stood up and, as was his custom, wanted to go to
bed with her; but she said, "Didn't I ask to be excused today?"

91 When he heard this he went off and lay down on another
bed. ²When he arose from his sleep, he said, "My Lady Mygdonia,
listen to the dream that I had: ³I saw myself reclining near King
Mizdai and a large table nearby. ⁴I saw an eagle come down from

88:7 ªCf. 117:5; Hb 13:8; APa 7.3:8
88:8 ªCf. 81:6
88:10 ª» 1:5

90:1 *it . . . with her*, reading αὐτόν for αὐτήν
("her"), and αὐτῇ for αὐτῷ ("with him"); see Bonnet, *Aaa* 2/2. 204 n. 23.

92:1 ªCf. Th (NHC
II,2) 22: 37,24–35;
APeMar 9(38):8

heaven—it snatched from me and the king two partridges, and took them off to its nest. [5]Again it came and hovered over us, so the king commanded a bow to be brought in. [6]This time the eagle snatched a pigeon and a turtle dove from right in front of us. [7]The king shot an arrow at him, and it passed through the bird from one side to the other; but it did him no harm, and the bird, uninjured, soared to its place. [8]When I woke up I was afraid and saddened, because I had tasted the partridge and it was now no longer permitted to my mouth."

[9]Mygdonia said to him, "Your dream is auspicious: you eat partridge every day, but this eagle has not tasted partridge until now."

92 In the morning, Carish went out and dressed—and tied his left sandal on his right foot.[a] [2]Pausing, he said to Mygdonia, "What's going on? First the dream, then this behavior!"

[3]Mygdonia responded, "This doesn't seem to be an ill omen, but quite auspicious; in fact, there will be a change from a foul practice to what is better." [4]He washed his hands and went to greet King Mizdai.

93 Mygdonia, too, arose, and went out to greet Judas Thomas the apostle. She found him conversing with the general and a large crowd. [2]He exhorted them, speaking about the woman who had received the Lord in her soul <and he asked>, "Whose spouse is she?" [3]The chief general said, "She is the wife of Carish the kinsman of King Mizdai, her husband is a harsh man, and the king usually does whatever he tells him. [4]More than that, he won't allow her to continue with this attitude she's expressing; after all, he has frequently sung her praises to the king, saying that there is no one like her when it comes to love. [6]So whatever you have said to her is foreign to her."

[7]The apostle said, "If the Lord truly and firmly has entered her soul and she has received the seed that has been sown, she won't

---

93:3 • *chief general* (ἀρχιστρατηπλάτης): Sifor, usually called a "general," is apparently promoted here and in 102:2.

91:4 *nest*, reading καλιάν ("dwelling, barn, nest," etc.; in the Greek Bible only at Gen 6:15[14] Sym.) for καρδίαν ("heart"), with Syr; see Bonnet, *Aaa* 2/2. 205 n. 14. The actual word occurs in the Greek text in 91:7.
91:5 *to be brought in*, reading ἐνεχθῆναι for ἀχθῆναι ("to be taken away"); see Bonnet, *Aaa*

2/2. 205 n. 16.
93:2 *Whose spouse . . .?* In P the elements of the dialogue are distributed differently: the commander asks whose wife it is, the apostle identifies her, and the commander comments on his character.

have any concern for transitory life. [8]She'll not fear death, nor will Carish be able to do her any harm, because the one she has accepted into her soul—if she really has accepted him—is more powerful."

94
When Mygdonia heard this she said to the apostle, "Truly, sir, I have accepted the seed that consists of your words,[a] and I shall bear the fruits that are like such a seed."

[2]"Souls praise you[a] and give thanks to you,[b] Lord," the apostle said, "for they belong to you. [3]Bodies give thanks to you, which you have deemed worthy to be dwellings of your heavenly gift." [4]He then said to all present,

> Congratulations to the chaste saints!
>> Their souls never condemn them;
>> having won them,
>> they are never separated from themselves.
> [5]Congratulations to the spirits of the chaste saints!
>> They have received the perfect heavenly crown
>> from the heavenly sphere assigned to them.
> [6]Congratulations to the bodies of the chaste saints!
>> They have been deemed worthy
>> to become temples of God,[a]
>> so that Christ might dwell in them.
> [7]Congratulations to you!
>> You have authority to forgive sins.[a]
> [8]Congratulations to you,
>> if you don't lose what has been given to you,
>> but bear it up with you as you depart rejoicing.
> [9]Congratulations to you, chaste saints!
>> It is your gift to ask and to receive.[a]
> [10]Congratulations, you who are gentle!
>> God has deemed you worthy
>> to be heirs of the heavenly kingdom.[a]
> [11]Congratulations, you who are gentle!
>> You have conquered[a] the evil one.[b]
> [12]Congratulations, you who are gentle!
>> You will see the face of the Lord.[a]

94:1 [a]Cf. Mt 13:23; AAnPas 44:4
94:2 [a]» 25:1
[b]» 15:2
94:6 [a]» 87:5
94:7 [a]Cf. Mt 9:6; 16:19; 18:18; Mk 2:10; Lk 5:24; Jn 20:23
94:9 [a]Cf. Mt 7:7; 21:22; Mk 11:24; Lk 11:9
94:10 [a]Cf. Mt 5:5
94:11 [a]Cf. 1Jn 2:14
[b]» 44:7
94:12 [a]Cf. Mt 5:8; Rv 22:4

94:4 • *Congratulations*... (or *Blessed*): A similar set of beatitudes, modeled on those of the Synoptic gospels but exalting sexual asceticism, appears in AcPaulThec 5–6; cf. AcPhil 5:25.

chaste saints: The adjective ἅγιος (routinely translated "holy") probably has the same connotations here as the noun ἁγιωσύνη in 58:9; 85:3.

94:13 ªCf. Mt 5:6
94:14 ªCf. Mt 5:9
95:8 ª» 10:3
96:3 ª» 20:4

¹³Congratulations, you who hunger for the sake of the Lord!ª
Rest is reserved for you:
your souls will rejoice hereafter.
¹⁴Congratulations, you who are peaceful,ª
to be released from sin and requital!

¹⁵When the apostle had finished speaking in the hearing of the entire crowd, Mygdonia was strengthened through the faith, glory, and majesty of Christ.

95 Carish, the king's kinsman and friend, came in for dinner and did not find his wife at home. ²He asked everyone in his household, "Where has your mistress gone?"

³One of them answered, "She went out to that stranger."

⁴When he heard this from his servant he was annoyed at the rest of his domestics, because they had not immediately told him what had happened. ⁵So he sat down to wait for her, and when she returned home that evening he said to her, "Where were you?"

⁶"I went to the doctor."

⁷"Is that stranger a doctor?" he asked.

⁸"Yes," she said, "he is a healer of souls.ª Most doctors heal mortal bodies, but he heals immortal souls."

⁹Hearing this, Carish was upset with Mygdonia because of the apostle, but out of fear he did not respond to her, because she was superior to him in both wealth and intellect. ¹⁰Off he went to dinner; but she went into her bedroom. ¹¹So he said to the servants, "Call her to dinner." But she did not wish <to go>.

96 When he heard that she did not want to leave her bedroom, he went in and said to her, "Why don't you want to eat dinner with me? ²I suppose you don't want to sleep with me either, as is our custom. ³I'm very apprehensive about this, because I've heard that that deceitful wizardª teaches that one shouldn't live together with his wife—he forbids what nature has seen fit to demand and the deity has instituted."

⁴While he spoke, Mygdonia remained silent. He then said to her, "Mygdonia, my mistress and consort, don't be led astray by empty,

---

94:14 • *requital:* There follows an obscure gloss, "of pure and impure animals."
95:11 • *But she did not wish <to go>* (ἡ δὲ οὐκ ἐβούλετο) exactly reproduces the wording of the young woman's refusal in 51:12; it is also reminiscent of Thomas's initial balking at the Lord's commission in 1:3: οὐκ ἐβούλετο δὲ ἀπελθεῖν. Finally, as a virtual *inclusio* to the whole narrative, in 169:1–3 Sifor and Vizan will choose to stay at Thomas's tomb because "they did not wish to go to the city."

deceptive words, nor by the magical practices that I've heard this
fellow does in the name of Father, Son, and Holy Spirit.[a] [5]For it has
never been heard of in this world that someone has raised up the
dead, as I hear rumors of him doing. [6]As for the fact that he neither
eats nor drinks,[a] don't think that it's for the sake of righteousness;
he does so simply because he doesn't own a thing. [7]What do you
think someone would do who doesn't even have enough bread for
the day? [8]It's because he's a pauper that he has only a single cloak.[a]
[9]As for the fact that he doesn't accept anything from anyone,[a] by
acting in this way he admits that he does <not truly> heal."

96:4 [a]» 27:10
96:6 [a]» 5:2
96:8 [a]» 20:6
96:9 [a]Cf. 20:6; 62:1
97:3 [a]» 58:9
98:2 [a]» 16:2
98:4 [a]» 25:3

97 While Carish was speaking, Mygdonia was as still as a stone,
but she was praying for day to dawn, so she could go out to the
apostle of Christ. [2]Carish withdrew from her presence and went off
to dinner dispirited, for he was anxious to sleep with her, as was his
custom. [3]When he had left, she knelt down and prayed, "My Lord
and Master, merciful Father, Savior Christ, grant me the power to
overcome the shamelessness of Carish and allow me to preserve
the holy chastity[a] in which you delight, that I, too, may find eternal
life for myself." [4]After her prayer she lay down on the bed with the
covers drawn over her.

98 When Carish finished dinner, he came in to her, but she cried
out and said, "You no longer belong with me, for my Lord Jesus,
who is with me and abides in me, is greater than you."

[2]He laughed: "You're making a good joke about that sorcerer,[a]
and you make a laughingstock of him who said, 'You have no life
with God unless you sanctify yourselves.' "

[3]Then he tried to sleep with her, but she did not permit it, cry-
ing bitterly, "I call on you, Lord Jesus, don't abandon me, because
I've taken refuge in you. [4]For as I've learned that you are the one
who seeks those bound in ignorance and saves those held by error,[a]
I now ask you, whose reputation I have heard and believed, to come
to my aid and save me from the shamelessness of Carish, so his foul-
ness may not dominate me." [5]Striking him with her hands, she fled

96:7 • *bread for the day:* Possibly an allusion to the Lord's prayer (see 144:1–4), in
which case ἡμερήσιον ("of the day," "for a day") is an interpretation of the dis-
puted term ἐπιούσιον (Matt 6:11; Luke 11:3).

96:9 *not truly heal*, reading μὴ ἐν ἀληθείᾳ
θεραπεύειν for τοῦ θεραπεύειν ("to heal"), with
Syr.

98:5 *him with her hands*, reading αὐτὸν ταῖς χερσί
for ἑαυτῆς τὰς χεῖρας ("her own hands"); Syr
"bound his hands."

98:5 ªCf. 99:9; 103:3;
Mk 14:51–52
99:7 ª» 16:2
99:9 ª» 98:5
99:10 ª» 16:2

away from him naked.ª ⁶As she was going out she tore the veil of the bedroom and, wrapping it around herself, she went to her nurse and slept there with her.

99 All night long Carish was despondent and kept slapping his face. ²He wanted to go immediately and report to the king about the misfortune that had overtaken him, but thought to himself, "If my great despondency forces me to go to the king now, who will grant me access to him? ³I know that it's my abusive language—the result of my arrogance, boastfulness, and haughtiness—that has ruined me. ⁴It has reduced me to this miserable state and separated my sister Mygdonia from me. ⁵If the king himself had stood before my doors at this hour, I would not have gone out to answer him. ⁶No, I'll wait here until dawn: I know that if I make any request of the king he'll grant it to me. ⁷I'll speak about the sorceryª of that stranger, and how in tyrannical style he casts important and respected people into a pit. ⁸It doesn't bother me that I've been deprived of intercourse with her, but I'm saddened for the woman herself and for the fact that her noble spirit has been brought so low. ⁹A beautiful woman—none of the servants ever criticized here—has run outside and fled nakedª from her own bedroom, and I don't know where she has gone. ¹⁰Perhaps, crazed by that sorcerer,ª she has gone out to the market seeking him in her madness; she seems to find pleasure in nothing but that man and what he says!"

100 After saying this, he began to lament: "Too bad for me, my consort, and too bad for you—I've been deprived of you all too soon. ²Too bad for me, my dearest love—you mean more to me than all my family. ³I've no son or daughter by you, in whom I might take consolation; you didn't even live with me a full year before the evil eye snatched you away from me. ⁴If a violent death had taken you, perhaps then I would still have been reckoned among kings and rulers, rather than suffer so much at the hands of a stranger! ⁵Perhaps he's a slave who ran away here to hurt me and harm my wretched

100:3 • *evil eye* (βάσκανος ὀφθαλμός), a malevolent power of envy or jealousy (sometimes stinginess), personal or impersonal. In the ʟxx, for Heb. *raʿ ʿayin* at Prov 23:6; 28:22; also Sir 18:18; 37:11. Similarly, πονηρὸς ὀφθαλμός in Sir 14:10; Matt 6:23; 20:15 (cf. Deut 15:9); Mark 7:22; *T. Iss.* 4:6.

99:7 *sorcery*, reading μαγείας for μανίας ("madness"), with Syr; see Bonnet, *Aaa* 2/2. 211 n. 24.
    how, reading πῶς for ἥτις ("which"), with Syr.

100:3 *a full year…*: U (followed here) and P differ in style through 100:10.

soul. ⁶May nothing hold me back until I destroy him and avenge this night! ⁷May I not be pleasing before King Mizdai if he does not give me justice by punishing this man. ⁸I'll also speak about General Sifor, who was the cause of her destruction. ⁹It was through him that the stranger appeared here and he is staying with him. ¹⁰There are many who visit him, and he teaches them his new doctrine,ᵃ saying that no one can live if he doesn't become detached, as he is, by giving up all his possessions."

101 While Carish brooded, day dawned. After being on watch through the night, he put on simple clothing, donned his sandals and went, downcast and despondent, to greet the king. ²When the king saw him he said, "Why are you grieved and why do you come with such an appearance? I see that your look is changed."

³Carish said to the king, "I have a strange business and a new desolation that Sifor has brought to India: a certain Hebrew wizard,ᵃ whom he keeps lodged in his own house, who doesn't leave his side. ⁴There are many who visit him: he teaches them a new Godᵃ and commands them to follow unheard-of laws. ⁵He says, 'It's impossible for you to enter the eternal life that I proclaim to you if you don't separate from your wives; women, too, must separate from their husbands.' ⁶Well, my poor wife went out to him and listened to his teachings. ⁷She believed them, left me at night, and ran away to the stranger. ⁸Send for Sifor and that wizardᵃ who is hidden in his house and execute them so that not all of our people will perish."ᵇ

102 When his friend Mizdai heard this he said, "Don't grieve or be despondent: I'll send for him and avenge you, and you'll again have your wife; I'll also avenge the others who can't do it themselves."

²The king went out to the judgment seat, and when he had taken his seat he ordered Sifor the chief general to be summoned. ³The king's emissaries went to his house and found him seated at the right hand of the apostle; Mygdonia was at his feet,ᵃ listening to him with all the crowd.

100:10 ᵃCf. Mk 1:27; Ac 17:19; APaTh 14:1
101:3 ᵃ» 20:4
101:4 ᵃ» 20:4
101:8 ᵃ» 20:4
ᵇCf. Jn 11:50
102:3 ᵃ» 9:3

100:7 • *give me justice*, literally, "that he may render justice to me through the head of the stranger"; see note on 21:11.
101:8 • *execute them*, literally, " bring (judgment) on their head"; see note on 21:11.

100:8 *I'll also speak* and *of her destruction* are added from Syr.

102:4 ᵃ» 20:4
102:8 ᵃ» 21:6
103:3 ᵃ» 98:5
103:5 ᵃ» 21:6
104:1 ᵃ» 20:4
104:4 ᵃCf. 120:6

⁴They approached and said to Sifor, "You're sitting here listening to vain words, while King Mizdai in his anger is seeking to destroy you on account of the deceiving wizardᵃ you brought into your house!"

⁵When Sifor heard this, he was dismayed, not because of the king's threat against him, but on account of the apostle, since the king had turned against him. ⁶He said to the apostle, "I grieve for you, for I told you from the start that this woman is the wife of Carish, the king's kinsman and friend. ⁷He will not allow her to do what she promised, and whatever he asks of the king, he grants him."

⁸"Don't be afraid," the apostle said to Sifor, "but believeᵃ in Jesus who defends us all. For we have been gathered to his place of refuge."

⁹When Sifor heard this, he put on his cloak and went to King Mizdai.

103 Now the apostle was questioning Mygdonia, "Why has your husband been angered, and why he is taking these steps against us?"

²She said, "Because I didn't give myself to that destructive activity of his. ³It was like this: late at night he wanted to subdue me and to make me subject to the passion that he serves, but he to whom I dedicated my soul saved me from my husband's hands—I ran away from him naked,ᵃ and slept by my nurse. ⁴I simply don't know what has happened to him, or why he has contrived these things."

⁵"These things won't harm us," the apostle said to her. "Only believeᵃ in Jesus and he will avert the anger, rage, and frenzy of Carish. ⁶He'll be your companion on the fearsome highway and will himself guide you to his kingdom. ⁷He'll lead you into eternal life by providing you with the boldness that does not perish nor change."

104 Sifor stood before the king, who asked him, "Who is that wizardᵃ that you have lurking in your house? Where does he come from and what does he teach?"

²Sifor answered the king, "You're not unaware, my king, of the grievous trouble my friends and I have had because of my wife—you know her, and many others remember her as well. ³And there is the matter of my daughter, more precious to me than all my property. ⁴What a lengthy trial I suffered! I became a curse and a mockery throughout our country.ᵃ ⁵I heard news of this man, went to him, and implored him; then I took him with me and brought him here. ⁶On the way I saw wonderful and strange things—even here many

have heard of the wild ass[a] and of the demon he expelled.[b] [7]He also healed both my wife and my daughter and now they are healthy. [8]He did not accept pay, but demands faith and holy chastity,[a] so that we might be partners with him in what he does. [9]He teaches this: Honor and fear one God,[a] the master of all, and Jesus Christ his Son, so that all may have eternal life. [10]What he eats is bread and salt and his drink is water from dusk to dusk.[a] [11]He prays constantly, and whatever he asks of God, God gives him. [12]He teaches that God is holy and powerful and that Christ is life and gives life. [13]So he encourages those who are present to approach him in holy chastity,[a] purity, love, and faith."

105
When King Mizdai heard this from Sifor, he sent many soldiers to General Sifor's house to bring Thomas the apostle and all who were found there. [2]When the soldiers who had been sent entered, they found him teaching a large crowd, and Mygdonia was seated at his feet.[a] [3]Astonished at the size of the crowd around him, they were afraid, and returned to their king and said, [4]"We didn't dare say anything to him, for there was a great crowd around him. [5]Mygdonia was sitting at his feet[a] listening to what he said."

[5]When King Mizdai and Carish heard this, Carish jumped up from before the king, took a large crowd with him, and said, "Listen, my king, I'll fetch him along with Mygdonia, now deprived of her senses thanks to him!" [6]He came to the house of General Sifor in great agitation, and found him teaching. [7]But he didn't catch Mygdonia, for she had returned to her house, knowing that her husband had been told she was there.

106
Carish said to the apostle, "Get up, evil one,[a] corrupter, and enemy[b] of my house. [2]Your magic will not harm me, because I'll set your magic on your own head."

[3]When he had spoken, the apostle turned to him and said, "Your threats will return to you; you'll not harm me in any way, for the Lord Jesus Christ, in whom I place my hopes, is greater than you, your king, and all your army."

[4]Carish took a turban from one of his servants and tied it around the neck of the apostle saying, "Drag him and bring him along: let's see whether God is able to save him from my hands!" [5]And dragging him along, they brought him to King Mizdai.

104:6 [a]Cf. 39–41
[b]Cf. 42–50
104:8 [a]» 58:9
104:9 [a]Cf. AAnMt 33:9; AJn 42:3; APaTh 9:2; 38:5; APa 7.1:7; 8.2:6; APeVer 22:8
104:10 [a]Cf. 20:6
104:13 [a]» 58:9
105:2 [a]» 9:3
105:5 [a]» 9:3
106:1 [a]» 44:7
[b]» 44:7

106:2 • *on your own head* is a Syriac idiom; see note on 21:11.
106:4 • *tied it around*, literally, "put it on."

106:7 ªCf. 2:11; 8:1;
Mt 26:63; 27:14;
Mk 15:2–5; Lk 23:9;
Jn 19:9

106:9 ªCf. Mt 22:15;
Mk 3:6; 12:13

107:1 ª» 27:15

ᵇ» 25:1

ᶜCf. Ac 5:41

107:2 ª» 15:2

107:3 ª» 16:2

ᵇ» 20:4

107:4 ªCf. Mt 11:28

ᵇCf. Mt 5:11

107:5 ªCf. Mt 10:22;
24:9; Mk 13:13; Lk
21:17

⁶So the apostle stood before the king, who said to him, "Tell me, who are you and by what power are you doing these things?" ⁷But the apostle remained silent.ª ⁸The king then commanded his servants to give the apostle a hundred and twenty-eight lashes and cast him bound into prison, and they bound him and led him away. ⁹Although the crowd worshiped him as a god, the king and Carish were considering how they might put him to death.ª ¹⁰They had it in mind to say that the stranger had insulted the king and was a deceiver.

107 The apostle went off to the prison in rejoicing and glad,ª and said, "I praise you,ᵇ Jesus, because you made me worthy not only of faith in you, but also of enduring much for your sake. ᶜ ²Therefore I thank you,ª Lord, because you have remembered me and given me endurance. ³I thank you, Lord, because for your sake I'm accused of being a sorcererª and a wizard.ᵇ ⁴Therefore <let me> receive some of the blessing of the humble, some of the rest of those who are weary,ª and some of the blessings of those whom men hate, persecute, and revile, saying vile things about them.ᵇ ⁵See, it's for your sake that I'm hated,ª it's for your sake that I've been separated from most people, and it's for your sake that people say that I am what I'm not."

108 As he prayed, all the prisoners looked on him and asked him to pray for them. So after praying, he sat down and began to recite this poem:

A Hymn of Judas Thomas
that he sang in the country of the Indians

When I was a little child
      and dwelt in my realm, in my father's house,
²and was at ease with rich delights
      of those who nourished me,
³then from the east, our native land,
      my parents furnished me and sent me out.

106:6 • by what power are you doing these things (ποίᾳ δυνάμει ταῦτα διαπράττῃ;)? Contrast Matt 21:23 = Mark 11:28 = Luke 20:2 ἐν ποίᾳ ἐξουσίᾳ ταῦτα ποιεῖς; (and see the continuation in Matt 21:24, 27; Mark 11:29, 33; Luke 20:8); but Acts 4:7 ἐν ποίᾳ δυνάμει . . . ἐποιήσατε τοῦτο ὑμεῖς;

107:4 *let me* is added from Syr.
108:1 *A Hymn:* Syr is translated, but important

divergences in Gr are noted; the verse numbers are those given in the standard editions.

⁴They took aplenty from our treasure's wealth
  and a package they prepared for me.
⁵It was large but light,
  so I could carry it myself:
⁶Gold from Beth-Elaye
  and unstamped silver from mighty Gazak,
⁷carnelians of India
  and from Beth Kushan, agates.
⁸They girded me with steel,
  which shatters iron.
⁹They removed the splendid <robe>
  that in their love they had made for me,
¹⁰and the woven scarlet tunic
  that was measured for my height.
¹¹They made a pact with me
  and inscribed it on my heart, lest it be forgotten:
¹²If you descend to Egypt
  and retrieve the pearl unique,
¹³in the middle of the sea,
  hard by the hissing serpent,
¹⁴you shall don your splendid <robe>
  and your tunic resting on it,
¹⁵and with your brother, our second in command,
  the heir you shall be in our realm.

109

¹⁶I left the east <and> down I went,
  while with me were two guides,
¹⁷for fearsome was the road, and hard,
  and I was young to travel it.
¹⁸I passed the border of Maishan,
  the lodging place of merchants from the east:

108:6 • *Beth-Elaye*, that is, "House of the Exalted Ones," a place to the east of Parthia; see Poirier, 1981: 260–61.
  from mighty Gazak: Gr etymologizes as τὴν μεγάλην θησαυρῶν ("of [or from] the great treasures"). Gazak is probably the name of a town in either Atropatene or Sogdia; see Poirier, 1981: 261–62.
108:7 • *Beth Kushan:* An area southeast of Sogdia, east of the Indus; see Poirier, 1981: 263–64.
109:18 • *Maishan:* Apparently the region around the mouth of the Tigris; see Poirier, 1981: 254.

108:9 *splendid robe:* Syr reads simply "splendor," possibly to be emended to "splendid (thing)," a metonymy for the splendid robe.

108:12 *retrieve*, i.e., "you bring it," emended from "he brought it down."

¹⁹I reached the land of Babel,
and entered Sarbug's walls.
²⁰To Egypt's heart did I descend,
and my companions left me.
²¹I went straight to the serpent
and lodged by his lair
²²to see if he might doze or sleep
and I might snatch the pearl from him.
²³Being single and alone,
I was a stranger to the lodgers at my inn.
²⁴Then I espied a kinsman,
noble born, from eastern stock,
²⁵a handsome youth and gracious,
an anointed one.
²⁶He came to me and joined me;
my intimate I made him,
²⁷the friend
with whom I shared my enterprise.
²⁸I warned him of Egyptians,
and of their contact with defilements.
²⁹Yet lest they reproach me for coming from abroad,
I put on their clothes
³⁰that I might take the pearl,
then against me rouse the serpent.
³¹Yet by some means they sensed
that I was not of their land.
³²With deceit they treated me,
and made me taste their food.
³³I forgot I was a royal son,
and I served their king.

109:19 • *the land of Babel:* This is often taken to be Mesopotamian Babylon, but Layton (1987: 372) suggests that it is the fortified garrison city in Egypt (Old Cairo). This Babylon would be the gateway to the heart of Egypt, the entry to which is recorded in this and the next verse. The name recurs in 111:50, 69.

Sarbug: Suggested sites for this enigmatic place-name include Mabboug, Borsippa, Shourouppak, a city in the epic of Gilgamesh, Babylon itself or a suburb; see Poirier, 1981: 255–60. It is later (111:50, 69 as emended) translated into Greek as "Labyrinth." Layton (1987: 373 n. 111d) identifies this as the temple complex of Sobk in Crocodilopolis. The "serpent" guarding the pearl would be the crocodile god, at least for Greek readers.

109:25 • *an anointed one:* This difficult form could be rendered "son of oil sellers" (so Wright, Klijn). More likely is "son of anointings," i.e., one who shares in the anointing of royalty; similarly Poirier, 1981: 422. Gr reads υἱὸν μεγιστάνων ("son of great ones"); cf. 143:3.

³⁴The pearl, too, I forgot—
  <the very thing> for which my parents had sent me out.
³⁵Through their heavy food,
  I fell into a deep sleep.

110

³⁶Of all these things that had befallen me
  my parents were aware, and they grieved for me.
³⁷In our realm it was proclaimed
  that all should come unto our gate,
³⁸kings, Parthian rulers,
  and all nobles of the east.
³⁹They formed a plan about me,
  lest I be left in Egypt.
⁴⁰They wrote to me a letter
  that each noble signed:
⁴¹"From your father, king of kings,ᵃ
  and your mother, of the east the queen,ᵇ
⁴²from your brother, second to us in command,
  to you, our son in Egypt, peace.
⁴³Awake and rise from sleep,ᵃ
  and hear our letter's words.
⁴⁴Recall you are a son of kings,
  observe your bondage and the one you serve.
⁴⁵Recall the pearl,
  for which to Egypt you were sent.ᵃ
⁴⁶Remember, too, your splendid robe,
  and recall your bright tunic,
⁴⁷which you will don and by it be adorned,
  when in the heroes' book
  your name has been proclaimed.

110:41 ᵃCf. 111:60; 112:86; 113:104
ᵇ» 7:10
110:43 ᵃ» 60:3
110:45 ᵃCf. 111:57

109:35 • *I fell into a deep sleep* (βάρει εἰς ὕπνον κατηνέχθην βαθύν): The sole NT occurrence of the idiom is in Acts 20:9, of Eutychus: καταφερόμενος ὕπνῳ βαθεῖ . . . κατενεχθεὶς ἀπὸ τοῦ ὕπνου.
110:41 • *king of kings:* The title was used in Iran in the Arsacid (ca. 250 B.C.E.–226 C.E.) and Sassanid (226–ca. 650) periods (Poirier, 1981: 240–44).

109:35 *their heavy food,* reading ⲁⲙⲓⲱⲓⲁⲥ (PSTS, s.v. ⲣⲓⲱⲓⲁⲥ [col. 4502; CSD, p. 608b] = τροφή in, e.g., Acts 14:17; 27:36) for ⲁⲙⲓⲉⲓⲁⲥ ("their oppressions"; PSTS, s.v. ⲣⲁⲓⲁⲥ [col. 1524; CSD, pp. 170b, 182b] = στενοχωρία in, e.g., Rom 2:9), with Gr.; but n.b. also PSTS, s.v. ⲣⲁⲟⲓⲁⲥ (col. 1513: τροφή, *cibus*).
110:47 *heroes' book:* Gr βιβλίον ζωῆς ("book of life"); cf. Rev 13:8; 17:8; 20:12; 21:27.

111:50 ªᴐ 109:19
111:57 ªCf. 110:45
111:60 ªCf. 110:41

⁴⁸And with your brother, our viceroy,
    you shall be together in our realm."

111
⁴⁹My letter is a letter
    that the king with his right hand did seal,
⁵⁰from the wicked men of Babel
    and harsh demons of Sarbug.ª
⁵¹It flew in eagle's form,
    the king of all the birds.
⁵²It flew and landed by my side,
    it then became all word.
⁵³At its voice and rustling sound
    I woke and rose up from my sleep.
⁵⁴ I took it up and kissed it
    and began to read it through.
⁵⁵As had been stamped on my heart,
    my letter's words were written.
⁵⁶I recalled I was a son of kings;
    my noble nature took command.
⁵⁷The pearl, too, I recalled,
    for which to Egypt I was sent.ª
⁵⁸I started to enchant him,
    that fearsome, hissing serpent.
⁵⁹I made him sleep and slumber,
    as I called o'er him my Father's name,
⁶⁰with his name who is second in command,
    and with that of my mother, of the east the queen.ª
⁶¹I seized on the pearl
    and to my father's house I turned to go again.
⁶²Their vile and filthy clothes
    I doffed and left in their land.
⁶³I went straight on the way by which I came,
    to our land's light, the East.
⁶⁴The letter that had awakened me
    I found before me on the way.

110:48 • *viceroy:* For attestation of the term in ancient near eastern titulature, see Poirier, 1981: 212–23.
111:56 • *my noble nature took command,* literally, "my nobility commanded its nature"; Gr is obscure, but probably "My freeborn <nature> sought my race."

111:50 *Sarbug:* Gr translates "Labyrinth"; see also 111:69.

⁶⁵As with its voice it roused me
  now with its light it led me,
⁶⁶as the royal silk before me
  in its appearance gleamed.
⁶⁷By its voice and by its guidance
  it urged me on in haste;
⁶⁸by its love
  it drew me on.
⁶⁹I exited and skirted Sarbug;^a
  I took my leave of Babel on my left.
⁷⁰I arrived at great Maishan,
  the harbor of the merchants,
⁷¹that sits
  on the shore.
⁷²The splendid <robe> that I had doffed,
  the tunic, too, in which it had been wrapped
⁷³from Hyrcania's height,
  my parents thither sent
⁷⁴by their treasurers' hand,
  whose fidelity they trusted with it.

112 ⁷⁵Since I remembered not its form—
  for in childhood I had left my father's house—
⁷⁶suddenly, when I confronted it,
  as if my mirror,^a the garment seemed like me.
⁷⁷I looked at the whole of it, complete,
  and in it faced myself entire,
⁷⁸for we were two in separation,
  yet we were also one in single form.
⁷⁹Again, the treasurers who had conveyed it to me,
  I saw to be thus:
⁸⁰Two they were and yet they were one form,
  for on them was inscribed one emblem of the king
⁸¹whose hands restored to me,
  through them, my deposit and my wealth,
⁸²my splendid decorated <robe>

111:69 ^a» 109:19
112:76 ^a» 14:3

111:70 • *Maishan:* The Greek may involve additional symbolism: Μαισαν is written as its homophone μέσον ("middle" or "midst"), which can designate the world; see 156:2.
112:78 • *we were also one:* For the notion that in the heavenly realm one becomes what one sees, see *Gos. Phil.* (NHC II,3) 38: 61,20 "People cannot see anything in the real realm unless they become it."

112:86 ª» 110:41
113:100 ªCf. 137:4;
144:5; 145:3; 171:1

adorned with colors bright,
[83]with gold and beryl stones,
    with carnelians and agates,
[84]with sardis of varied hue.
    Also it was worked throughout its height,
[85]and with stones of adamant
    all its seams were joined.
[86]The image of the king of kings[a]
    was painted in relief all over it,
[87]and like a sapphire stone
    its colors, too, were varied.

113
[88]Again I saw that through it all
    insight's stirrings moved.
[89]I saw as well that it was ready,
    as if to speak.
[90]The sound of gentle tones I heard,
    that whispered with its outer folds:
[91]"For this most valiant servant
    they raised me up before my Father.
[92]I, too, perceive inside myself
    that, like his labors, so my stature grows."
[93]Then with its royal motions
    it stretched out to me,
[94]and from its givers' hands
    it rushed that I might take it.
[95]Then, too, my love provoked me
    that I should run to meet and take it.
[96]So I reached out and took it,
    with its colors' beauty I adorned myself,
[97]and in my brilliantly colored tunic
    I wrapped myself completely.
[98]I donned it and was lifted up
    unto the gate of peace and adoration.
[99]I bowed my head and I adored
    the glory of my Father, who had sent me out,
[100]for his commands I had performed,[a]
    and what he promised me he did.

112:87 *like a . . . stone,* reading ܟܐܦܐ for ܟܦܐ
("stone ").
113:90 *its outer folds,* reading ܣܝܦܬܗ (PSTS, s.v.

ܚܘܬ [col. 2345; CSD, p. 336b]) for the obscure
form ܡܣܚܘܬܗ.
113:91 *this,* reading ܗܕܐ for ܐܢܐ ("I ").

[101]And at gates of princes
  I mingled with his nobles,
[102]for he rejoiced in me and took me in
  and I was with him in his realm,
[103]and with the voice of praise
  all his servants gave him glory.
[104]He also promised me that I would present myself
  at the portal of the king of kings with him,[a]
[105]and with my present and my pearl
  I would with him appear before our king.

[106]Here ends the hymn that Judas Thomas the apostle pronounced in prison.

114 Carish went home happy, thinking that his wife would be with him and would be as she had been before hearing the divine word and coming to believe in Jesus. [2]But when he arrived, he found her with her locks shorn and clothing torn—at the sight of which he could only say: [3]"My Lady Mygdonia, what dread disease has seized you? Why have you done this to yourself? [4]I've been your husband since you were a young woman, ever since the gods and the laws granted me authority over you. [5]So what is this insanity? You've become a laughingstock throughout the whole nation. [6]Lay aside concern for that sorcerer;[a] let me eliminate his face, so you'll see him no more."

115 Hearing this, Mygdonia gave in to grief—she mourned and lamented. [2]Again Carish said, "Have I sinned so much against the gods that they've afflicted me with so great a malady? What enormous wrong did I commit that they've brought me so low? [3]I beg you, Mygdonia, not to strangle my soul with this pitiable vision of you, with this squalid appearance, and not to burden my heart with anxieties about you. [4]I'm Carish, your husband!—someone the whole nation honors and respects. [5]So what am I to do? I don't know where to turn. What plan shall I devise? Must I suffer

113:104 [a]» 110:41
114:6 [a]» 16:2

113:101 • *princes:* On this title, sometimes translated "satraps," see Poirier, 1981: 227–33.
113:106 • *Here ends . . . in prison:* At this point, Syr adds a long "Song of Praise of the Apostle Thomas"; see the Appendix.

113:103 *of praise,* reading ܪܩܘܒܚܐ (= ܪܩܘܒܚܐ = δόξα) for the obscure ܪܩܘܒܝܚܐ.

115:8 ᵃCf. 8:10
116:1 ᵃCf. 6:1
116:6 ᵃ» 16:2

in silence? ⁶But who can bear it when people seize his treasure? Who would put up with this 'good' behavior of yours? ⁷What's left for me? Your fragrance is in my nostrils and your bright face is set in my eyes, but my soul is taken away—the exquisitely beautiful body that I delighted to look on is destroyed. ⁸The sharp-eyed sight is blinded, my right hand is cut off,ᵃ my joy is turned to sorrow, my life to death. ⁹Light walks in darkness; let none of my kinsmen, from whom no help has come to me, see me. ¹⁰Neither shall I worship any more the gods of the east who have encompassed me with such evils. ¹¹I won't pray to them ever again nor offer sacrifice to them, now that I'm deprived of my spouse. ¹²What else would I ask from them? All my honor has been taken away. ¹³I'm a ruler, second only to the authority of the king, but Mygdonia has rejected me, she has deprived me of all these things."

116 While Carish was making this lugubrious speech, Mygdonia sat beside him in silence, looking at the floor.ᵃ ²He approached her again and said, "My Lady, most dear Mygdonia, remember that I chose and selected you out of all the women in India as the most beautiful, although I could have married others who were much more beautiful. ³No; I lie, Mygdonia. I swear by the gods that your equal is not to be found in the whole of India. ⁴Too bad for me, because you don't want to say even a single word to me. ⁵Insult me, if you please, so that I might be worthy of just one word from you. ⁶Look at me, since I'm surely more handsome than that sorcerer:ᵃ I have wealth and honor and everyone knows that no one is my equal. ⁷You are family and kindred to me, and look, you've been taken from me."

117 When Carish had spoken, Mygdonia said to him, "The man I love is better than you and your possessions. ²Your property is from the earth and returns to the earth, but the man I love is heavenly and will bring me with him to heaven. ³Your wealth will vanish and your beauty will disappear, along with your clothes and your many works; you'll be alone with your excesses. ⁴Don't remind me of your activities. For I pray to the Lord that you be forgotten,

---

115:6 *this 'good' behavior:* The Greek is probably ironic; Syr "Could I bear your lovely beauties which are always before me?"
115:7 *is taken way,* reading the third person plural, grammatically equivalent to the passive voice ("they took" = "he/she/it was taken"), for the

participle.
115:9 *let none . . . see,* reading βλεπέτω for βλέπετε; see Bonnet, *Aaa* 2/2. 226 n. 5.
116:6 *I have,* reading ἔχω for σὺ εἶ ("you are"), with Syr; alternatives in Bonnet, *Aaa* 2/2. 227 n. 7.

so that the pleasures of old and the physical intimacy, which will depart as a shadow, will not be remembered.[a] [5]Jesus alone remains forever,[a] along with the souls that hope in him; Jesus himself will release me from your shameful actions that I performed with you."

[6]When he heard this, Carish, emotionally drained, turned to go to sleep and said to her, "Think the matter over tonight. [7]If you want to be with me as you used to be and no longer see that sorcerer,[a] I"ll do whatever you wish. [8]And if you abandon your fixation on him, I'll have him released from prison. [9] He may then go abroad and I'll not cause you any grief, for I know that you think very highly of him. [10]You're not the first person this sort of thing has happened to—he's led astray many others with you, but they've woken up and come to their senses. [11]Don't totally disregard my words and disgrace me among the inhabitants of India."

118 After saying this, Carish fell asleep. [2]Mygdonia took ten denarii and went off unnoticed to bribe the guards,[a] so as to visit the apostle. [3]Judas Thomas, coming along the road, met her. [4]When she saw him she was frightened, thinking that he was one of the ruling nobles, for a great light preceded him. [5]She said to herself as she fled, "You're lost, you poor wretch; you'll never again see Judas the apostle of the Living One,[a] and you still have not received the holy seal."[b] [6]In her flight she ran to a narrow alley, where she hid and said: "It's better to be caught by humbler folk, whom one can persuade, than to fall into the hands of this powerful ruler who would despise bribes."

ACT 10 MYGDONIA RECEIVES BAPTISM

119 While Mygdonia pondered these things in solitude, Judas came and stood over her. [2]When she saw him she was afraid and fainted away out of fright, but he stood over her, took her hand, and said to her, [3]"Don't be afraid, Mygdonia. Jesus won't forsake you, nor will the Lord to whom you have dedicated your soul overlook you. [4]His merciful rest won't abandon you, and he who is beneficent

117:4 [a] » 169:5
117:5 [a] » 88:7
117:7 [a] » 16:2
118:2 [a]Cf. APaTh 18:1
118:5 [a] » 60:3
    [b] » 49:3

118:6 *to be caught*, reading ἁλίσκεσθαι for ἀναλίσκεσθαι ("to be consumed"), with Syr; see Bonnet, *Aaa* 2/2. 229 n. 3.

120:1 ᵃ» 49:3
120:6 ᵃCf. 104:4
120:10 ᵃCf. Jn 2:1–11
121:2 ᵃ» 25:4

and good won't abandon you, on account of his beneficent goodness. ⁵So get up from the ground, you who were once entirely above it. ⁶See the light, because the Lord doesn't allow those who love him to walk in darkness. ⁷Observe him who accompanies his servants, because he is their ally amidst dangers."

⁸Mygdonia stood up, approached him, and said, "Where did you go, my Lord? Who is it that led you out of prison to see the sun?"

⁹Judas Thomas said to her, "My Lord Jesus is more powerful than all powers, kings, and rulers."

120 Mygdonia then said, "Give me the seal ᵃ of Jesus Christ and I shall receive a gift from your hands before you depart this life." ²She took him along, entered the courtyard, and woke her nurse, saying to her, ²"My mother and nurse Narkia, you have performed for me all sorts of services and vain acts of refreshment from my childhood until this time, and I owe you a temporal debt of gratitude for them. ⁴Now do me this favor, so you may receive an eternal requital from him who bestows great blessings."

⁵"What do you wish, my daughter Mygdonia, and what is your pleasure?" Narkia responded. ⁶"The stranger has not allowed you to grant the rewards which you previously promised me, and you've made me a mockery in all the nation.ᵃ ⁷What new thing do you charge me to do now?"

⁸Mygdonia said, "Share with me in eternal life, so that I may receive perfect food from you. ⁹Gather up some bread and a drink of water and bring them to me, out of respect for my freeborn state."

¹⁰The nurse said, "I'll provide you with many loaves of bread and, instead of water, jugs of wine,ᵃ and I'll do your bidding."

¹⁰Mygdonia said to her nurse, "I don't want the jugs of wine, nor do I need that many loaves. ¹¹Bring me only a drink of water, a single loaf, and some oil."

121 When Narkia had brought these things, Mygdonia stood before the apostle with her head uncovered. ²He took the oil and poured it on her head,ᵃ saying,

Holy oil given for our sanctification,
secret mystery in which the cross was revealed to us:
³You it is who discloses covered parts;
you it is who humiliates stubborn deeds.

120:2 *Narkia*: In Greek the name is Marcia.   120:8 *water*: Syr "wine"; cf. 152:3.

121:7 ªCf. 18:4
ᵇ» 27:10
121:9 ª» 49:3
121:10 ªCf. Rv 1:7
121:12 ª» 1:5
122:4 ª» 48:4
123:2 ª» 20:4

⁴You it is who reveals hidden treasures;
  you are the offshoot of beneficence.
⁵Let your power come;
  let it be established in your servant Mygdonia
  and heal her through this freedom.

⁶When the oil was poured, he ordered her nurse to disrobe her and put on her a linen garment. ⁷There was a water fountain nearby,ª and the apostle went up into it and baptized Mygdonia in the name of the Father, the Son, and the Holy Spirit.ᵇ ⁸When she had been baptized and clothed, he broke bread, took the cup of water, made her a sharer in the body of Christ and in the cup of the Son of God; ⁹and he said, "You have received your sealª and acquired eternal life for yourself."

¹⁰Immediately from above a voice was heard saying, "Yes, Amen."ª

¹¹When Narkia heard this voice, she was astonished and asked the apostle that she, too, might receive the seal. ¹²The apostle gave it to her and said, "May the care of the Lord be with you,ª as with the others."

122 Afterward the apostle returned to the prison, where he found the gates opened and the guards still sleeping. ²Thomas said, "Who is like you, O God, you who withhold your loving care and concern from no one? Who is merciful like you, who have saved your possession from evils? ³You are the life that overcame death, the repose that cut off toil. ⁴Glory to the only-begotten of the Father.ª Glory to the merciful one sent from Mercy."

⁵When he had said this, the guards were awakened and saw all the doors opened and those who had been incarcerated <asleep>. ⁶They said among themselves, "Didn't we secure the doors? How is it that they are now open and the prisoners are <still> in there?"

123 At dawn, Carish came to Mygdonia <and her nurse>, and found them praying and saying:

  ²New Godª who has come here to us through the stranger,
  God hidden from the inhabitants of India;

123:1 • *God . . .* : With these repeated petitions invoking the deity, cf. AcJohn 75.

122:5 *asleep* is added from Syr.
123:1 *and her nurse* is added from Syr; the nurse's presence is presupposed by the sequel.

123:4 ª » 15:8
123:7 ª » 16:2

3God, who revealed your glory through your apostle Thomas,
  God, whose fame we heard of and in whom we believed;
4God, to whom we have come to be saved;
  God, who out of love of and pity for humanity
  have come down to our smallness,ª
5God, who sought us when we did not know you;
  God, who holds the heights
  and who does not avoid the depths:
  Avert from us the mad rage of Carish.

6When Carish heard this he said to Mygdonia, "You rightly call me wicked, crazed and base, for if I had not put up with your disorderliness and indulged your libertinism, you would not have cried out against me and mentioned my name before God. 7Believe me, Mygdonia, there is no benefit to be had from that sorcerer,ª and he is unable to do what he has promised. 8Whatever I promise, I'll do right before your eyes, so that you may believe and accept my words and be with me as you used to be."

124 He approached and begged her again, "If you obey me, I shall no longer have any grief. 2Remember that day when you first met me. 3Tell the truth: Wasn't I more handsome to you at that time than Jesus is now?"
    4Mygdonia replied:

That time had its qualities, this time has its own;
    that was a time of beginning, this of ending.
5That was a time of temporary life, this of eternal;
    that was a time of transitory joy,
    this of joy that abides forever.
6That was a time of day and night,
    this of day without night.
7You knew that past marriage which does not last;
    this marriage lasts forever.
8That intercourse leads to destruction;
    this to eternal life.
9Those members of the bridal party
    are transitory men and women;
    the present ones remain forever.

124:7 *which does not last,* reading οὐδὲ μένον for
ὧδε καὶ μόνον ("here and only"), with Syr.

[10]That marriage stands on earth <in constant turmoil>;
  this one makes love of humanity drop down like dew.
[11]That bridal chamber is removed again;
  this remains forever.[a]
[12]That bed is covered with spreads;
  this with love and faith.
[13]You are a groom who departs and is destroyed;
  Jesus is the true bridegroom,
  who remains forever, immortal.[a]
[14]That unveiling festival involves sums of money,
  and clothes that grow old;[a]
  this involves living words that never end.[b]

124:11 [a]» 6:14
124:13 [a]Cf. 14:7
124:14 [a]» 36:11
[b]Cf. Mt 24:35; Mk
13:31; Lk 21:33
126:5 [a]» 12:2

125 When Carish heard this, he went off to the king and told him everything. [2]The king ordered Judas to be brought in, to sentence him and have him executed. [3]But Carish said, "Hold off a little, my king—frighten the man first and persuade him to convince Mygdonia to be with me again as she used to be."

[4]Mizdai sent for the apostle of Christ and had him brought in. [5]All the prisoners were saddened because the apostle was leaving them; they grieved for him and said, "Even this bit of consolation which we had they have taken away from us."

126 Mizdai said to Judas, "Why do you teach this new teaching, which both gods and mortals hate, since it has nothing useful about it?"

[2]Judas replied, "What do I teach that is base?"

[3]Mizdai said, "You teach that it's not possible to live well in the sight of the God you proclaim, <except for those who live purely>."

[4]"King, you speak the truth," Thomas said. "This is what I teach. But tell me, aren't you annoyed at your bodyguards when they wear soiled clothing? [5]So, if you, an earthly king who returns to earth, demand that your subordinates behave properly, do you declare that I teach improperly when I say it's necessary for those who serve my king to be reverent and clean, removed from all grief and care, from children,[a] useless wealth, and worthless worry? [6]You desire that your subjects follow your way of life and your customs,

---

126:1 • *this new teaching* (τὴν νέαν ταύτην διδασκαλίαν) is reminiscent of Mark 1:27 (no Synoptic parallel), where the phrase is διδαχὴ καινή; see also note on 20:6.

124:10 *in constant turmoil* is added from Syr.   **126:3** *except . . . purely* is added from Syr.

126:7 ªCf. 28:4
127:7 ª» 29:1
128:2 ªCf. APeVer
17:37

and if they scorn your commands you punish them. ⁷How much more necessary is it for those who believe in God to serve him with reverence, purity, and constancy, released from all bodily pleasures—adultery, prodigality, thievery, drunkenness, gluttony,ª and foul practices?"

127 When Mizdai heard this he said, "I release you. Go and convince Mygdonia, the wife of Carish, not to seek a divorce from him."

²Judas responded, "Don't delay if you're going to do something <to me>. ³If she has really accepted what she has been taught, neither iron, nor fire, nor anything stronger than these will be able to harm her, or to remove him who is contained in her soul."

⁴Mizdai said to Judas, "One potion is the antidote of another and venom is the antidote of the viper's sting; if you wish, you can provide an antidote for these spells and create peace and harmony in this marriage. ⁵If you do so, you'll spare yourself—and you've not yet had enough of life, have you? ⁶Realize that if you don't persuade her I'll remove you from this life, which is dear to all."

⁷Judas said, "This life is given on loan,ª and this period of time ends, but the life that I teach is imperishable. Beauty and apparent youth are soon gone."

⁸"I've given you sound advice," the king said to him, "but you don't know what's good for you."

128 When the apostle left the king, Carish spoke up and made a request: "Please, sir," he said, "I've never done any wrong against you or any other person or the gods. ²Why do you inflict such a great evil on me? Why have you brought such chaos into my home?ª ³What benefit do you derive from this? If you think that you'll have some profit, tell me what it is and I'll readily provide it. ⁴Why drive me crazy and bring yourself to ruin? If you don't persuade her, I'll kill you and then take my own life. ⁵But if, as you say, there is, after

---

127:2 • *Don't delay …* (μὴ μέλλε …): A relatively infrequent meaning of μέλλειν (in the Greek Bible only at 4 Macc 6:23; 9:1; Acts 22:16 "Why do you wait?"). Here the request is possibly an ironic reversal: in the NT, another "Judas" is charged to "do quickly" his work of betrayal (John 13:27).

127:7 • *on loan* (κατὰ χρῆσιν δέδοται) presumably continues the metaphorical figure begun in 29:1.

127:2 *to me* is added from Syr.
127:6 *from this,* reading ἀπὸ ταύτης τῆς for the

obscure ἀπὸ τῆσαι; see Bonnet, Aaa 2/2. 236 n. 3.

129:3 ᵃ» 4:6
130:4 ᵃCf. Jn 1:5

departure from this world, both life and death, along with condemnation, vindication, and judgment, I too shall go there with you to be judged. ⁶And if the God you proclaim is just and justly inflicts punishments, I know that I can exact justice from you, for you've harmed me, though you suffered no wrong from me. ⁷Yet even here I'm able to defend myself and inflict on you what you have done to me. ⁸Be persuaded, then; come home with me, and convince Mygdonia to be with me as she was before she laid eyes on you."

⁹Judas responded: "Believe, my child, that if people loved God as much as they love one another, they would ask and receive everything from him, with nothing forcing him."

129 While Thomas was speaking, they entered the home of Carish and found Mygdonia seated and Narkia standing by her with her hand on Mygdonia's cheek. ²She said, "Mother, may the remaining days of my life be cut off for me, may all my hours be as one hour, and may I depart this life, that I might the sooner go and see that handsome man, whose reputation I've heard. ³He is alive and gives life to those who believe in him, where there is neither day and night, nor light and darkness, nor good and evil, nor rich and poor, male and female, free and slave,ᵃ nor anyone who is haughty and who holds the lowly in subjection."

⁴As she spoke, the apostle stood next to her. She immediately arose and bowed to him.

⁵Carish said to him, "Do you see how she fears you, honors you, and willingly does whatever you command?"

130 As he was speaking, Judas said to Mygdonia, "My daughter Mygdonia, obey what your brother Carish tells you."

²Mygdonia said, "If you couldn't even name the thing, are you going to force me to endure the act itself? ³I used to hear from you that this life is of no use, pleasure here is temporary, and these possessions don't abide. ⁴You also used to say that anyone who turns away from this life will receive eternal life, anyone who hates the life of day and night will behold the light incomprehensible,ᵃ and anyone who looks beyond these goods will find others that are eternal. ⁵But now is it out of fear that you say these things to me? ⁶Who, having accomplished something and having been praised,

130:3 *of no use* (χρησιμαία οὐκ ἔστιν), or, omitting οὐκ ("no, not"), "is a loan" (cf. 127:7), with Syr; see Bonnet, *Aaa* 2/2. 238 n. 7.

130:5 *that you say these things to me* is added from Syr.

130:8 ª» 37:7
130:9 ªCf. Mt 13:44;
Th (NHC II,2) 109:
50,31–51.3
130:11 ª» 16:2
131:3 ª» 58:9
131:4 ª» 49:3
131:5 ªCf. 47:4
132:2 ªCf. Eph 4:24;
Col 3:10; AAnPas
7:3–10

changes it? [7]Who builds a tower and then razes it to the ground? [8]Who digs a well in an arid place[a] and then fills it in? [9]Who, having found a treasure, does not use it?"[a]

[10]When Carish heard this he said, "I'll not imitate you, nor shall I be rushed into destroying you, nor, even though I have the authority, shall I have you bound. [11]Yet I certainly shall not allow you to speak with this sorcerer.[a] [12]If you do <not> obey me, I know what I must do."

131 Judas left the house of Carish, went to the home of Sifor and took up residence there with him. [2]Sifor said, "I'll prepare a room for Judas to teach in." [3]He did so and said, "My wife, daughter and I shall live hereafter in holy chastity,[a] purity, and single-mindedness. [4]I ask to receive the seal[a] from you, so that we may become worshipers of the one true God and might be numbered among his lambs and sheep."

[5]Judas said, "I'm afraid to say what I'm thinking; I know something, but it's not possible for me to divulge what I know."[a]

132 He began to speak about baptism:
This baptism is the remission of sins. [2]It gives birth to the light poured out; it gives birth to the new person[a] and mixes a new spirit into the person's soul; it thus triply generates the new person and involves a share in the remission of sins.

[3]Glory to you, the ineffable one who shares in baptism.
Glory to you, the invisible power in baptism.
[4]Glory to you, renewal,
     through which are renewed the baptized,

132:1 • *is the forgiveness of sins* (ἁμαρτιῶν ἐστιν ἄφεσις): Unlike the very similar expression in Mark 1:4; Luke 3:3, here baptism is specified as the forgiveness itself, not as the means to that end ("*for* forgiveness"); similarly, in 133:5, of the eucharistic bread. Cf. *Barn.* 11:1, where baptism "brings" (φέρον) forgiveness. In AcThom 132:1, a translator may have understood the Syriac preposition ‎ܠ (intended to stand for εἰς, perhaps) as the marker of the copula / predicate.

130:7 *Who builds a tower* is added from Syr; cf. Isa 5:1–7; Luke 14:28.
130:8 *an arid place*, reading διψαλέῳ for δαψιλαίῳ ("fertile"); see Bonnet, *Aaa* 2/2. 238 n. 15. Cf. 37:7 ἐν ταύτῃ τῇ χώρᾳ τῇ διψαλέᾳ ("in this parched place").
130:12 *if you do not obey*: Syr involves an ellipse: "If you obey me, <fine,> but if not, I know...."
132:1 *This baptism...*: U and P differ here for several lines, and there has been substantial corruption.
132:2 *new*, reading καινήν for καινοῦν ("renewing") or possibly καὶ νοῦν ("and mind"); see Bonnet, *Aaa* 2/2. 239 n. 14.
     the person's soul, reading τοῦ ἀνθρώπου for τοὺς ἀνθρώπους ("people"), and τῇ ψυχῇ for τὴν ψυχήν.
132:3 *to you... who shares*, reading κοινωνουμένῳ (or κοινωνοῦντι) for κοινωνούμενον.

those who come in contact with you
in a loving disposition.

[5]After saying this he poured oil on their heads and said,[a]

[6]Glory to you, merciful love,[a]
Glory to you, name of Christ,
Glory to you, power founded on Christ.

[7]He ordered that the basin be brought in and baptized them in the name of the Father, the Son, and the Holy Spirit.[a]

133 After they had been baptized and clothed, he set bread on the table, blessed it, and said, [2]"Bread of life, those who eat of which remain incorruptible, bread that fills hungry souls with your blessing: [3]You are the one who has been deemed worthy to receive a gift, that you might become for us forgiveness of sins,[a] that those who eat of you might be immortal.[b] [4]We pronounce over you the name of the Mother,[a] of an ineffable mystery, and of hidden authorities and powers: we pronounce over you your name, Jesus." [5]And he said, "May the power of the blessing come and let the bread be consecrated, so that all souls who partake of it might be released from their sins." [6]Then he broke it and gave it to Sifor, and his wife and daughter.

ACT 11 TERTIA, WIFE OF MIZDAI

134 When King Mizdai had released Judas and finished his dinner, he went home. [2]He told his wife what had happened to his kinsman Carish: [3]"See," he said, "what happened to that poor man; you yourself know, my sister Tertia, that nothing is more lovely to a man than the wife he delights in. [4]It happened that the wife of Carish went to that sorcerer[a] who, as you heard, was visiting the land of India. [5]She succumbed to his spells and separated from her own husband. [6]He doesn't know what to do—when I wanted to destroy

132:5 [a]» 25:4
132:6 [a]» 50:2
132:7 [a]» 27:10
133:3 [a]Cf. 132:1
[b]Cf. 113:151†; 135:7;
IEph 20:2
133:4 [a]» 7:10
134:4 [a]» 16:2

133:5 • *let . . . consecrated* (ἐνιδρύσθω), or "established"; the term appears again in the invocation in 157:10.

133:4 *Mother:* Syr "Father."

134:7 ᵃ» 16:2
135:2 ᵃ» 38:2
135:7 ᵃCf. 113:151†;
133:3
135:9 ᵃ» 36:11

the scoundrel, he wouldn't agree to it. [7]Why don't you go and advise her to return to her husband, and keep herself away from the sorcerer'sᵃ empty words?"

135
Tertia arose early and went to the home of Carish, <the kinsman of> her husband. [2]She found Mygdonia lying on the ground in a wretched state—covered with ashes and sackcloth and praying that the Lord might forgive her previous sinsᵃ and that she might soon depart from life. [3]Tertia said to her, "Mygdonia, my dearest sister and companion, what is this all about? [4]What illness has overtaken you? Why do you act so crazily? Come to your senses, return and be restored. [5]Approach your large family and spare your true husband, Carish. Don't do anything that's alien to your noble status."

[6]Mygdonia replied, "Tertia, you haven't yet heard the herald of life; he hasn't yet come into your hearing. [7]Nor have you yet tasted the medicine of lifeᵃ and the release from sorrows. [8]Standing in this time-bound life, you don't recognize eternal life and salvation, and you know nothing about an imperishable communion. [9]You stand clothed in robes that grow old,ᵃ and you don't desire those that are eternal. [10]You think highly of this vanishing beauty, but you don't give a thought to the soul's squalor. [11]You're wealthy, and have an abundance of servants, <but you haven't set your own soul free from slavery>. [12]You preen yourself with the adulation that comes from the multitude, but you don't redeem yourself from the sentence of death."

136
Hearing this from Mygdonia, Tertia said, "Please, my sister, lead me to that stranger who teaches these marvelous things, so that I, too, may go, hear him, be taught to worship the God that he preaches, share in his prayers, and become a participant in everything about which you have spoken."

135:3 • *what is this all about?* literally, "what is this hand?"
135:7 • *medicine* (φάρμακον): This is the word that Mizdai earlier used for Thomas's spells, but here with a positive sense.

135:1 *the kinsman of* is added from Syr.
135:7 *medicine of life* (τὸ τῆς ζωῆς φάρμακον): Syr "the words of the preacher of life." The Greek phrase is found already in Sir 6:16, of "a faithful friend" who is "an elixir of life" (rsv). A similar expression in Ignatius *Eph.* 20:2 describes the eucharist as "one bread, *the medicine of immortality* (φάρμακον ἀθανασίας)"; the same epithet is

applied to the Christian life in general in Clement of Alexandria *Prot.* 106.1 "Excellent is *the medicine of immortality!*" But the specific expression in AcThom 135:7 seems not to have been anticipated in early Greek-speaking Christian authors. It eventually reappears in, e.g., in Serapion *Euch.* 13.15 (refs. in *LPGL*, s.v. φάρμακον [p. 1472a–b]).
135:11 *but … slavery* is added from Syr.

²"He is in the house of General Sifor," Mygdonia said to her, "for he has become the cause of all those who are being saved in India."ᵃ

³When Tertia heard this, she went in haste to Sifor's house to see the new apostleᵃ who was visiting there. ⁴When she entered, Judas said to her, "What have you come to see,ᵃ a stranger, poor, despicable, and beggarly, having no wealth nor even any possession? ⁵But I do have one certain thing that neither king nor rulers can take away, something that does not waste away nor decay: ⁶Jesus, savior of all humanity, the Son of the living God,ᵃ who gave his life for all who believe in him, flee to him, and are known to be in the number of his servants."

⁷Tertia responded, "May I become a participant in this life which you promise that all who gather together in God's lodging will receive!"

⁸The apostle said, "The storeroom of the holy king has been openedᵃ and those who partake worthily in the goods therein find rest, and as they attain rest they come to rule.ᵇ ⁹Yet no one unclean or base comes to it first; he knows what is inside our heartsᵃ and he knows the depths of our thought, and it's not possible for anyone to hide from him.ᵇ ¹⁰If you, then, truly believe in him, you will be deemed worthy of his mysteries, and he himself will magnify you, enrich you, and make you heir of his kingdom."

137 When Tertia heard this she went back home in joy, and found her husband waiting without his dinner. ²Seeing her, Mizdai said, "Where have you been today to make such a lovely entrance? And why did you come on foot? ³Such behavior hardly befits your noble standing."

⁴Tertia replied, "I must thank you for sending me to Mygdonia. I went and heard about a new life and I saw the new apostleᵃ of the God who gives life to those who believe in him and fulfill his commands.ᵇ ⁵So I ought to pay you back for this favor and give you good advice in exchange for yours. ⁶You'll be a great king in heaven if you listen to me and fear the God who is proclaimed by the stranger, and keep yourself in holy chastity for the living God. ⁷For this kingdom is passing awayᵃ and your life of ease will turn

136:2 ᵃ» 39:6
136:3 ᵃ» 82:1
136:4 ᵃCf. Mt 11:7–9; Lk 7:24–26
136:6 ᵃ» 10:8
136:8 ᵃCf. Mt 13:52
ᵇCf. 142:13
136:9 ᵃ» 80:3
ᵇCf. Ps 43(44):21; Hb 4:12–13
137:4 ᵃ» 82:1
ᵇCf. 113:100; 145:3; 171:1
137:7 ᵃCf. 1Cor 7:31

136:8 • *rest . . . rule:* A well-known phrase, attested in, e.g., Thom (NHC II,*2*) 2: 32,15–19; 2; Clement of Alexandria *Strom.* 2.9.45,5; 4.14.96,3.

136:6 *for all . . . who are known to be,* reading γινωσκομένοις for the nominative singular γινωσκόμενοι; Syr has γινομένοις ("who become"); see Bonnet, *Aaa* 2/2. 243 n. 5.

servants: Possibly emend δούλων ("servants") to προβάτων ("sheep"), with Syr; in Syriac the two words are not very dissimilar: ܥܒܕܐ ("servant"), ܥܢܐ ("sheep").

138:3 ª» 16:2

into tribulation, but go, go to that man, believe him, and you'll live forever."

⁸When Mizdai heard this from his spouse he struck his face with his hands, rent his garments, and said, ⁹"May the soul of Carish not find rest, because he has wounded me to my very soul, and may he not have hope, because he has taken away my hope." ¹⁰He went out, agitated.

138 He found his kinsman Carish in the marketplace and said, "Why did you cast me, your friend, into hell? Why did you make me empty and punish me with no gain for yourself? ²Why did you harm me, though you derived no benefit? Why did you kill me, when you didn't even get life for yourself? ³Why did you do me injustice though you didn't find justice for yourself? Why didn't you let me destroy that sorcererª before he ruined my house with his sinfulness?"

⁴All the while, Carish kept silent. But finally he said, "What happened to you?"

⁵"He has used his sorcery on Tertia!" said Mizdai.

⁶They both went off to General Sifor's house and found Judas sitting and teaching. ⁷All present made way for the king—all except Judas, who did not rise; but Mizdai knew that he was the man and, taking hold of his chair, he threw him down. ⁸Then he took the chair in his hands and struck Judas on the head, wounding him. ⁹He handed him over to his soldiers, saying, "Take him and drag him away, roughly and without any restraint, so that the violence done him might be plain to everyone." ¹⁰They dragged him away to the place where Mizdai administered justice, and there he stood, held by Mizdai's soldiers.

ACT 12 VIZAN, SON OF MIZDAI

139 Vizan, son of Mizdai, came to the soldiers and said, "Give me this fellow so that I can converse with him until the king arrives." ²They turned him over, and Vizan led him to the place where the king administered justice.

139:2 *Vizan:* In Greek the name is Vazanes.

³Vizan spoke: "Don't you know," he said, "that I'm a son of King Mizdai, and that it's possible for me to tell the king what I want and he'll let you live? ⁴Tell me, then, who is your God and what power do you hold to and worship? ⁵If it's some magical power or skill, speak up, teach it to me, and I'll have you released."

⁶Judas said <this> to him:

> You're the son of Mizdai the king, a king of this world;
>> I'm a servant of Jesus Christ, an eternal king.
> ⁷It's possible for *you* to tell your 'father'
>> to save those whom you wish in this temporal life,
>> in which people don't remain permanently
>> even if you and your 'father' grant it.
> ⁸*I* ask my Lord and cry out to him for people
>> and he gives them a new life, lasting forever.
> ⁹*You* boast over possessions,
>> slaves, clothes, luxury, and polluted beds;
> *I* boast of poverty, love of wisdom, humility, fasting, prayer,
>> of communion with the Holy Spirit
>> and with my brothers and sisters who are worthy of God;
>> I also boast of eternal life.
> ¹⁰*You* have taken refuge in a person like yourself,
>> unable to save his own soul from judgment and death;
> *I've* taken refuge in the living God,
>> in the Savior of kings and rulers, the judge of all.ᵃ
> ¹¹*You're* probably here today, but not tomorrow;
> *I've* taken refuge in the one who remains forever,
>> who knows all our times and seasons.

¹²If you wish to be a servant of such a God, you shall be so swiftly. ¹³Show that you will be a servant worthy of him in these matters: first in holy chastity,ᵃ which is the chief of all goods;ᵇ ¹⁴then in communion with the God I proclaim, in love of wisdom, simplicity, love, faith, hopeᵃ in him, and the simplicity of pure food.

139:10 ᵃCf. Hb 12:23

139:13 ᵃ» 58:9

ᵇCf. 85:4

139:14 ᵃCf. 1Cor 13:13

139:8 *lasting*, reading διαμένον for δεόμενος ("asking" or "when asked"), with Syr.

139:11 *who knows*, reading the accusative γινώσκοντα for the genitive γινώσκοντος; see Bonnet, *Aaa* 2/2. 246 n. 22.

139:14 *in communion*, reading the dative article τῇ (with κοινωνίᾳ) for the nominative ἡ; see Bonnet, *Acta* 2/2. 246 n. 26.

   hope: Syr ܣܒܪܐ (PSTS, s.v. [col. 2513; p. 359b]: "hope, trust, confidence, expectation"); Gr εὐαγγέλιον ("gospel"). The conceptual difference cannot be great, however, since the Peshitta often translates εὐαγγέλιον with the cognate Syriac ܣܒܪܬܐ (PSTS, s.v. [col. 2513; CSD, p. 359b]: "tidings, good tidings, the Gospel"]), e.g., in Matt 4:23; 9:35; Rom 10:16); cf. Ps.-Clement *Rec.* 1.64:2 (in parallel with the Latin *euangelium*).

   simplicity: Syr ܦܫܝܛܘܬܐ (= ἁπλότης); Gr ἑνότης ("unity").

140:9 ᵃCf. 1Cor 1:25
140:12 ᵃCf. 18:4
140:13 ᵃCf. APaTh 22:5
141:1 ᵃCf. 18:4; 140:12
141:6 ᵃ» 39:6
ᵇ» 9:5
ᶜCf. 142:11; Mt 16:28; Mk 9:1; Lk 9:27

140 Persuaded by the Lord, the youth was seeking a pretext to let Judas escape; but while he pondered the problem, the king arrived. ²The soldiers took Judas and led him away. Vizan went out with him and stood by him. ³The king took his seat and ordered Judas to be brought in with his hands bound behind him. ³When he had been brought in, he stood in the center of things. ⁴The king said, "Tell me who you are and with what power you do these things."

⁵Judas responded, "I'm a person, just like you. I do these things by the power of Jesus Christ."

⁶Mizdai said, "Tell me the truth before I have you executed."

⁷Judas said, "You don't have authority over me as you believe, and you won't do me any harm."

⁸When Judas said this, King Mizdai grew angry. He gave an order to heat up some slabs and to set him on them barefoot. ⁹When the soldiers were untying his sandals he said, "The wisdom of God is better than the wisdom of all humankind.ᵃ ¹⁰Lord King, let your kindness resist their wrath!"

¹¹They brought in the slabs that looked like fire and made the apostle stand on them. ¹²But immediately water was sent out from the earth in abundance,ᵃ so that the slabs were submerged. ¹³Those who were holding him let him go and fled away.ᵃ

141 When the king saw the abundant watersᵃ he said to Judas, "Ask your God to rescue me from this death, so that I might not die in a flood."

²The apostle prayed and said:
O you who have fettered this natural element,
brought it to a single place,
and scattered it to different regions;
³O you who bring order out of disorder;
O you who grant great and magnificent wonders
through the hands of your servant Judas;
⁴O you who have pity on my soul
that I might always receive your light;
⁵O you who give wages to those who have labored;
O Savior of my soul, who restore it to its own nature
that it might not share in harmful things;
⁶O you who are ever the cause of life,ᵃ
cause this element to cease, lest it rise up and destroy,
for there are someᵇ of those standing hereᶜ
who will believe in you and live.

[7]When he had offered up his prayer the water was gradually absorbed and the place became dry. [8]When Mizdai saw this he commanded him to be brought to the prison, "until I investigate how he ought to be treated."[a]

142

As Judas was being led to the prison, everyone followed him; Vizan, the king's son, walked at his right and Sifor at his left. [2]When they entered the prison he sat down, along with Vizan and Sifor, who ordered his own wife and daughter to be seated. [3]They, too, had come to hear the word of life,[a] but they knew that because of his excessive rage Mizdai would kill him.

[4]Judas began to speak:

<You> who freed my soul from the servitude that afflicts so many, because I gave myself to be sold, now I rejoice and exult, knowing that the times have been fulfilled for me to enter and receive you.
> [5]Now I am being released from the cares of the earth,
> I finish with hope and receive truth;
> [6]Now I am being released from grief and put on joy alone,
> I am becoming free of care or grief, to live in repose;
> [7]Now I am being released from servitude
> and have been called to freedom;
> [8]Now I have transcended times and seasons
> and have been exalted above them;
> [9]Now I am receiving from the one who requites,
> who gives without counting,
> because his wealth suffices for his gift;
> I shall not again be stripped bare.
> [10]Now I am going to sleep,
> but I shall awake[a] and not be laid to sleep again;
> [11]Now I am dying, but I shall come to life
> and not taste death[a] again.

141:8 [a]Cf. 21:7; 164:1; Ac 24:25; APaTh 17:5; AAnGE 4:10

142:3 [a]Cf. Phl 2:16; 1Jn 1:1

142:10 [a]Cf. Ps 3:5

142:11 [a]» 141:6; Th (NHC II,2) 1: 32,12–14; 85: 47,29–34

142:4 • *the times have been fulfilled* (ἐπληρώθησαν οἱ χρόνοι): Cf. Mark 1:15 πεπλήρωται ὁ καιρός (no Synoptic parallel); Gal 4:4 τὸ πλήρωμα τοῦ χρόνου; Eph 1:10 τοῦ πληρώματος τῶν καιρῶν. Instead of this phrase P has ὁ καιρὸς ἤδη τῆς ἀναλύσεώς μου παρέστιν, which is virtually identical in wording to 2 Tim 4:6.

142:4 *you* is added from Syr; P supplies "the imperishable crown" (cf. 158:8, see note; 1 Cor 9:25; 1 Pet 5:4).
142:9 *because*, reading the accusative with διά

τό for the genitive of the articular infinitive τοῦ ἐξαρκεῖν ("so that his wealth *might* suffice"), with Syr.

142:13 ªCf. 136:8

143:3 ªCf. 109:25

ᵇ» 10:3

143:6 ªCf. APeVer 7:5

ᵇCf. 2:7; Mt 13:55;
Mk 6:3; AAnMt 12:3;
APeVer 14:11

143:7 ª» 15:8

ᵇ» 28:2

143:8 ªCf. Jn 20:24–
29; 1Jn 1:1

ᵇCf. Mt 17:1–13; Mk
9:2–13; Lk 9:28–36;
2Pt 1:17–18; AJn 90:1

143:10 ªCf. 167:4; Mt
17:24–27

[12]Now they rejoice, anticipating that I shall come
  and be among their kinsfolk
  and be placed as a blossom in their garland.
[13]Now I reign[a] in the kingdom
  in which I have hoped from here.
[14]Now the insolent fall before me,
  because I have put them to flight.
[15]Now peace has come,
  which all people welcome.

143 While the apostle spoke, all those present listened intently, thinking that this was the time for him to depart from this life. [2]Again he said,

Entrust to the one who heals all things, visible and invisible, the salvation of the souls who ask aid of him:
[3]He is a freeborn one, <offspring> of kings;[a]
  he is the healer of his own possessions.[b]
[4]He is the one reproached by his own slaves;
  he is the Father of the height,
  Lord of nature, and judge.
[5]He is exalted above every greatness,
  the only-begotten son of the depth.
[6]He is called son of the virgin Mary,[a]
  and was known as son of Joseph the carpenter.[b]
[7]He is the one whose smallness[a] <we have beheld>
  with our bodily eyes,[b]
  and whose greatness we have received in faith—
  indeed, we have seen it in deeds.
[8]His human body we have felt with our hands,[a]
  his appearance we saw transformed for our eyes,
  but his heavenly form we were unable to see
  on the mountain.[b]
[9]He it is who overthrew the rulers
  and constrained death.
[10]He is truth that is not deceived;
  and he has paid the poll tax
  for himself and his disciples.[a]
[11]When the ruler saw this he was frightened,
  and the powers with him were troubled.

142:12 *kinsfolk*: Syr has "joy," but Gr may echo the *Hymn of the Pearl* (109:24).

143:7 *we have beheld* is added from Syr; cf. John 1:15–18.

¹²The ruler bore witness about who he was
 and where he was from,
 but he did not know the truth,
 since he is alien to the truth.ᵃ
¹³Having authority over the world and its pleasures,
 its possessions and its delight.
¹⁴<He rejects> all of them,
 and commands his subjects not to use them.

144 When he finished these remarks, he stood up and prayed as follows:ᵃ

Our Father in the heavens,
 your name be revered;
²Impose your imperial rule,
 enact your willᵃ on earth as you have in heaven.
³<Give us the enduring bread of the day.>
 Forgive our debts
 to the extent that we have forgiven those in debt to us.
⁴And don't subject us to test after test,
 but rescue us from the evil one.
⁵My Lord and my God,ᵃ hope, confidence, and teacher:
 you taught me to pray this way;
 so now I say this prayer and fulfill your command.ᵇ
 Be with me until the end.
⁶You it is who sowed life in me from childhood,
 and preserved me from corruption.

143:12 ᵃCf. Jn 18:38
144:1 ᵃCf. Mt 6:9–13; Lk 11:2–4
144:2 ᵃ» 3:1
144:5 ᵃ» 10:1
 ᵇCf. 171:1

144:1–4 • *Our Father:* With four small differences, the Greek is identical to that of the modern critical text of Matt 6:9–13: (1) the form ἐλθάτω ("impose"; literally, "let . . . come") for ἐλθέτω in Matt 6:10 (a minor difference in spelling, as in variant readings of the parallel verse, Luke 11:2); (2) the article τῆς before γῆς ("*the* earth," as in many mss in Matt 6:10); (3) the absence of the petition for bread (see note on 144:3); and (4) τὰς ὀφειλάς ("debts," as in Rom 13:7; in the singular in Matt 18:32; 1 Cor 7:3; *Did.* 8:2), a synonym for Matthew's τὰ ὀφειλήματα.
144:5 • *to pray this way* or *to pray thus* (οὕτως): Likewise, in the NT gospels the Lord's Prayer is not merely overheard but is specifically taught to the disciples; Matt 6:9 "Pray then *like this* (οὕτως)"; Luke 11:2 "When you pray, say"; cf. *Did.* 7:1; 8:2 οὕτω προσεύχεσθε (before the Lord's Prayer); 9:1 οὕτως εὐχαριστήσατε.

143:14 *He rejects* is added from Syr.
144:3 *Give us the enduring bread . . . :* This petition is supplied from Syr.

144:4 *rescue us from the evil one:* U and P differ considerably from here to the end of chap. 149; the translation follows U except in chap. 147.

144:7 [a]Cf. Th (NHC
II,2) 29: 38,31–39,2;
85: 47,29–34; 110:
51,4–5

144:9 [a]Cf. AJn 113:1

145:1 [a]» 15:2; 25:1

145:3 [a]Cf. 113:100;
137:4; 144:5; 171:1

145:4 [a]Cf. Mt 25:35–
39; 2Cor 11:23–29

145:7 [a]Cf. Mt 13:19;
Mk 4:15; Lk 8:12

146:1 [a]Cf. Mt 13:32;
Mk 4:32; Lk 13:19;
Th (NHC II,2) 20:
36,26–33

146:3 [a]Cf. Mt 25:14–
30; Lk 19:11–27

146:4 [a]Cf. Mt
18:23–25

146:5 [a]Cf. Lk
14:18–20

[b]Cf. Mt 22:13

146:6 [a]Cf. Mt 22:2, 11

146:7 [a]» 7:4; Lk
12:35–36

[7]You it is who brought me into the poverty of this world,
  and invited me to true wealth.[a]
[8]You it is who made yourself known to me,
  and showed me that I am yours.
[9]I have abstained from touching a woman,
  so that what you require of me might not be found dirty.[a]

145 My mouth isn't able to thank you,[a] my mind isn't able to conceive of your love for me—you who, when <I wanted to> become rich and have many possessions, showed me in <your> deed that great wealth on earth is loss. [2]But I believed in your revelation and remained in this world's poverty until the time when you, who are true wealth, appeared, filled your people who are worthy of wealth, and released them from want, care, and greed. [3]I therefore have now brought your work to completion and fulfilled your commandment.[a] [4]I've become poor, needy, a stranger, a slave, one despised, a prisoner, hungry, thirsty, naked, and weary.[a] [5]Don't let my confidence be disappointed; don't let my hope in you be put to shame. [6]Don't let my labors be in vain; don't let my prayers and constant fasts go for nothing; and don't let my deeds done for you be diminished. [7]Don't let the devil snatch the seed of grain from the earth.[a]

146 Instead, have it send its roots deep and its spreading branches into heaven,[a] so that its fruits might be displayed on earth and those who are worthy of you may be delighted with it. [2]Look, the monies and possessions that you've given me—I've put in the bank; give them back to me with interest as you promised. [3]With your one talent I have earned another ten; have them added to my account, as you've ordered.[a] [4]I've forgiven the debt of those who owed me a talent; don't have it requested back from me—you've forgiven me that debt <of mine>.[a] [5]At your invitation I've come to dinner, leaving behind field and wife;[a] don't have me cast outside,[b] but let me blamelessly taste of the meal. [6]Let me appear worthy and not go into the outer darkness, bound hand and foot.[a] [7]My lamp with a bright gleam waited for the master, and received him when the wedding banquet[a] was

---

146:2 • *I've put in the bank:* The money that Thomas received from Jesus (chap. 3) has apparently been invested in the mission.
146:3 • *talent*, that is, "mina" (μνᾶ), as in Luke 19:13–25.

145:1 *I wanted to* is added with Syr and P.

over; don't let me find it in danger of being snuffed out when the oil gives out. [8]Let my eyes look for you and my heart rejoice because I've fulfilled your will and done your command,[a] so that I may be compared to your active and reverent servant who in his prudent diligence neglects nothing. [9]For I stayed on watch all night and grew weary guarding my house against a break-in by thieves.[a]

147

¹<I've girded my loins with truth[a]
 and bound sandals on my feet
 that I might not ever see them loosened.
[2]I've put my hands to the yoked plow[a] and not turned back,[b]
 that my furrows might not be made crooked.
[3]The field has become white and the harvest is imminent,[a]
 that I might receive my reward.
[4]I've made my antiquated garment grow old[a]
 and completed the toils on toils that lead me to repose.
[5]I've kept the first, second, and third watch,
 to see your face and worship your holy radiance.
[6]I've torn down the barns
 and left them deserted on the earth,
 that I might be filled from your treasuries.
[7]I've dried up the flowing fountain inside me,
 that I might live and repose
 at your inexhaustible fountain.
[8]The prisoner you entrusted to me I slew,
 that the one who is released by me
 might not lose his confidence.
[9]That which is inside I have made outside,
 and that which is outside <inside>,
 and all of your fullness has been fulfilled in me.
[10]I've not turned back, but advanced forward,
 that I might not be ashamed.
[11]I've brought the dead to life and overcome the Living One[a]
 and filled up what was lacking,[b]
 that I might receive the crown of victory[c]

146:8 [a] » 171:1
146:9 [a] Cf. Mt 24:42–44, 45–51; Lk 12:39–40
147:1 [a] Cf. Lk 12:35; Eph 6:14, 15
147:2 [a] Cf. 3:6
[b] Cf. Lk 9:62
147:3 [a] Jn 4:35
147:4 [a] » 36:11
147:11 [a] » 60:3
[b] Cf. Col 1:24; 1Ths 3:10
[c] » 85:2

146:7 *don't let me find it:* So P and Syr; U "he did not find it."

 gives out is supplied from P.
146:8 *so that I may be compared to* is supplied from P and Syr.

 who … nothing follows Syr; the Greek of U is badly corrupt.

147:6 *the barns:* So Syr; P "the worst people."
147:9 *inside* is added from Syr; cf. Thom (NHC II,2) 22: 37,24–35.
147:1–12 *<I've girded my loins …>:* The paragraph is added from P and Syr. U has only "Let my furrows not become crooked. My fields have become white; they await the harvest."

148:4 ªCf. 167:4

148:6 ªCf. 1Mcc 9:55;
Rm 3:19; 2Cor 11:10;
Hb 11:33

149:3 ª» 36:15

and that the power of Christ
might be brought to perfection in me.
   [12]I've received shame on earth;
grant me a requital and recompense in heaven.>

148 May wicked, base, and evil ones not harm the servant who is meek and easy to despise. [2]The great and the haughty will not dare to resist on account of your encompassing power, Jesus; they flee and go into hiding, since they cannot even bear to look. [3]But suddenly they fall on their subjects, and then the fate of these wicked children cries out and discloses them; that is why no one is able to overlook them. [4]May I pass by their ranks in peace,ª with peace and joy accompanying me. [5]May the devil not see me as I stand before the judge, but may his eyes be blinded by the light that you have established. [6]May his blasphemous mouth be stopped up,ª because he doesn't have anything harmful against me.

149 When he had been released, he said other things to those about him: "Believe in the savior of those who have labored in their service to him. [2]My soul rejoices, because my time is near to receive him. [3]In his beautyª he leads me to speak about what his beauty is like, though I'm completely incapable of speaking of it adequately. [4]You who are the light of my poverty, who fill up what I lack, and who nourish my neediness, be with me until I come and receive you forever and ever."

ACT 13 VIZAN AND OTHERS
RECEIVE BAPTISM

150 The youth Vizan made a request of the apostle, saying, "I beg of you, apostle of God, allow me to depart and I'll persuade the

---

148:1 • *evil ones* are probably hostile supernatural powers blocking the way to the road on high.

148:2 *great and the haughty*, reading nominatives for the accusatives μέγαν καὶ ὑψούμενον, with Syr.

148:3 *their*, reading αὐτῶν for αὐτοῦ ("his"), with P. *them* is supplied from P, which reads "and

rebukes them."

148:6 *because … against me* follows Syr, closely paralleled by P; U is corrupt.

149:4 *you who are*, reading ὁ ὤν for νοῶν ("of minds"), with Syr.

prison guard to let you come home with me, that I might receive the seal[a] from you and become your servant and one who keeps the commands of the God you proclaim. [2]Even prior to this I've conducted myself according to your teachings, when my father forcibly married me to a woman named Manashar. [3]I am now twenty-one years old and I've already been married for seven years. [4]Before entering into marriage I did not know any other woman; now I'm reckoned useless to my father, because I've had no son or daughter by this woman. [5]My wife has lived with me for all of this time with modesty, and today, if she were healthy and had heard you, I know that I, too, would have found rest and she would have received eternal life. [6]But she is in danger and is being tormented with affliction. [7]So I shall persuade the guard, if you promise to come with me; for I live alone, by myself. [8]And you can heal this wretched woman straight away."

[9]When Judas the apostle of the Most High heard this he said to Vizan, "If you believe, you'll see the wonders of God and how he saves his servants."

151 While they were speaking, Tertia, Mygdonia, and Narkia stood in the door of the prison. [2]Having given the guard three hundred and sixty-three silver staters, they came before Judas. [3]They found Vizan, Sifor, his wife and daughter, and all the prisoners seated, listening to the apostle's discourse. [4]As they stood there near him, he said to them, "Who let you come to us? Who opened the sealed door so that you could get out?"

[5]Tertia said to him, "Didn't you open the doors for us and tell us to enter the prison, telling us to do so, so that we might take our brothers and sisters who are there, and then the Lord will show his glory in us? [6]And when we drew near the doors you were separated from us, I know not how, and secretly preceded us here. [7]Where we heard the noise of the doors, <we assumed that> you had locked us out. [8]So we gave money to the guards and entered. [9]Now we are here, begging you to be cooperative and let us take you into exile until the king's anger subsides."

[10]Judas responded, "Tell us first how you were locked up."

152 "You were with us," she said to him, "and had not left us for a single hour, yet you ask us how we were locked up? [2]Well, if

---

150:2 *Manashar:* In Greek the name is Ἀνισάρα ("Anisara," as here) or Μνησάρα ("Mnesara"); see   154:4; 155:2; 156:11; 158:12.

152:3 ᵃ» 20:4
152:5 ᵃCf. Mt 10:28;
Lk 12:4–5
152:8 ᵃ» 49:3
153:1 ᵃ» 34:2
153:3 ᵃCf. Phl 4:13
1Tm 1:12
153:7 ᵃ» 60:3

you want to hear the tale, listen: ³When King Mizdai sent for me he said to me, 'That wizard[a] has not yet prevailed over you, since, as I understand it, he enchants people with oil, water, and bread, and he has not yet worked his magic on you. ⁴But believe me, I'll punish you by keeping you under lock and key, and I'll destroy that man, for I know that if he hasn't given you oil, water, and bread, he can't control you.' ⁵I then said to him, 'You have authority over my body. Do what you will, but I'll not destroy my soul for you.'[a] ⁶When he heard this, he locked me in the house. ⁷Carish brought Mygdonia and shut her up with me, but you led us out and brought us to this spot. ⁸Now give us the seal[a] quickly, so that the hopes of Mizdai, who has been plotting all of this, may be frustrated."

153 When he heard this, the apostle said, "Glory be to you, Jesus of many forms.[a] ²Glory to you who appear according to the measure of our humanity. ³Glory to you who encourage us, empower us,[a] grant us favor, support us, stand by us in all dangers, and make our weakness strong."

⁴While he was speaking, the guard came and said, "Douse the lights, so you won't be reported to the king."

⁵Then, when they had put their lights out and had gone to sleep, the apostle addressed the Lord: "Now, Jesus, it is time for your swift coming; look—the children of darkness make us sit in their darkness. ⁶Let us shine, then, because we're in the light of <your> nature."

⁷Suddenly the whole prison was bright as day. While everyone in the prison slept in a deep sleep, only those who had come to believe in the Lord were awake.[a]

154 Judas then said to Vizan, "Go ahead and prepare what is required."

²Vizan said, "Who will open the doors of the prison for me? The guards locked them and went to sleep."

³"Believe in Jesus," said Judas, "and you'll find the doors opened." When he went to leave them, everyone else followed behind him.

⁴When Vizan had gone some distance, his wife, Manashar, met him on her way to the prison. She recognized him and said, "My brother Vizan, is it you?"

152:7 • *Carish brought Mygdonia . . . :* Carish thus acts on the threat in 130:10.

152:3 *bread:* Syr adds wine; cf. 120:8.
152:8 *plotting,* reading βουλευομένου for

βουλομένου ("wishing"), with Syr.
153:6 *your* is added from Syr.

5"Yes," he replied, "is it you, Manashar?"

6"Yes," she said.

7Vizan said to her, "How is it that you're walking here, especially at this ungodly time? How were you able to get up?"

8She replied, "This youth gave me his hand and raised me up and I had a dream that I was going where the stranger was sitting and I became completely well."

9"What youth is with you?" said Vizan.

10She said, "Don't you see him—leading me by the hand on the right?"

155

While they were conversing, Judas, along with Sifor, his wife and daughter, Tertia, Mygdonia, and Narkia, came to Vizan's house. 2When Vizan's wife, Manashar, saw him she did obeisance and said, "Have you come to be our savior from the troublesome disease? 3You're the one I saw in the night giving this youth to lead me to the prison; your gentleness didn't let me grow weary, and you yourself came to me."

4After speaking she turned around and saw the youth no longer. 5When she did not find him, she said to the apostle, "I'm unable to walk by myself; the youth you gave me isn't here."

6Judas said, "Hereafter Jesus will lead you by the hand."

7Then she came to him at a run. When they entered the house of Vizan, the son of Mizdai the king, though it was still night, abundant light surrounded and shone on them.

156

Then Judas began to pray, saying:

> Friend and ally, hope of the sick, confidence of the humble,
> > Refuge[a] and lodging of those who have fallen asleep,
> 2Voice come from on high,[a]
> > Consoler who dwells in the midst,[b]
> 3Lodging and harbor of those
> > who go through the rulers' realms,
> > Physician[a] who accepts no pay;[b]
> 4You who were crucified by men on behalf of many,

156:1 [a]» 10:2

156:2 [a]Cf. 48:1; Rv 19:5; AAnMt 3:1; AAnGE 28:15

[b]Cf. 48:1

156:3 [a]» 10:3

[b]» 20:5

156:2 • *in the midst:* For *the midst* (μέσον) as the world, see 111:70; also *Od. Sol.* 22:1–2: "He who brought me down from the height, . . . and gathered the things that were *in the middle*"; Irenaeus *Adv. haer.* 1.7.1; *Gos. Truth* (NHC I,3) 19,19; 20,8–9; 26,4–5.

156:2 *Voice come from on high:* So Syr; Gr "Then a voice came from sleep." For Christ as the heavenly voice, see also 10:9; 48:1.

156:4 ª» 10:9

156:8 ª» 50:2

156:10 ªCf. Mt
4:1–11; Mk 1:12–13;
Lk 4:1–13

156:12 ª» 25:3

156:14 ªCf. 10:3

You are he who descended into Hades with great power;[a]

[5]You, whose sight the powers of death could not bear,

You ascended with great glory,

leading all who have taken refuge in you.

[6]You prepared for them a way,

and all those you liberated followed in your footsteps.

[7]Bringing them into your own flock,

you mingled them with your sheep.

[8]Son of mercies,[a] you who were sent to us

from the perfect fatherland above;

[9]Lord of all possessions, who enslave your servants

so that they might live;

[10]You who fill creation with your own wealth,

You who became needy and fasted for forty days,[a]

You who satisfy souls thirsty for your goods:

[11]Be with Vizan, the son of Mizdai, and Tertia and Manashar,

Gather them to your fold

and include them in your number.

[12]Be their guide in a place of error,[a]

Be their physician in a place of illness.

[13]Be their rest in a place of weary people.

Sanctify them in an unclean place.

[14]Be the physician of their bodies and souls.[a]

Make them your holy temples,

and let your holy spirit dwell in them.

157 After he prayed in this way, the apostle said to Mygdonia, "Undress your sisters."

[2]She undressed them, tied loincloths around them and led them in. [3]Vizan had entered first, and they came after him. [4]Judas took oil in a silver vessel and made this invocation over it:

[5]O fruit more beautiful than the other fruits,

to which no other fruit can be compared;

[6]Altogether merciful one,

heated by the force of the word;

[7]Power of the wood,

clothed with which people overcome their adversaries;

[8]You who crown the victors,

symbol and joy of those who are weary;

156:13 *unclean*, reading μιάρας for μιᾶς ("one"),
with Syr.

9You who proclaimed to people their salvation,
  you who showed forth light in darkness;
10You whose leaves are bitter,
  but who are well formed with fruit most sweet;
11You who are rough to the sight, but smooth to the taste,
  you who seem to be weak, but in an abundance of power
  bear the power that contemplates all things!

12After saying this he added: "Jesus, let your victorious power come and let it be established in this oil, as your power was established in the wood akin to you, the power whose word those who crucified you could not endure. 13Therefore, let the gift come, through which you breathed on your enemies and made them retreat and fall prone,[a] and may it dwell in this oil on which we invoke your holy name."

14When he had said all this, he poured <oil>[a] first on the head of Vizan, then on the heads of the women, saying, "In your name, Jesus Christ, may it become for these people remission of sins,[b] defense from the hostile one,[c] and salvation for their souls." 15He ordered Mygdonia to anoint the women, but he himself anointed Vizan. 16When he finished the anointing he led them down to the water in the name of the Father, Son, and Holy Spirit.[a]

158

When they emerged he took bread and a cup, blessed them, and said,

2We eat your holy body that was crucified for us,
  and we drink for our salvation your blood
  that was shed for us.
3Therefore, let your body become our salvation
  and your blood produce remission of sins.[a]
4In return for the gall that you drank on our account,
  let the gall of the devil be removed from us.
5In return for the vinegar that you drank for us,
  let our weakness be empowered.
6In return for the spittle that you received on our account,
  may we receive the dew of your beneficence.
7By the reed with which they beat you on our account,
  may we receive the perfect dwelling.

157:13 [a]Cf. Jn 18:6;
Ac 1:18
157:14 [a]» 25:4
[b]» 50:8
[c]» 44:7
157:16 [a]» 27:10
158:3 [a]» 50:8

157:12 *added:* The word περιωχείμας is gibberish; something like "added" or "continued" is required.

your: Here and in the next clauses reading σοῦ for αὐτοῦ ("his").

158:8 ªCf. Mt 27:29;
Mk 15:17; Jn 19:2, 5
158:10 ªCf. Jn 19:41
158:14 ª» 21:6
159:3 ª» 15:8
159:4 ª» 73:7
159:5 ªCf. Hb 11:6

[8]Because you received a crown of thorns on our account,ª
     may we who love you put on an unfading crown.
[9]In return for the shroud in which you were wrapped,
     let us gird ourselves with your unconquerable power.
[1] In return for the new tombª and the burial,
     may we receive renewal of soul and body.
[11]Because you arose and came back to life,
     may we arise to life
     and stand before you in just judgment.

[12]He broke the eucharistic bread and gave it to Vizan, Tertia, Manashar, and Sifor's wife and daughter and said, "May this eucharist bring you salvation, joy, and health of soul."
[13]And they said, "Amen."
[14]Then a voice was heard saying, "Amen. Fear not, but only believe."ª

THE MARTYRDOM OF THOMAS

159 Afterwards Judas went off to prison. He did not go alone; Tertia, Mygdonia, and Narkia went off to prison as well. [2]Judas said to them, "My daughters, servants of Jesus Christ, listen to me: In my last day I'm bringing my preaching to a conclusion for you; I'll not speak again in the body. [3]Now I am being taken up to my Lord Jesus who has had pity on me, who humbled himself to my smallnessª and brought me into the service of greatness and deemed me worthy to be his servant. [4]I rejoice that the time of releaseª from here is near, that I my go and receive my reward completely. [5]For my paymaster is just;ª he knows how one ought to give recom-

---

158:8 • *unfading crown*: στέφανον ἀμαράντινον, as in 1 Pet 5:4; also as v.l. in 142:4 (see note, and cf. 85:2). The phrase is often connected with martyrdom, and recurs, e.g, in AcAndGE 18b:33 "Athletes of virtue, . . . the Judge prepares the imperishable crown for you"; *Acts Eupl.* 2, where Euplus receives "*the unfading crown* from Christ our God"; *Acts Matt.* 24, where Matthew is greeted in heaven by "twelve men . . . with golden and never-fading crowns (ἀμαραντίνους καὶ χρυσοῦς στεφάνους) on their heads" (ANF 8. 532b; cf. Rev 9:7).
159:1 • *Afterwards . . .*: P has a different and smoother version of the martyrdom.

159:2 *daughters*: Several mss add καὶ ἀδελφαῖς
("and sisters"); see also 157:1.

pense. ⁶He is not envious, but is generous to those who are good, confident in his wealth, because it is unfailing.

160:1 ᵃCf. 11:5
ᵇCf. Jn 1:20
160:3 ᵃ» 166:1
ᵇ» 171:1
160:5 ᵃ» 36:15
161:1 ᵃ» 49:3
162:1 ᵃ» 16:2
162:5 ᵃ» 16:2

160 "I am not Jesus, but a servant of Jesus;ᵃ I am not Christ,ᵇ but one who ministers before him. ²I am not a son of God, but I pray to be considered worthy by God. ³Abide in the faith of Jesus Christ, await the hope of the Son of God, don't shrink back in tribulations, and don't doubt when you see me tortured, in chains, and at the point of death,ᵃ for in these things I fulfill what has been commanded me by the Lord.ᵇ ⁴Even if I don't wish to die, perhaps I shall be able to do so; yet what is apparently death is nothing but only release from and dissolution of the body. ⁵I accept that gladly, that I might go and receive that beautiful one,ᵃ the merciful one, for I've become quite worn out in service to him and in what I've done through his grace; now he surely will not abandon me. ⁶As for you, see to it that that one who worms his way into and destroys the mind does not draw near you, for the one you have received is stronger. ⁷Therefore, expect his coming, so that when he comes he might take you. You'll see him when you depart."

161 When he finished this speech to them, he entered into the dark house and said, "Savior, who endured many things because of us, let these doors be as they were and let them be sealedᵃ with their seals." ²Leaving the women he went away to be locked up. They grieved and cried, knowing that King Mizdai was going to have him killed.

162 Judas went off and found the guards quarreling and saying, "What sin have we committed against that sorcerer?ᵃ ²With magical skill he has opened the doors of the prison and he wants to set all the prisoners free. ³But let's go tell the king about his wife and his son."

⁴As the guards were saying these things Judas listened in silence. ⁵At dawn they arose and went off to King Mizdai and said, "Master, release that sorcererᵃ or command that he be imprisoned elsewhere. ⁶Though we locked up at the appropriate time those your good fortune has kept as prisoners, when we got up we found the doors opened. ⁷Moreover, your wife and your son along with the rest of those people don't desert the man."

161:1 *let them be sealed*, reading σφραγίσθωσαν for σεμναὶ ἔσθωσαν ("let them be holy"), with Syr.

163:8 ªCf. 9:5; 164:1
164:1 ª» 141:8
ᵇCf. 163:8
164:2 ªCf. Jn 19:17;
Ac 7:58; Hb 13:12

[8]When the king heard this he came to examine the seals that he had set on the doors, and he found the seals as they had been. [9]He said to the guards, "Why are you lying? These seals remain sound. How is that you say that Tertia and Mygdonia have gone off into the prison?"

[10]"We told you the truth," the guards said.

163

After this the king entered the prison and sent for Judas. [2]When he came they stripped him and girded him with a loincloth and stood him before the king.

[3]Mizdai said to him, "Are you slave or free?"

[4]"I'm a slave," said Judas, "and you have no authority over me whatsoever."

[5]"How is it," asked the king, "that you ran away from servitude and came to this land?"

[6]Judas answered, "I came here to save many,ª and through your hands I shall depart from this body."

[7]Mizdai said to him, "Who is your master? What is his name? Where does he live?"

[8]"My Lord," said Thomas, "is both my master and yours, since he is Lord of heaven and earth."

[9]"And who might that be?" said Mizdai.

[10]"You cannot hear his true name at this time," Judas said, "but I can tell you the name applied to him for a time, 'Jesus Christ.' "

[11]Mizdai said, "I did not rush to kill you; on the contrary, I delayed. But you have increased your deeds so that your sorceries have been heard throughout the land. [12]Now I shall bring it about that your sorceries will perish with you and that our nation will be cleansed of them."

[13]Judas said, "These sorceries that you say will follow me will never depart from those who are here."

164

As they were speaking, Mizdai deliberated about the manner in which he would put him to deathª—for he was afraid of the crowd standing about—many people believed in him,ᵇ including some prominent nobles. [2]He stood up and took Judas outside the city,ª a few armed soldiers following him. [3]The remaining crowds thought that the king wanted to learn something from him, and they stood and waited for him. [4]When the king and his party had gone three stadia, the king handed him over to four soldiers and one of the officers, commanding them to take him to a mountain and spear him while he himself returned to the city.

165 The people present ran to Judas, eager to snatch him away.[a] [2]He, however, was taken away—soldiers surrounding him, two on each side holding spears, the officer holding him by the hand and leading him to punishment. [3]As they went along, Judas said, "O for your hidden mysteries[a] that are fulfilled in us at the end of life! [4]O wealth of your grace, that doesn't permit us to experience bodily suffering! [5]See how four men have taken me, since I'm made up of four elements. [6]One leads me, since I am from a single source,[a] to which I am going away. [7]Yet now I've learned that my Lord, since he was from that single source, to whom I'm going away, who is always invisibly with me—[8]he was struck by only one man, but I, since I am made up of four elements, I am struck by four men."[a]

166 When they arrived at the place where they were going to spear him,[a] Judas said to those who held him, "Listen to me now, because I'm standing at the point of departure from the body.[b] [2]May the eyes of your mind[a] not be darkened, neither may your ears be blocked so as not to hear what I've said. [3]Believe in the God I proclaim, and be freed from spiritual arrogance. [4]Conduct yourselves with the behavior suitable for free people, for good repute among other people and for life with God."

167 He then said to Vizan, "Son of the earthly king, but servant of Jesus Christ, give to those who carry out the command of King Mizdai what is due them so that, free of them, I might go off and pray."

[2]When Vizan persuaded the soldiers, Judas turned to prayer, which ran like this: "My Lord and my God,[a] and my hope, redeemer, leader, and guide[b] through all ways, be with all who serve you and guide me who am coming to you today. [3]Let no one <else> take my soul,[a] which I've entrusted to you. [4]Let the toll-keepers not see me,[a]

165:1 [a]Cf. AAnPas 52:4; APa 2:12; 5.2:15; APeMar 7(36):8

165:3 [a]» 10:5

165:6 [a]Cf. 20:4

165:8 [a]Cf. 32:2

166:1 [a]Cf. AAnPas 52:1

[b]Cf. 160:3; 2Tm 4:6; 2Pt 1:14

166:2 [a]» 28:2

167:2 [a]» 10:1

[b]» 10:2

167:3 [a]Cf. Mt 10:28; Lk 12:4–6

167:4 [a]Cf. 167:4

[b]» 29:1

165:2 • *to punishment* involves a double entendre: πρὸς τιμήν can also mean "to honor" (cf. 3:3); P Syr "supporting him."

166:2 *I've said*, reading εἶπον for εἴπειν ("to speak").
167:2 *Judas turned to prayer*: In several mss (PFSLZ) the following prayer is not found. These mss record instead the prayer uttered by Thomas in chaps. 144–48, but without the Lord's Prayer.
167:4–5 *Let the toll-keepers not see me . . .*: Syr lacks these petitions, and instead has Thomas pray for deliverance from sinners.

167:6 ᵃCf. 171:1
167:8 ᵃCf. Jn 11:42
168:1 ᵃ» 171:1
169:1 ᵃ» 95:11
169:2 ᵃCf. Mt 28:6; Mk 16:6

and let not the toll collectors extort anything from me.ᵇ ⁵Let the serpent not see me and the children of the dragon not hiss at me. ⁶Look, Lord, I've fulfilled your task and have completed what you have commanded.ᵃ ⁷I've been a slave; therefore today I receive freedom. You, then, give this to me in perfection. ⁸I say this, not out of doubt, but so that those who need to hear me may do so."ᵃ

168 When he had prayed, he said to the soldiers, "Come and complete the task of the one who sent you."ᵃ ²At once the four struck and killed him, and all the brothers <and sisters> wept. ³Clothing him with beautiful garments and many linens, they placed him in the tomb where the kings of old used to be buried.

169 Sifor and Vizan did not wish to go down into the cityᵃ but they spent the whole day there in vigil. ²Judas appeared to them and said, "I am not here,ᵃ so why do you sit and guard me? I have ascended and received what I had hoped for. ³Stand up, then, and go; not long from now you will be brought to me."

⁴Mizdai and Carish, despite their forceful insistence, did not persuade Tertia and Mygdonia to change their minds. ⁵Judas appeared to the women and said, "Don't forget what happened before. Jesus, who is holy and living, will himself aid you." ⁶The people around Mizdai and Carish, since they did not persuade them, allowed them to do as they wished.

167:4 • *toll collectors,* that is, sentinels guarding the gates to the various levels of the heavenly realm. Cf. *Apoc. Paul* (NHC V,2) 19,16; 22,20; *1 Apoc. Jas.* (NHC V,3) 33,8; *Ep. apost.* 12.
168:1 • *complete the task of the one who sent you* (πληρώσατε τὸ πρᾶγμα τοῦ πέμψαντος ὑμᾶς): Thomas's exhortation is doubly ironic, in that (1) the condemned man is urging on his executioners, and (2) his wording imitates that of his Lord (Jesus), of fulfilling the Father's work, in John 4:34; 17:4 (and see refs. at 76:5 above). The choice of both verb and object differs, however: John has τελειοῦν and ἔργον (cf. AcThom 168:1 in mss PQ et al.: τελέσατε τὰς ἐντολὰς τοῦ πέμψαντος ὑμᾶς).
169:3 • *stand up* (ἀναστάντες) involves a play on words: Thomas, who is ascended (169:2 ἀνῆλθον). charges the believers to "arise" and walk (περιπατεῖτε); cf. Matt 9:5; Mark 2:9; 5:42; Luke 5:23; John 5:8–9; Acts 3:8.
   not long from now (μετ᾽ οὐ πολύ): The exact temporal phrase occurs in Acts 27:14 (also in Marcus Aurelius *Med.* 12.21; Ps.-Clement *Hom.* 6.1.2; 12.18.2); but Acts 1:5 has the very similar expression, οὐ μετὰ πολλὰς ταύτας ἡμέρας, which is taken up in the AcPaulMart 6:4 (the last two words are reversed; cf. also AcPaulThec 23:2) and the derivative AcPetPaul 85(64).
169:5 • *don't forget what happened before* (μὴ ἐπιλάθεσθε τῶν προτέρων): Contrast Isa 43:18 μὴ μνημονεύετε τὰ πρῶτα καὶ τὰ ἀρχαῖα μὴ συλλογίζεσθε; but see also Isa 46:9 μνήσθητε τὰ πρότερα ἀπὸ τοῦ αἰῶνος, and cf. AcThom 117:4.

169:7 ª» 16:9
170:7 ª» 16:9
171:1 ªCf. 113:100;
137:4; 144:5; 145:3;
146:8; 160:3; 167:6;
168:1
ᵇ» 76:5

⁷All the believersª who were there were gathered together, for Judas, as he was being led off to be executed on the mountain, had made Sifor a presbyter and Vizan a deacon. ⁸The Lord came to their aid and through them made faith abundant.

170 After much time had passed, it happened that one of the sons of Mizdai was possessed by a demon. ²Since the demon was quite strong, no one was able to offer healing. ³Mizdai considered the matter and said, "I'll go and open the tomb, take a bone from the apostle of God, touch it to my son and I know that he'll be healed." ⁴He went to do what he had intended.

⁵Judas appeared to him and said, "Since you did not believe in one who was alive, how can you want to believe in one who is dead? ⁶But fear not. Jesus Christ has compassion on you because of his abundant mercy." ⁷Mizdai did not find the bones—one of the believersª had stolen them and brought them to the western regions. ⁸But taking <even the> dust from where the bones of the apostle had lain, he touched it to his son and said, "I believe in you, Jesus, now that he has left me—he who always troubled people so they might not see your spiritual light." ⁹When he attached it to his son and believed, he became well. ¹⁰When his son became well in this manner, he was brought to Sifor with bowed head, together with all the other believers. ¹¹He urged all the believers to pray for him so that he might receive mercy from our Lord Jesus Christ.

171 So were completed the deeds of Judas Thomas the apostle which he did in India, as he fulfilled the commandª of the one who sent him,ᵇ to whom be glory forever and ever. Amen.

170:3 • *take a bone* (ἄρας ὀστοῦν): Regard for "relics" of various sorts is anticipated in the NT by the healing power of Paul's σουδάρια ἢ σιμικίνθια (Acts 19:12; cf. already Matt 9:20–21; Mark 5:27–28; Luke 8:44; Acts 5:15); more remotely in 2 Kgs 2:14 (the mantle of Elijah) and 2 Kgs 13:21 (the bones of Elisha). As early as the *Martyrdom of Polycarp*, widely regarded as reflecting authentic tradition from the 150s c.e., the holy man's bones (ὀστᾶ) are revered as "more precious than precious stones, and finer than gold," and become the focus of a shrine or cult center (*Mart. Pol.* 18:2–3). Here in AcThom 170 Mizdai's plan is literally to "hang" or "suspend" (κρεμάσω, given above as "touch") the bone on or from his son; this choice of verb (repeated in 170:8) presumably prompted mss M and S to add "the throat [or neck] of."

APPENDIX

10:7(a) [a]Cf. 48:5(e)†;
70:3(h)†; 113:121†
[b]Cf. 1Cor 1:24
[c]Cf. 48:5(d)†;
70:3(m)†; 113:110†
10:7(b) [a]Cf. 70:3(d)†;
80:4(d)†; 113:107†,
111†, 130†, 140†
10:7(f) [a]Cf. 48:5(a)†
[b]Cf. Jn 5:28; 11:43
10:7(h) [a]Cf. 113:127†,
144†

As already indicated in the Introduction, the Greek and Syriac recensions differ in greater and lesser ways at numerous points in the narrative. These differences can be variously accounted for, from the accidents of Greek and Syriac idiom to distinct and quite conscious theological preferences. Many of the smaller differences are reported in the notes to the main body of the translation. In a few places, however, the Syriac tradition stands alone in preserving poetic, sometimes possibly liturgical, material that apparently lacks a direct relation to the extant Greek. Several of these poetic or hymnic pieces are reproduced here.

1

10 [7(a)]You became the Christ, and put on the first man,[a]
You are the power, wisdom,[b] understanding,
will,[c] and rest of your Father.
[7(b)]In him you are hidden in glory,
and by him you are revealed in your works.[a]
[7(c)]You are one,
<but> of two names.
[7(d)]You appeared in weakness,
so that those who saw you
thought that you were someone in need of help.
[7(e)]Yet you showed the glory of your divinity
through the condescension of your spirit
to our humanity.
[7(f)]You threw down the evil one[a] from his fortress,
and called out to the dead with your voice[b]
and they came alive.
[7(g)]You promised to those who live and hope in you
an inheritance in your kingdom.
[7(h)]You became an ambassador
sent from the heights above,
to perform the living and perfect will
of him who sent you.[a]

10:7(a) • *You became the Christ, . . . :* Wright, 1871: 1. ܡܚܠ [179] (Syriac text); 2. 154–55 (ET); ET also in Klijn, 2003: 42–43; Schneemelcher-Wilson, 1991: 2. 406 n. * (Drijvers).

⁷⁽ⁱ⁾Glorious are you,^a Lord, in your power,
    and your rule works to renew all your creatures
    and the works that your divinity has brought about.
^{7(j)}No one can annul your majestic will,
    or stand up against the nature of your dignity,
    so <exalted> are you.

2

48

^{5(a)}Jesus, right hand of the Father,^a
    who has thrown down the evil one^b to the lowest limit,
^{5(b)}and has gathered his possessions
    into one blessed congregation;
^{5(c)}Jesus, king over all,
    who keeps all things under <your> control;
^{5(d)}Jesus, who are in the Father and the Father is in you,^a
    yet you are one in power, will,^b glory, and real being;
^{5(e)}who for our sake were named with names,^a
    and are the Son,
    and put on a body;^b
^{5(f)}Jesus, who became a Nazir,
    and your grace provides for all like God.

3

70

^{3(a)} Glorious are you,^a God of Truth^b and Lord of all creation,
    because you willed with your will
    and <so> make all your works,

10:7(i) ^a Cf. 70:3(a)†
48:5(a) ^aCf. *Ep. apost.* 19:11
^bCf. 10:7(f)†
48:5(d) ^aCf. Jn 14:10; *Ep. apost.* 17:4, 8; AcJn 100
»Cf. 10:7(a)†
48:5(e) ^aCf. 70:3(c)†
^b» 10:7(a)†
70:3(a) ^aCf. 10:7(i)†
^bCf. 39:7

10:7(i) • *Glorious are you* (ܐܢܬ ܡܫܒܚ): Cf. 113:107† "You are to be glorified."
48:5(a) • *Jesus, right hand . . .*: Wright, 1871: 1. ܝܡ̣ܝ-ܠܝ [216–17] (Syriac text); 2. 187–88 (ET); ET also in Klijn, 2003: 120–21; Schneemelcher-Wilson, 1991: 2. 407 (Drijvers).
48:5(d) • *real being* (ܐܝܬܘܬܐ), or "essence" (Wright, Klijn). The term translates ὑπόστασις in Heb 1:3 (rsv "nature"; BADG, s.v. [p. 847a] "real being").
48:5(f) • *a Nazir* (so Wright, Klijn) or "Nazirite" (Drijvers). Klijn: "In the Syriac church the Naziraeans were living an ascetic life " (2003: 122).
70:3(a) • *Glorious are you . . .*: Wright, 1871: 1. ܡܝ-ܢܝ̣ܠ [239–40] (Syriac text); 2. 207–8 (ET); ET also in Klijn, 2003: 148–49; Schneemelcher-Wilson, 1991: 2. 408 n. * (Drijvers).
    all creation, literally, "all natures" (so Wright, Klijn); see also 70:3(l).

70:3(b) ªCf. 39:17

70:3(d) ª» 10:7(b)†

70:3(e) ªCf. 59:4; 113:111†, 115†

70:3(h) ª» 10:7(a)†

70:3(k) ªCf. 48:5(e)†
ᵇ» 27:10

70:3(m) ª» 10:7(a)†

70:3(p) ªCf. 39:9

70:3(r) ªCf. Jn 12:28; 2Ths 1:12; Rv 15:4

3(b)and finish all your creaturesª
and bring them to the control of their nature,
3(c)and set the fear of you on all of them,
so that they might be subject to your command.
3(d)And your will trod the way
from your hiddenness to manifestation,ª
and made provision for every soul that you made.
3(e)And it [*or* he] was spoken
by the mouths of all the prophets,ª
in all <manner of> visions, sounds, and voices.
3(f)Israel did not obey
because of their evil inclination.
3(g)But because you are Lord of all,
you take care of all your creatures:
3(h)This is why you spread out your mercy on us
in the one who came by your will
and put on the bodyª—your creature,
3(i)the one you willed and formed by your glorious wisdom,
whom you set up in your secrecy,
but set forth in your revelation.
3(j)To this one you gave the name "Son":
this one is your will, the power of your thought.
3(k)This is why you exist with various namesª—
Father, Son, and Spiritᵇ—
3(l)for the ruling of your creatures,
for the nourishing of all creation,
3(m)while you are one in glory,
power, and will.ª
3(n)You are divided, but not separated;
one, though divided.
3(o)and everything holds together in you
and is subject to you,
because everything is yours.

3(p)I trust you, Lord, and at your command I have taken control of these dumb animals:ª 3(q)so that you might show your ministering power <over> us and them. 3(r)And <this> is <also> necessary, that your name be glorifiedª in us and in these dumb animals.

70:3(r) <*also*> *necessary:* One Syriac ms adds "so that you might serve us and them with what is needed."

4

80 4(a)What I am to call you, this I do not know—
noble <one>, silent, quiet yet speaking,
4(b)seer who is in <every> heart,[a]
seeker who is in <all> understanding—
4(c)Glory be to you, gracious one;
Glory be to you, living word;
4(d)Glory be to you, the hidden one[a]
who has many forms.[b]

5

SONG OF PRAISE OF THE APOSTLE THOMAS

113 107You are to be glorified, Father,
Lord of all, self-existent, ineffable,
hidden[a] in the radiance of your glory
from all created things.
108You are to be praised, the Son, the firstborn of life,
who are from the exalted Father, the Word of life.[a]
109You are to be glorified, the one Father,
who show yourself with wisdom in all creatures
and in all worlds.
110You are to be praised, Son of light—
wisdom and power and knowledge[a]—
who are in all worlds.
111You are to be glorified, exalted Father,
who arose from hiddenness into manifestation[a]
through all your prophets.[b]

80:4(b) [a]Cf. 1Chr 28:9; Ps 139:23; Prv 20:27; Jer 17:10
80:4(d) [a]» 10:7(b)†
[b]» 44:3
113:107 [a]» 10:7(b)†
113:108 [a]» 142:3
113:110 [a]» 10:7(a)†
113:111 [a]» 10:7(b)†
[b]» 70:3(e)†

80:4(a) • *What I am ...*: Wright, 1871: 1. ܐܘܢ [249] (Syriac text); 2. 216 (ET); ET also in Klijn, 2003: 158; Schneemelcher-Wilson, 1991: 2. 408 n. * (Drijvers). This sequence fills out the doxology ("Glory to you, ...") that already constitutes Thomas's prayer.
113:107 • *You are to be glorified ...*: Wright, 1871: 1. ܐܘܢ-ܝ [279–83] (Syriac text); 2. 245–51 (ET); ET also in Klijn, 2003: 195–98. Klijn categorically states of this hymn that "it does not belong to the original Acts" (2003: 195). The doxological invocation, "You are to be gloried (ܬܫܒܘܚܬܐ)" recalls "Glorious are you" in 10:7(i)†.

113:115 ª» 70:3(e)†
113:121 ª» 10:7(a)†
113:122 ªCf. Ps 104:4;
Hb 1:7

[112]You are to be praised, Son of mercy,
by whom all things were fulfilled
in wisdom and in silence.
[113]You are to be glorified, supreme Father,
born of your firstborn in silence
and the stillness of meditation.
[114]You are to be praised, adored Son,
who arose from the Father, in his likeness,
in peace and in glory.
[115]You are to be glorified, good Father,
who revealed the mystery of your firstborn
to the prophets[a]
by the Spirit of holiness.
[115]You are to be praised, tested Son,
who revealed the glory of the Father to your apostles
in all the nations.
[116]You are to be glorified, serene Father,
who forever made your majesty holy in your firstborn,
the giver of life to your creation.
[117]You are to be praised, lovely Son,
who arose from the radiance of the Father,
and have delivered our souls by your innocent blood.
[118]You are to be glorified, omnipotent Father,
who dwell in your glorious light
and are veiled in your glory,
but manifested to all in your grace.
[119]You are to be praised, perfect Son,
who are sown in the living earth
yet existed before the world with your holy Father.
[120]You are to be glorified, the feeder of all,
who are in all worlds, on high and in the depths,
so that there is no place that is without you.
[121]You are to be praised, Son, adored fruit,
who arose over all <creation> in mercy,
and put on <our> humanity,[a]
and whom our adversary killed.
[122]You are to be glorified, infinite Father,
who made the outpourings of your Spirit your angels,
and a flaming fire your ministering spirits.[a]
[123]You are to be praised, Son of light,
who are borne by the Spirit
and clothed in the light of the Father
on holy clouds.

¹²⁴You are to be glorified, Father who gives life to all,
    who gathered up the worlds for your glory
    by the hand of your dear <One>,
    so that they might make <their> praise arise to you.
¹²⁵You are to be praised, Son of life,
    whose gift the Father gives richly to the holy,
    through which they go out and come in
    by the peaceful road.
¹²⁶You are to be glorified, Father who gives life to all,
    who have revealed the mysteries of your Son
    by the Spirit to his saints
    in quietness and rest.
¹²⁷You are to be praised, Son, fruit of the Father,
    who hid your chosen ones under your wings,
    and have fulfilled the will of your Father,[a]
    and redeemed your beloved ones.
¹²⁸You are to be glorified, good Father,
    who give life to all creatures by your dear <Son>,
    in mercy and in grace,
    through his death by crucifixion.
¹²⁹You are to be praised, firstborn Son,
    who feed all things created with your body,
    and blot out our sins with the mark of your wounds
    and the sprinkling of your blood upon us.[a]
¹³⁰You are to be glorified, good Father,
    who dwell in the pure heart,
    in the mind of your worshipers,
    and in outward form are hidden from all,
    yet are revealed to us in your Christ.[a]
¹³¹You are to be praised, the Son, the Word,
    proclaiming your coming in quietness,
    who put on our humanity[a]
    and deliver us by your living and innocent blood.
¹³²You are to be glorified, living Father,
    who have given life to our mortality,
    for we had strayed from your way—

113:127 [a]Cf. 10:7(h)†; 113:141†
113:129 [a]Cf. 113:153†
113:130 [a]» 10:7(b)†
113:131 [a]» 10:7(a)†

113:128 • *by your dear <Son>*, literally, "by the hand of your dear <Son>."
through his death by crucifixion (ܡܗܒܠܝܨܠܝ ܐܠܡܘܬܗ): Cf. Phil 2:8 "even death on a cross."

113:133 ªCf.
113:151†; 133:3;
135:7
113:134 ªCf.
113:148†; Phl 1:11
ᵇCf. 2Cor 5:18–19
113:135 ªCf. Jn
14:6–7, 9
113:137 ªCf. 113:147†
113:138 ªCf. Ps 8:1, 9

we were dead, perished,
    but your mercy was upon us.
¹³³You are to be praised, beloved Son,
    who have given life to our mortality,
    and turned back our going astray,
    and have become the medicine of lifeª for us
    by your life-giving body
    and the sprinkling of your living blood.
¹³⁴You are to be glorified, Father,
    exalted by all mouths and by all tongues,ª
    who have been reconciled to us by your Christ,ᵇ
    and whom we have tasted through your fruit
    <in that we> have become children of your peace.
¹³⁵You are to be praised, Son, peacemaker,
    who have healed our wounds
    and convinced <us in> our stubbornness,
    and gathered <us in> our wandering,
    and schooled us in your truth—
    through you, we have come to know your Father.ª
¹³⁶You are to be glorified, omnipotent Father,
    who sent us your living and life-giving fruit;
    and by the blood of his cross he brought together
    your mercy and your creatures.
¹³⁷You are to be praised, Son, Word of light,
    who have arisen from on high
    and satisfy us with knowledge of you;
    who have cleansed us of our impurity,
    and give life to our mortality by your sign,
    the radiant cross.ª
¹³⁸You are to be glorified, Father of all praises,
    and your great name is to be exalted in all worlds;ª
    for you have not counted our sins against us
    but have given us life through your Christ,
    who is the life of your will.
¹³⁹You are to be praised, Son,
    voice conceived out of knowledge,
    our holy priest who has made atonement for us
    by your pure and holy offering,

113:134 *of your peace* (ܫܝܢܟ): ܫܝܢܐ translates εἰρήνη ("peace") at Matt 10:34; Jas 3:18; but ܫܠܡܐ is the more common term, e.g., in Matt 5:9, 47; 23:7; 27:29; Mark 12:38; Luke 1:28, 29; 8:48; 10:6; 20:46; John 14:27; 16:33. For "peace," Klijn's ET has the misprint "place" (2003: 197).

and have poured out your living blood
　　on behalf of sinners.
[140]You are to be glorified, exalted Father,
　　who are hidden from all worlds
　　but revealed to all your worshipers[a]
　　according to your will.
[141]You are to be praised, Son of life,
　　who fulfill the will of your Father,[a]
　　who have reconciled your creatures
　　so that through you they worship him who sent you,
　　and have become partakers of your mysteries.
[142]You are to be glorified, exalted Father,
　　by every knee which bows to you
　　in heaven and on earth, through your beloved <Son>.[a]
[143]You are to be praised, adored and perfectly merciful Son,
　　through whom peace and hope
　　have come to <all> creatures,
　　so that they may know <their> creator.
[144]You are to be glorified, Father giving life to all,
　　the riches of whose mercy never give out
　　through the abundance of your gifts,
　　but at all times it is your desire it is to give to us.
[145]You are to be praised, Son, fruit:
　　you are the gate of light and the way of truth,[a]
　　and you have made us run in thy footsteps
　　so that we may arrive at the house
　　of your exalted Father.[b]
[146]You are to be glorified, peaceable Father,
　　who have given us peace by our life-giver,
　　and revealed to us your glorious and holy mysteries
　　by the hearing of your teaching.
[147]You are to be praised, only Son of the Father,[a]
　　whose mercy has come upon us,
　　because you have signed us
　　with your living and life-giving cross.[b]
[148]All mouths and all tongues glorify the Father
　　and worship the Son[a]

113:140 [a]» 10:7(b)†
113:141 [a]Cf. 10:7(h)†; 113:127†
113:142 [a]Cf. Phl 2:10–11
113:145 [a]Cf. Jn 14:6
[b]Cf. Jn 14:2
113:147 [a]Cf. Jn 1:14
[b]Cf. 113:137†
113:148 [a]» 113:134†

113:143 • *adored ... Son* (ܟ̈ܪܐ ܣ̇ܓܝ̈ܐ): Klijn (2003: 198) has the misprint "adorned Son."
113:146 • *by our life-giver*, literally, "by the hand of our life-giver."

113:149 ªCf. 1Pt 3:19
113:151 ª» 131:133†
113:152 ªCf. Mt
13:16; Lk 10:23–24
113:153 ªCf. 113:129†
113:154 ªCf. Jn 20:28

and praise your Holy Spirit,
the worlds and the creatures—
those hidden and those manifest.
[149]Your angels glorify you in the highest through your Christ,
who in the underworld
became the peace and hope of the dead,[a]
those who came to life and were raised up.
[150]We beseech you, our Lord and our life-giver,
<to grant> all that you have said and promised:
fill with us your grace
and raise us up to your peaceful place.
[151]For you are our life-giver,
You are our Paraclete,
You are the medicine of our life,[a]
You are our sign of victory.
[152]We are blessed, Lord, who have known you;[a]
we are blessed, who have come to believe in you.
[153]We are blessed through your wounds and your blood[a]
<wounds borne and blood spilled> on our behalf.
[154]We are blessed, because you are our great hope;
we are blessed, because you are our God,[a]
for ever and ever. Amen.

BIBLIOGRAPHY

TEXTS AND TRANSLATIONS

Acta Apocrypha Armenica: see Tchérakian, below.

Allberry, C. R. C., ed., with a contribution from Hugo Ibscher, *A Manichaean Psalm-Book* (Manichaean Manuscripts in the Chester Beatty Collections 2/2; Stuttgart: Kohlhammer, 1938).

Bedjan, Paul, ed., *Acta martyrum et sanctorum Syriace* (7 vols.; Paris / Leipzig: Harrassowitz, 1890–97; reprinted Hildesheim: Olms, 1968) 3. 1–175. Of importance for reporting variant readings in the Syriac manuscript Cod. Berol. Sachau 222, along with readings from Brit. Lib. 14645.

Bonnet, Max, ed., *Acta Thomae: Graece partim cum novis codicibus contulit partim primus edidit latine recensuit praefatus est indices adiecit* (Supplementum codicis apocryphi 1; Leipzig: Mendelssohn, 1883).

———, ed., "La Poème de l'ame: Version greque remaniée par Nicétas de Thessalonique," *Analecta Bollandiana* 20 (1902) 159–64. Nicetas's text has been reedited in Poirier, 1981: 365–75.

———, ed., "*ΠΡΑΧΕΙΣ ΤΟΥ ΑΓΙΟΥ ΑΠΟΣΤΟΛΟΥ ΘΟΜΑ*," in Richard Adelbert Lipsius and idem, eds., *Acta apostolorum apocrypha* (2 vols. in 3 parts; Leipzig: Mendelssohn, 1898–1903; reprinted Hildesheim: Georg Olms, 1959; also reprinted 1972) 2/2. 99–291. The standard critical edition. A new edition is anticipated in the Brepols Corpus Christianorum Series Apocryphorum.

Budge, E. A. W., "The Preaching of Saint Thomas in India," "The Martyrdom of Thomas in India," and "The Acts of Saint Thomas in India," in idem, *The Contending of the Apostles (Maṣḥafa Gadla Ḥawâryât)* (London: Oxford University Press, 1899–1902; English trans. rev., 1935; reprinted Amsterdam: Philo, 1976) 1. 265–87, 287–95, 336–81 (Ethiopic text); 2. 265–86, 287–95, 335–84 (English translation).

Burkitt, Francis Crawford, ed., "Fragments of the Acts of Judas Thomas from the Sinaitic Palimpsest," Appendix VII in Agnes Smith Lewis, *Select Narrations of Holy Women from the Syro-Antiochene or Sinaitic Palimpsest as Written Above the Old Syriac Gospels by John Stylite, of Beth-Mari-Qanun in A.D. 778* (2 vols.; Studia Sinaitica 9–10; London: Clay, 1900) 1. 23–44. A preliminary edition of the text published more fully by Lewis (see below).

Cureton, W., ed. and trans., *Ancient Syriac Documents Relative to the Establishment of Christianity in Edessa and the Neighbouring Countries* (London: Williams & Norgate, 1864; reprinted Amsterdam: Oriental, 1967; Piscataway, N.J.: Gorgias, 2005).

De Bruyne, Domitien, "Epistula Titi, discipuli Pauli, de dispositione sanctimonii," *Revue bénédictine de critique, d'histoire et de littérature religieuses* 37 (1925) 47–72.

Dihle, Albrecht, "Neues zur Thomas-Tradition," *Jahrbuch für antike und Christentum* 6 (1963) 54–70.

Elliott, J. K., "The Acts of Thomas," in idem, *The Apocryphal New Testament: A Collection of Apocryphal Christian Literature in an English Translation* (Oxford: Clarendon, 1993) 439–511. Announced by the publisher as the successor to the venerable translation of M. R. James (see below). Includes additional bibliography of modern translations and studies.

Erbetta, Mario, ed. and trans., "Gli Atti di Tommaso," "Martirio del santo ed illustre apostolo Tommaso," and "Gli Atti Latini di Tommaso: i Miracoli e la Passione (Ps. Abdia)," in idem, *Gli apocrifi del Nuovo Testamento* (3 vols. in 4 parts; Casale Monferrato: Marietti, 1966–81; 2d ed., 1975–82; reprinted 1992) 2. 307–71, 371–374, 375– 91.

Fabricius, Johann Karl (1668–1736), *Codex apocryphus Novi Testamenti* (3 vols. in 2 parts; Hamburg: Schiller, 1703; 2d ed.; Hamburg: Schiller und Kisner, 1719–46). A foundational set of texts and commentaries: vols. 1–2 = 986 pp.; vol. 3 = 1036 pp. Schneemelcher: the work "has retained its value down to modern times" (in Hennecke-Schneemelcher, 1962–65: 1. 66; Schneemelcher, 1991–92: 1. 66).

Festugière, André-Jean, *Les actes apocryphes de Jean et de Thomas: Traduction française et notes critiques* (Cahiers d'orientalisme 6; Geneva: Cramer, 1983).

Hennecke, Edgar, ed., *Neutestamentliche Apokryphen in Verbindung mit Fachgelehrten in deutscher Überlieferung und mit Einleitungen* (Tübingen/Leipzig: Mohr-Siebeck, 1904). *Acts of Thomas*: introduction by Hennecke, translation by Georg Schimmelpfeng: 473–544.

In subsequent editions:

2d German ed., 1924; *Acts of Thomas*—introduction by Walter Bauer, translation by Richard Raabe: 256–89;

3d German ed., 1959–64 (2 vols.; ed. with Wilhelm Schneemelcher); *Acts of Thomas*—introduction and translation by Günther Bornkamm: 2. 297–372;

English translation of the 3d ed.: Edgar Hennecke and Wilhelm Schneemelcher, eds., R. McL. Wilson, trans. ed., *New Testament Apocrypha* (2 vols.; London: Lutterworth; Philadelphia: Westminster, 1962–65): 2. 425–531;

4th German ed., 1968–71 = a corrected reprint of the 3d ed. (no corresponding English translation published);

5th ed., 1987–89 (ed. by Schneemelcher); *Acts of Thomas*—introduction and translation by Han J. W. Drijvers: 2. 289–367;

English translation of the 5th ed.: Wilhelm Schneemelcher, ed., R. McL. Wilson, trans. ed. (rev. ed.; Cambridge: Clark; Louisville: Westminster/John Knox, 1991): 2. 322–411;

6th German ed., 1990–91 = a corrected reprint of the 5th ed. (no corresponding English translation published).

Howard, George, trans., *The Teaching of Addai* (Society of Biblical Literature Texts and Translations 16; Early Christian Literature Series 4; Chico, Calif.: Scholars Press, 1981).

James, Montague Rhodes, ed., "Acta Thomae (ex Cod. Brit. Mus. Add. 10,073)," in idem, *Apocrypha Anecdota: Second Series* (Texts and Studies 5/1; Cambridge: Cambridge University Press, 1897; reprinted Nendeln, Liechtenstein: Kraus, 1967) xxxii–xlv, 27–63.

———, trans., "The Acts of Thomas," in idem, *The Apocryphal New Testament: Being the Apocryphal Gospels, Acts, Epistles, and Apocalypses* (Oxford: Clarendon, 1924; corrected and augmented ed. 1953; often reprinted) 364–438. For more than half a century this was the standard English translation.

Jansma, T., *A Selection from the Acts of Judas Thomas* (Semitic Study Series NS 1; Leiden: Brill, 1952).

Klijn, A. F. J., *The Acts of Thomas: Introduction - Text - Commentary* (Supplements to Novum Testamentum 5; Leiden: Brill, 1962; 2d ed., 2003).

Layton, Bentley, trans., "The Hymn of the Pearl," in idem, *The Gnostic Scriptures: A New Translation with Annotations and Introductions* (Anchor Bible Reference Library; New York: Doubleday; London: SCM, 1987) 366–75.

Leloir, Louis, ed. and trans., *Écrits apocryphes sur les apôtres: Traduction de l'édition arménienne de Venise*, vol. 2: *Philippe, Barthélemy, Thomas, Matthieu, Jacques frère du Seigneur, Thaddée, Simon, Listes d'apôtres* (Corpus Christianorum Series Apocryphorum 4; Turnhout: Brepols, 1992).

Lewis, Agnes Smith, *Acta Mythologica Apostolorum Transcribed from an Arabic MS in the Convent of Deyr-es-Suriani, Egypt, and from MSS in the Convent of St. Catherine, on Mount Sinai: With Two Legends from a Vatican MS by Ignazio Guidi, and an Appendix of Palimpsest Syriac Fragments of the Acts of Judas Thomas from Cod. Sin. Syr. 30* (Horae semiticae 3; London: Clay, 1904) 198–228.

Migne, J.-P., "Thomas (Histoire de saint Thomas, d'après l'Histoire apostolique d'Abdias)," and "Voyages et martyre de saint Thomas l'Apôtre," in *Dictionnaire des apocryphes, ou Collection de tous les livres apocryphes relatifs à l'Ancien et au Nouveau Testament: Pour la plupart traduits en français, pour la première fois, sur les textes originaux, enrichie de préfaces, dissertations critiques, notes historiques, bibliographiques, géographiques et théologiques = Troisième et dernière Encyclopédie théologique*, vols. 23–24 (2 vols.; Paris: Migne, 1856–58; reprinted Turnhout: Brepols, 1989) 2. cols. 987–1015, 1015–46.

Moraldi, Luigi, ed. and trans., "Atti di San Tomaso," in idem, *Apocrifi del Nuovo Testamento* (2 vols.; Classici delle religioni [24], Sezione 5: Le altre confessioni cristiane; Turin: Unione Tipografico-Editrice, 1971; and reprinted) 2. 1225–1350.

Pick. Bernhard, trans., "The Acts of Thomas," in idem, *The Apocryphal Acts of Peter, Paul, John, Andrew, and Thomas* (Chicago: Open Court, 1909; reprinted Eugene, Or.: Wipf & Stock, 2006) 222–362.

Piñero, Antonio, and Gonzalo del Cerro, eds. and trans., "Hechos de Tomás," in idem, *Hechos apócrifos de los Apóstoles* (2 vols.; Madrid: Biblioteca de Autores Cristianos, 2004–2005) 863–1199.

Poirier, Paul-Hubert, *L'Hymne de la Perle des Actes de Thomas* (Homo religiosus 8; Louvain-la-Neuve: Centre de l'histoire des religions de Louvain-la-Neuve, 1981) 325–48.

Poirier, Paul-Hubert, and Yves Tissot, eds. and trans., "Actes de Thomas," in François Bovon, Pierre Coltrain, and Jean-Daniel Kaestli, eds., *Ecrits apocryphes chrétiens* (2 vols.; Bibliothèque de la Pléiade 442, 516; Paris: Gallimard, 1997–2005) 1. 1323–1470.

Tchérakian, Chérubin, ed., *Ankanon Girkh Arakhelakankh [= Non-Canonical Apostolic Writings]*, vol. 3: *Thankgaran Haykakan Hin ew Nor Deprutheankh [= Ancient and Modern Treasures of Armenian Literature 3]* (Venice: Òazar, 1904). A production of the Mekhitarists, a religious order dedicated to the educational development of the Armenian people. This volume is cited as *Acta Apocrypha Armenica* in Klijn, 1962: 9 n. 3.

Thilo, Johann Karl (1794–1853), *Acta S. Thomae apostoli ex codd. Pariss. primum edidit et adnotationibus illustravit* (Leipzig: Vogel, 1823). Günther Bornkamm: "an obsolete edition of the text, which is however distinguished by a discerning commentary, valuable even today" (Hennecke-Schneemelcher-Wilson, 1963–65: 2. 425).

Tischendorf, Constantin von, ed., "ΠΡΑΧΕΙΣ ΤΟΥ ΑΓΙΟΥ ΑΠΟΣΤΟΛΟΥ ΘΟΜΑ," in idem, *Acta apostolorum apocrypha ex triginta antiques codicibus Graecisvel nunc primum eruit vel secundum atque emendatius edidit* (Leipzig: Avenarius und Mendelssohn, 1851) 190–242. The immediate predecessor to the Bonnet (1883) and Lipsius-Bonnet (1898–1901) editions (see above).

Walker, Alexander, trans., "The Acts of the Holy Apostle Thomas," and "The Consummation of Thomas the Apostle," in idem, *Apocryphal Gospels, Acts, and Revelations* = Alexander Roberts and James Donaldson, eds., *Ante-Nicene Christian Library*, vol. 16 (Edinburgh: T&T Clark, 1870) 389–422; 423–28. Reprinted in Roberts and Donaldson, eds., A. Cleveland Coxe, American ed., *The Ante-Nicene Fathers: Translations of the Writings of the Fathers Down to A.D. 325*, vol. 8: *The Twelve Patriarchs, Excerpts and Epistles, the Clementina, Apocrypha, Decretals, Memoirs of Edessa and Syriac Documents, Remains of the First Ages* ("Authorized Edition"; Buffalo: Christian Literature Company, 1886; New York: Scribner, 1925; reprinted often) 535–49; 550–52.

Wright, W., ed. and trans., "The Acts of Judas Thomas (or the Twin) the Apostle," in idem, *Apocryphal Acts of the Apostles Edited from Syrian Manuscripts in the British Museum and Other Libraries* (2 vols.; London: Williams & Norgate, 1871; reprinted Amsterdam: Philo, 1968) 1. ܥܠ-ܩܡܒ [172–333] (Syriac text); 2. 147–298 (English translation).

STUDIES AND OTHER WORKS CITED

Adam, Alfred, *Die Psalmen des Thomas und das Perlenlied als Zeugnisse vorchristlicher Gnosis* (Beihefte zur Zeitschrift für die neutestamentliche Wissenschaft 24; Berlin: Töpelmann, 1959).

Attridge, Harold W., "The Acts of Thomas," in *The Anchor Bible Dictionary* (6 vols.; Garden City, N.Y.: Doubleday) 4. 531–34.

———, "The Original Language of the *Acts of Thomas*," in idem, John J. Collins, and Thomas Tobin, eds., *Of Scribes and Scrolls: Studies on the Hebrew Bible, Intertestamental Judaism, and Christian Origins Presented to John Strugnell on the Occasion of His Sixtieth Birthday* (Lanham, Md.: University Press of America, 1990) 241–50.

Barnard, Leslie W., "The Origins and Emergence of the Church in Edessa During the First Two Centuries A.D.," *Vigiliae christianae* 22 (1968) 161–75.

Bauer, Johannes Baptist, "Die Thomasakten," in idem, *Die neutestamentlichen Apokryphen* (Die Welt der Bibel 2; Düsseldorf: Patmos, 1968) 76–78.

Bauckham, Richard, "The Parable of the Vine: Rediscovering a Lost Parable of Jesus," *New Testament Studies* 33 (1987) 84–101.

Bornkamm, Günther, *Mythos und Legende in den apokryphen Thomas-Akten: Beiträge zur Geschichte der Gnosis und zur Vorgeschichte des Manichäismus* (Forschungen zur Religion und Literatur des Alten und Neuen Testaments 49, NF 31; Göttingen: Vandenhoeck & Ruprecht, 1933).

Botte, Bernard, "Le rîte de baptême dans l'Église syrienne," *L'Orient syrien* 1 (1956) 137–55.

Bousset, Wilhelm, "Manichäismus in den Thomas-Akten," *Zeitschrift für die neutestamentlichen Wissenschaft* 18 (1917–18) 1–39.

Bovon, François, ed., *Les actes apocryphes des apôtres: Christianisme et monde païen* (Publications de la Faculté de Théologie de l'Université de Genève 4; Geneva: Labor et Fides, 1981).

———, Ann Graham Brock, and Christopher R. Matthews, eds., *The Apocryphal Acts of the Apostles: Harvard Divinity School Studies* (Religions of the World; Cambridge, Mass.: Harvard University Press / Harvard University Center for the Study of World Religions, 1999).

Bremmer, Jan N., ed., *The Apocryphal Acts of Thomas* (Studies on Early Christian Apocrypha 6; Louvain: Peeters, 2001). Conference papers (Rijksuniversiteit, Groningen, 1998) and extensive bibliography.

Brock, Sebastian, "Clothing Metaphors as a Means of Theological Expression in Syriac Tradition," in Margot Schmidt, ed., *Typos, Symbol, Allergorie bei den östlichen Vätern und ihren Parallelen im Mittelalter: Internationales Kolloquium, Eichstätt 1981* (Eichstätter Beiträge 4; Regensburg: Pustet, 1982) 11–40.

———, "Eusebius and Syriac Christianity," in Harold W. Attridge and Gohei Hata, eds., *Eusebius, Christianity, and Judaism* (Detroit: Wayne State University Press; Studia post-Biblica 42; Leiden / New York: Brill, 1992) 212–34.

———, *The Holy Spirit in the Syrian Baptismal Tradition* (Kottayam, Kerala: Deepika, 1979; 2d ed.; Syrian Churches Series 9; Kottayam, Kerala: Jyothi, 1998).

———, "Studies in the Early History of the Syrian Orthodox Baptismal Liturgy," *Journal of Theological Studies* NS 23 (1972) 16–64.

———, "The Syrian Baptismal Ordines (with Special Reference to the Anointings)," *Studia liturgica* 12 (1977) 177–83.

Brown, Leslie Wilfrid, *The Indian Christians of St. Thomas: An Account of the Ancient Syrian Church of Malabar* (Cambridge: Cambridge University Press, 1956; 2d ed., 1982).

Brown, Peter, *The Body and Society: Men, Women, and Sexual Renunciation in Early Christianity* (Lectures on the History of Religions NS 13; New York: Columbia University Press, 1988; London: Faber & Faber, 1989).

Burkitt, Francis Crawford, "Another Indication of the Syriac Origin of the Acts of Thomas," *Journal of Theological Studies* 3 (1902) 94–95.

———, "The Name Habban in the Acts of Thomas," *Journal of Theological Studies* 2 (1901) 429.

———, "The Original Language of the Acts of Judas Thomas," *Journal of Theological Studies* 1 (1900) 280–90.

Burrus, Virginia, *Chastity as Autonomy: Women in the Stories of Apocryphal Acts* (Studies in Women and Religion 23; Lewiston: Edwin Mellen, 1987).

Bussagli, Mario, "The Apostle Thomas and India," *East and West* NS 3 (1952) 88–94.

Colpe, Carsten, "Die Thomaspsalmen als chronologischer Fixpunkt in der Geschichte der orientalischen Gnosis," *Jahrbuch für Antike und Christentum* 7 (1964) 77–93.

Culianu, Ioan P., "Erzählung und Mythos im 'Lied von der Perle,'" *Kairos* 21 (1979) 60–71.

Czachesz, István, *Commission Narratives: A Comparative Study of the Canonical and Apocryphal Acts* (Studies on Early Christian Apocrypha 8; Louvain: Peeters, 2007).

Davies, Stevan L., *The Revolt of the Widows: The Social World of the Apocryphal Acts* (Carbondale: Southern Illinois University Press; London: Feffer & Simons, 1980).

Devos, Paul, "Actes de Thomas et Actes de Paul," *Analecta Bollandiana* 69 (1951) 119–30.

Dihle, Albrecht, "Neues zur Thomas-Tradition," *Jahrbuch für Antike und Christentum* 6 (1963) 54–70.

Drijvers, H. J. W., *Bardaisan of Edessa* (Studia semitica neerlandica 6; Assen: Van Gorcum, 1966).

———, "Jews and Christians in Edessa," *Journal of Jewish Studies* 36 (1985) 88–102.

Fiaccadorii, G., "Tommaso in Etiopia," *Studi Classici e Orientali* 34 (1984) 298–307.

Franzmann, M., "The Parable of the Vine in *Odes of Solomon* 38.17–19? A Response to Richard Bauckham," *New Testament Studies* 35 (1989) 604–8.

Geerard, Maurice. "Acta Thomae," in idem, *Clavis apocryphorum Novi Testamenti* (Corpus Christianorum; Brepols: Turnhout, 1992) 146–52.

Gingras, George E., *Egeria: Diary of a Pilgrimage* (Ancient Christian Writers 38; New York: Newman, 1970).

Gunther, John J., "The Meaning and Origin of the Name 'Judas Thomas,' " *Muséon: Revue d'études orientales* 93 (1980) 113–48.

Gutschmid, Alfred von, "Die Königsnamen in den apokryphen Apostelgeschichten: Ein Beitrag zur Kenntnis des geschichtlichen Romans," *Rheinisches Museum für Philologie* neue Folge 19 (1864) 161–83, 380–401; reprinted in idem, *Kleine Schriften* (ed. Franz Ruehl; 5 vols.; Leipzig: Teubner, 1889–94) 2. 332–64.

Hamman, Adalbert Gautier, "Sitz im Leben des actes apocryphes du Nouveau testament," in F. L. Cross, ed., *Papers Presented to the Fourth International Conference on Patristic Studies Held at Christ Church, Oxford, 1963*, vol. 2: *Patres apostolici, historica, liturgica, ascetica, et monastica* (Studia patristica 8 = Texte und Untersuchungen 93; Berlin: Akademie, 1966) 62–69.

Hennecke, Edgar, and Erwin Preuschen, "Thomasakten," in Hennecke, ed., *Handbuch zu den Neutestamentlichen Apokryphen* (Tübingen: Mohr-Siebeck, 1904) 562–601. Cited as Hennecke, 1904b. Detailed notes on text and translation. The volume was published as a companion to the first ed. of Hennecke, *Neutestamentliche Apokryphen* (1904; see above).

Huxley, George Leonard, "Geography in the Acts of Thomas," *Greek, Roman, and Byzantine Studies* 24 (1983) 71–80.

Jonas, Hans, "Response to G. Quispel's 'Gnosticism in the New Testament,' " in J. Philip Hyatt, ed., *The Bible in Modern Scholarship: Papers Read at the 100th Meeting of the Society of Biblical Literature, December 28–30, 1964* (Nashville: Abingdon, 1965) 279 – 93; reprinted as "The Hymn of the Pearl: Case Study of a Symbol, and the Claims for a Jewish Origin of Gnosticism," in Jonas, *Philosophical Essays: From Ancient Creed to Technological Man* (Englewood Cliffs, N.J.: Prentice-Hall, 1974) 277–90.

Junod, Eric, "Actes apocryphes et hérésie: le jugement de Photius," in Bovon, *Les actes apocryphes*, 11–24.

———, "Créations romanesques et traditions ecclésiastiques dans les actes apocryphes des apôtres: L'Alternative Fiction romanesque—vérité historique: une impasse," *Augustinianum* 23 (1983) 271–85.

———, "Origène, Eusèbe, et la tradition sur la répartition des champs de mission des apôtres (Eusèbe, *Histoire ecclésiatique* III,1,1 – 3)," in Bovon, *Les actes apocryphes*, 233–48.

Kaestli, Jean-Daniel, "Les scènes d'attribution des champs de mission et de départ de l'apôtre dans les actes apocryphes," in Bovon, *Les actes apocryphes*, 249–64.

——, "L'utilisation des actes apocryphes des apôtres dans le manichéisme," in Martin Krause, ed., *Gnosis and Gnosticism: Papers Read at the Seventh International Conference on Patristic Studies (Oxford, September 8th–13th, 1975)* (Nag Hammadi Studies 8; Leiden: Brill, 1977) 107–16.

Kirsten, E., "Edessa," *Reallexikon für Antike und Christentum* 4 (1959) 552–97.

——, "Edessa, eine römische Grenzstadt des 4. bis 6. Jahrhunderts im Orient," *Jahrbuch für Antike und Christentum* 6 (1963) 144–72.

Klijn, A. F. J., "Baptism in the Acts of Thomas," in Jacob Vellian, ed., *Studies on Syrian Baptismal Rites* (Syrian Churches Series 6; Kottayam: CMS Press, 1973) 57–62.

——, "The Influence of Jewish Theology on the Odes of Solomon and the Acts of Thomas," in *Aspects du judéo-christianisme: Colloque de Strasbourg, 23–25 avril, 1964* (Bibliothèque des centres d'études supérieuses specialisés; Paris: Presses universitaires de France, 1965) 167–79.

——, "The so-called Hymn of the Pearl," *Vigiliae christianae* 14 (1960) 154–64.

——, "Das Thomasevangelium und das altsyrische Christentum," *Vigiliae christianae* 15 (1961) 146–59.

Koester, Helmut, "*Gnomai Diaphoroi*: The Origin and Nature of Diversification in the History of Early Christianity," in James M. Robinson and idem, *Trajectories through Early Christianity* (Philadelphia: Fortress, 1971) 114–57.

Kruse, H., "The Return of the Prodigal: Fortunes of a Parable on its Way to the Far East," *Orientalia* 47 (1978) 163–214.

LaFargue, Michael, *Language and Gnosis: The Opening Scenes of the Acts of Thomas* (Harvard Dissertations in Religion 18; Philadelphia: Fortress, 1985).

Lemm, Oskar von, "Koptische apokryphe Apostelakten," *Mélanges asiatiques tirés du Bulletin Impériale des Sciences de Saint Pétersbourg* 10 (1890) 99–171.

Lipinski, Matthias, *Konkordanz zu den Thomasakten* (Bonner biblische Beiträge 67; Frankfurt am Main: Athenäum, 1988).

Lipsius, Richard Adelbert, "Die Acten des Thomas," in idem, *Die apokryphen Apostelgeschichten und Apostellegenden: Ein Beitrag zur altchristlichen Literaturgeschichte* (2 vols. with Ergänzungsband; Braunschweig: Schwetschke, 1883; reprinted Amsterdam: APA-Philo, 1976) 1. 225–347.

Magne, J., "Le Chant de la Perle à la lumière des écrits de Nag Hammâdi," *Cahiers du cercle Ernest-Renan pour libres recherches d'histoire du christianisme* 100 (1977) 26–36.

Marcovich, Miroslav, "The Wedding Hymn of Acta Thomae," *Illinois Classical Studies* 6/2 (1981) 367–85.

Ménard, Jacques-E., "Le Chant de la Perle," *Revue des sciences religieuses* 42 (1968) 289–325.

Murray, Robert, "The Characteristics of the Earliest Syriac Christianity," in Nina G. Garsoïan, Thomas F. Mathews, and Robert W. Thompson, eds., *East of Byzantium: Syria and Armenia in the Formative Period* (Dumbarton Oaks Symposium 1980; Washington, D.C.: Dumbarton Oaks Center for Byzantine Studies, 1982) 3–16.

Nagel, Peter, "Die apokryphen Apostelakten des 2. und 3. Jahrhunderts in der manischäischen Literatur: Ein Beitrag zur Frage nach den christlichen Elementen im Manichäismus," in Karl-Wolfgang Tröger, ed., *Gnosis und Neues Testament: Studien aus Religionswissenschaft und Theologie* (Gütersloh: Mohn, [1973] 1975) 149–82.

Payne Smith, J. (Mrs. Margoliouth), ed., *A Compendious Syriac Dictionary Founded Upon the Thesaurus Syriacus of R. Payne Smith, D.D.* (Oxford: Clarendon, 1903, and reprinted). A highly-regarded abridgment of the huge *Thesaurus Syriacus* (see next entry); referred to in this volume by the siglum CSD.

Payne Smith, R., *Thesaurus Syriacus* (2 vols.; Oxford, Clarendon, 1879-1901; reprinted Hildesheim: Olms, 2006). A *Supplement* was issued in 1927. Identified by the siglum PSTS.

Peterson, Eric, "Einige Bemerkungen zum Hamburger Papyrus-Fragment der Acta Pauli," *Vigiliae christianae* 3 (1949) 142–62.

Plümacher, E., "Apokryphe Apostelakten," in A. F. Pauly and G. Wissowa, eds., *Paulys Real-Encyclopädie der classischen Alterthumswissenschaft, Supplementband* 15 (1978) 11–70.

Poirier, Paul-Hubert, "The Writings Ascribed to Thomas and the Thomas Tradition," in Turner and McGuire, *Nag Hammadi Library After Fifty Years*, 295-307.

Scholten, Clemens, *Martyrium und Sophiamythos im Gnosticizismus nach den Texten von Nag Hammadi* (Jahrbuch für Antike und Christentum, Ergänzungsband 14; Münster: Aschendorff, 1987).

Segal, Judah B., *Edessa, 'The Blessed City'* (Oxford: Clarendon, 1970; reprinted Piscataway, N.J.: Gorgias, 2001).

Sfameni Gasparro, Giulia, "Atti apocrifi e tradizione encratita: Discussione di una recente formula interpretative," *Augustinianum* 23 (1983) 287–307.

———, *Enkrateia e antropologia: Le motivazioni protologiche della continenza e della verginità nel cristianesimo dei primi secoli e nello gnosticismo* (Studia ephemeridis Augustinianum 20; Rome: Institutum Patristicum Augustinianum, 1984).

Söder, Rosa, *Die apokryphen Apostelgeschichten und die romanhafte Literatur der Antike* (Würzburger Studien zur Altertumswissenschaft 3; Stuttgart: Kohlhammer, 1932; reprinted Darmstadt: Wissenschaftliche Buchgesellschaft, 1969).

Spittler, Janet E., *Animals in the Apocryphal Acts of the Apostles: The Wild Kingdom of Early Christian Literature* (Wissenschaftliche Untersuchungen zum Neuen Testament 2/247; Tübingen: Mohr-Siebeck, 2007).

Tissot, Yves, "Les Actes de Thomas: Exemple de recueil composite," in Bovon, *Les actes apocryphes*, 223-32.

———, "Encratisme et actes apocryphes," in Bovon, *Les actes apocryphes*, 109–19.

———, "L'encratisme des *Actes de Thomas*," *Aufstieg und Niedergang der römischen Welt* 2.25.6 (Berlin / New York: De Gruyter, 1980) 441-30.

Turner, John D., and Anne McGuire, eds., *The Nag Hammadi Library After Fifty Years: Proceedings of the 1995 Society of Biblical Literature Commemoration* (Nag Hammadi and Manichaean Studies 44; Leiden / New York / Cologne: Brill, 1997).

Whitaker, E. C. *Documents of the Baptismal Liturgy* (Alcuin Club Collections 42; London: S.P.C.K., 1960; 2d ed., 1970; 3d ed., rev. and exp. as Alcuin Club Collections 79 by Maxwell E. Johnson: London: S.P.C.K., 2003).

Wilkinson, John, *Egeria's Travels to the Holy Land: Newly Translated with Supporting Documents and Notes* (rev. ed.; Jerusalem: Ariel; Warminster: Aris and Phillips, 1981; 3d ed., 1999).

Wire, Antoinette Clark, "The Social Functions of Women's Asceticism in the Roman East," in Karen L. King, ed., *Images of the Feminine in Gnosticism* (Studies in Antiquity and Christianity; Philadelphia: Fortress, 1988; reprinted Harrisburg, Pa.: Trinity Press International, 2000) 308–24.

Ysebaert, Joseph, *Greek Baptismal Terminology: Its Origins and Early Development* (trans. F. M. Foran Hedlund; Graecitas Christianorum primaeva 1; Nijmegen: Dekker & Van de Vegt, 1962).

INDEX

OLD TESTAMENT

Entries marked with a dagger (†) refer to the Appendix that follows the main text.

OLD TESTAMENT APOCRYPHA

OLD TESTAMENT PSEUDEPIGRAPHA

APOSTOLIC FATHERS

NEW TESTAMENT APOCRYPHA

NAG HAMMADI AND RELATED WRITINGS

OTHER EARLY CHRISTIAN WRITINGS

156 *Index*

OTHER GREEK AND ROMAN AUTHORS